I0132187

George E. Shelley

A Handbook to the Birds of Egypt

George E. Shelley

A Handbook to the Birds of Egypt

ISBN/EAN: 9783337244224

Printed in Europe, USA, Canada, Australia, Japan

Cover: Foto ©Andreas Hilbeck / pixelio.de

More available books at **www.hansebooks.com**

A

HANDBOOK

TO THE

BIRDS OF EGYPT.

BY

G. E. SHELLEY, F.G.S., F.Z.S., ETC.,

LATE CAPTAIN GRENADIER GUARDS,

FELLOW OF THE ROYAL GEOGRAPHICAL SOCIETY,

AUTHOR OF 'CONTRIBUTIONS TO THE ORNITHOLOGY OF EGYPT,'

ETC. ETC.

LONDON:

JOHN VAN VOORST, PATERNOSTER ROW.

MDCCCLXXII.

PRINTED BY TAYLOR AND FRANCIS,
RED LION COURT, FLEET STREET.

TO

LIEUT.-COLONEL SHELLEY,

MY COMPANION

IN MY ORNITHOLOGICAL TRIPS

TO EGYPT,

IN REMEMBRANCE OF

MANY HAPPY HOURS SPENT IN

COLLECTING THE MATERIALS

FOR THE PRESENT VOLUME,

This Work is Dedicated

BY HIS AFFECTIONATE BROTHER,

G. E. SHELLEY.

PREFACE.

The object of this book is explained by its title; and the Introduction so fully refers to the circumstances under which it was undertaken, that I feel there is no need for prefatory remarks, except as a means of expressing my thanks to the brother ornithologists who have so kindly aided me in the production of my work.

G. E. S.

CONTENTS.

PART I.

CHAPTER I.

PREPARATORY DETAILS, AND SPORT IN THE DELTA.

CHAPTER II.

CHAPTER III.

FROM CAIRO TO ASSOUAN.

CHAPTER IV.

THE FAYOOM.

PART II.

LIST OF PLATES.

INTRODUCTION.

The Nile has now become such a popular winter resort, and so many of my countrymen go there, not only to visit the famous ruins along its banks, but also to enjoy the magnificent climate, that I have been induced to publish the present volume in the hope that it may satisfy a requirement which appears to me to be very generally felt by visitors to Egypt, viz. for some book upon the sport and collecting to be obtained in that country.

Few parties that one meets upon the Nile are without a gun; and it is seldom that there is not some one among them who is anxious to make a collection of the many varieties of birds which are sure to be met with. The boating trip is admirably adapted for making a collection, as there is invariably much time left on hand while the vessel is delayed by adverse winds; even at other times its progress is frequently not so rapid as to prevent the traveller from keeping pace with the boat, if he chooses to land for the sake of sport, which may generally be obtained along the banks of the river.

I shall commence with a short account of my personal

experiences in Egypt, in order to give the reader some idea of the nature of the country and the best localities for the ornithologist and sportsman to visit. I shall then give a more complete list than has been hitherto published, with a description of each species, of the birds which are undoubtedly to be found in Egypt between the Mediterranean and the Second Cataract, to which limits my observations have been confined.

In the following pages the greater portion of the information given is derived from my own personal observation, the result of three ornithological tours which I have made in Egypt, and from a collection of nearly a thousand skins which are now in my possession.

In my descriptions of the birds, I have endeavoured to point out the characters by which they may be most easily recognized, and have placed in italics the characteristic points by which allied species may be distinguished from one another.

I have given plates of a few of the most interesting species which have come under my notice; some of these have never been figured before; and in order to facilitate the naming and classification of the specimens when brought home, I have referred at the end of each description to some good figure of the species, selecting as often as possible from the four following works:—Gould's 'Birds of Asia,' his 'Birds of Europe,' and the works on the latter subject by Messrs. Sharpe and Dresser, and Dr. Bree.

CHAPTER I.

PREPARATORY DETAILS, AND SPORT IN THE DELTA.

February 4th.—It was a bright and cloudless morning on which we entered the harbour of Alexandria; and as the large vessel was brought up to her moorings, numberless small boats flocked around, like sea-gulls to some dead monster of the deep, all anxious to carry away something for themselves. These boats form a curious sight, manned as they are by seamen in the dress of diverse races; for here, at Alexandria, the human tides from east and west meet, and the amalgamation of costume gives a strange appearance to the scene.

The first boat that approaches has a crew of native marines in fez caps and tunics of white sail-cloth, which contrast strongly with the deeply bronzed, weather-beaten faces of the wearers. In the stern sit two dignitaries in yellow and red turbans and flowing garments, the chief of the party being clad in a shabby greenish-black frock-coat and trousers, with a loose fez on his head; they have the sullen, cunning expression of countenance which distinguishes the Turk from the Egyptian. These are the government authorities, who have come to see that there is no contagion on board the vessel. As soon as they have expressed themselves satisfied on this point, all the other boats' crews begin struggling and fighting among themselves, occasionally with blows, but more generally in high discordant tones, each considering himself aggrieved by the others. Now we have to select one of these boats to convey us and our luggage on shore; so we take one with a dragoman, or guide, who can speak a few words of English. He is dressed in a short jacket very much embroidered, loose sky-blue lower garments, much resembling a bag, through which his feet protrude, decked in red leather shoes and cotton socks, which hang loosely about his feet. His complexion is a sallow bronze, his eyes are narrow, dark, and deep-set, and the only hair upon his face is a neat black moustache. He is a Syrian by birth, a dragoman by profession, and a rogue by nature. Into his hands do we confide ourselves, knowing how impossible it is to do any thing for ourselves in this land of "backsheesh." We are not detained long at the Custom-house—the only contraband articles being fire-arms and ammunition, with both of which we are well supplied. They are, however, passed, unchallenged of course, with a knowing look, on our presenting a well-known and never-failing passport; and we then proceed to the Hotel Abbat, one of the most comfortable hotels in Alexandria.

Here it soon becomes known that we are going up the Nile, and shall require a dragoman; consequently we are speedily set upon by this Egyptian species of harpy, each individual ready to take us by the day, month, or tour, upon such terms as they all endeavour to prove clearly would make them losers rather than gainers by the transaction. Their estimates generally varied from £400 to £600 for a tour of three months or for the journey to the Second Cataract and back—a perfectly absurd price for two people. Sooner, almost, than we had settled in our own minds that a certain man might suit, that very man seemed allotted to us by general consent; his prices were at once the most moderate; his testimonials excellent, and all appeared willing to say a good word for him.

It is not advisable to ask a dragoman whom you think likely to suit for his terms at the outset, as he might be tempted to name such a sum that he cannot afterwards reduce it to your idea of the correct thing without appearing such a rascal as to give you a distaste for him at once. The better plan is to form an estimate from the demands of the others, and from what information you can pick up from the Consul and residents, as to the cost of such a boat as you require; then make your offer, say £100 per month, or £200 to the Second Cataract and back, with twelve days' stoppages, *all backsheesh included*, and the contract not to commence till the day of starting. If you intend going into Palestine after the Nile tour, it is advisable to hire a Syrian dragoman; otherwise an Egyptian is perhaps preferable, as being quieter and less likely to fall out with the crew. Prices differ according to the season and number of visitors to the Nile; *i.e.* the prices of the boats. The actual feeding, attendance, and paying of backsheesh, a dragoman will probably be ready to undertake for from £50 to £60 a month for two, £60 to £70 for three, and in similar proportion for a larger number. This would include a cook and one or two servants to wait upon the party.

The boat, which should be one of the best you can find, should not cost more than £40 or £50 per month; this includes a Reis or captain, a second captain and crew of ten men. Wines and drinkables are not included in a contract; they can be got either at Alexandria from Goodman and

Goridge, or at Cairo from Ablitt, the latter of whom I employed. When laying in your supplies, arrange that such articles as are not damaged shall be taken back on your return. Good powder can be best obtained at Alexandria; shot anywhere. Having decided on your dragoman, you get the contract duly drawn up at the Consulate, and there signed and sealed.

At Alexandria there is but little to be done or seen. Of course the strange dresses of the East first attract attention; and then the native bazars are never-failing objects of interest, composed as they are of dirty little shops in series of the dirtiest of narrow lanes, swarming with flies and children; the very ground we walk on is formed of the refuse from the stalls, which, being trodden under foot instead of being carried away, becomes in wet weather, which is not uncommon at Alexandria, the most abominable mud, reaching to the ankles. Leaving this scene, we next emerge upon the Grand Square. This part of the town looks much more European than Egyptian; here are situated most of the hotels; and here the donkey-boys, sharp-looking young Arabs, pounce down upon the lately arrived European, and, driving their donkeys alongside, keep up an incessant chatter. "This very good donkey, this Billy Barlow." "Mister, this Jim Crow—won the Derby, take you to Pompey Pillar, show you every thing." "How 's your poor feet? walking bad for you." And so they continue till we go to mount; then comes a hustle, each boy endeavouring to thrust his own donkey under us; and the matter has generally to be decided by a free use of the stick.

Now we are off sight-seeing. That which perhaps first amuses us most is to see our long-legged friend perched upon a very small donkey, his knees nearly up to his nose; then there trots the ragged little donkey-boy, a true Aladdin, perfectly at his ease without saddle or bridle; then the stately Ali Baba, in flowing robes, red slippers, and turban, jogs quietly along, followed by a small boy bearing his pipe in one hand and a stick to keep his donkey up to its pace in the other. Away we trot through the European quarters; en route a fresh-blown Briton from the west attracts our attention at the door of the Hotel d'Orient, surrounded by a group of dragomans and town-guides, who are giving him such information as each imagines he may require, to impress him with a sense of their individual usefulness, while, from a respectful distance, a small Arab shoe-black keenly watches his soiled boots, ready to pounce down as soon as the larger birds of prey have done with him. Thus the European in the East is daily passed on from the "Harpies" of dragomans to the local guides, or "Vultures, and from them by the donkey-boys, or minor "birds of prey," to the little unclothed urchins, the "Jackdaws" of the place, who, hoping against hope, cry for "backsheesh" until their unmeaning clamour is lost in the distance. On we go by the bright shops and the cafés, differing in no respect from European ones, save that those who sit at the tables, chiefly Greeks and Italians, wear the red fez. Turning out of the square, we pass the British Consulate on our way to the Ramleh station, close to which stands a much-worn obelisk. This is Cleopatra's Needle; and the companion to it lies on the ground half covered with rubbish. These two obelisks are the sole remains of the ancient grandeur of the Cæsareum to be seen at the present day. From this spot the view is pretty, over the bright blue sparkling Mediterranean, bathing the eastern side of the Old Town, which extends on a narrow neck of land out to the Pharos rock.

At the Station we quit our donkeys and go by rail to Ramleh, to visit our Consul Colonel Stanley, who, after a most hospitable reception, gives us some useful information about the best snipe-grounds in the Delta, which proves of much service to us in the course of our tour. Ramleh is a charming place, consisting of a number of small country residences occupied by Europeans who have business in Alexandria, which can be reached in a few minutes by train. Here reside all who can avail themselves of the healthy situation (with a fine sea-breeze), instead of remaining pent up in the dull and, at times, strong-smelling and unwholesome town; for certainly Egypt to the new comer puts forth its most unpleasant aspect in the Europeanized town of Alexandria. At Ramleh the Khédive had a palace, which was burnt down when just finished, in the spring of 1870; when asked what should be done, his reply was "Rebuild it;" and they are now at work fulfilling his orders.

Between Ramleh and Alexandria, the land, for the most part, lies waste and barren. Here some Roman fortifications are still to be traced, and numerous ancient graves, which have long since been rifled in search of antiquities. By the edge of the sea, and just below the water, may be seen tombs excavated in the rock, which has all the appearance of an ancient limestone formation, but which is evidently a recent deposit; for the bones which have been washed from the graves form portion of the matrix. At first sight such a formation may appear uninteresting, as it only contains bones from the neighbouring tombs (known as Cleopatra's Baths); but it really opens another page in the history of Egypt, and is one of the few proofs possessed by us that the Delta has sunk within historic times; for it is self-evident that graves could never have been dug below the sea-level; and that these square excavations, lined with human bones now cemented by nature into a solid limestone rock, were once tombs, cannot be doubted.

February 5th.—We ride off after an early breakfast, and find the streets frightfully muddy from the rain which fell during the night, the black mud in places rising over our donkeys' hocks as we scamper along on our way to Pompey's Pillar. In answer to our inquiries as to whether it often rained at Alexandria, our dragoman said that formerly the climate was as dry as in other parts of Egypt, until Europeans settled there and brought their wet weather with them. He finished by saying that he did not know whether that was really the case, but such was the belief among the native inhabitants.

Passing out of the town by one of the western gates through the city walls, and riding past an Arab burial-ground, we come to "Pompey's Pillar," a single column nearly one hundred feet high. It was erected by Diocletian, and has nothing whatever to do with Pompey. Though of fine proportion, in its present position it is utterly unmeaning, and is certainly disappointing. We continue our ride on to the river to look at some "dahabeahs" which are moored to the bank; and here we first make acquaintance with the Nile boats. Although the general plan in all these boats is much the same, there are, in the arrangements on board, some apparently trivial matters which are of the greatest importance for the comfort of the traveller who has to live in them perhaps for months; and nothing should be be more careful about, after suiting himself with a dragoman, than in the selection of his boat. He should pay special attention to the fitting of the windows, as up to the end of February the nights are chilly; and he must of course assure himself that the new paint does not cover old and rotten woodwork, as is too frequently the case: he should also see that the ropes, sails, and masts are strong and in good order; or he may be delayed at some disagreeable place, to suit the convenience of the captain, while they are being repaired.

The dahabeah has a raised cabin occupying the stern-half of the vessel; this cabin contains a double-bedded room aft, then four or more rooms along each side of the passage which runs through the centre, one of them containing a bath, on which a bed can be made up if required, then the sitting room, in front of which, on each side of the passage, are other rooms for the dragoman's supplies. The fore part of the boat is devoted to the crew, who sleep on the deck. The mainmast stands near the bows, with the kitchen just in front of it; in the stern, near the helm, is another small mast. Over the cabin is the quarter-deck; on this the crew need never come, save the second captain, who steers, as the mainsail is worked in front of the cabin and all the rigging is forward.

February 7th.—We start by the midday train for Cairo, thankful to have left Alexandria, as certainly the most disagreeable part of the Nile tour is the time spent in that town, so remarkable in ancient history, so uninteresting at the present day. Steaming along the side of Lake Mareotis, our hopes of sport rise as we watch the flocks of water-fowl scattered here and there over its surface, the Plovers and Curlews flying round, and the Herons wading in its muddy margin, while the lazy Kite flaps slowly along over the cultivated land, where large flocks of the Buff-backed Heron feed fearlessly, close to the dwellings of the natives, who never molest them. These birds are often pointed out as the Sacred Ibis; but, alas! that bird is no longer to be met with, or at all events is extremely rare, in the country where once it was worshipped.

We now cross the Mahmoodeeh Canal, which was begun by Mohammed Ali in 1819, and finished within the year, but was done, like most Egyptian undertakings, hurriedly, and badly, with an utter disregard of life. It is said that 250,000 men were employed upon the work, out of which 20,000 died within the year. As we approach Cairo we see the stately Pyramids, those gigantic monuments of Egypt, rising in solemn grandeur over the intervening landscape, and the range of the Mokattam Mountains, which overhang Cairo, that most truly characteristic of oriental cities. On our arrival we put up at the New Hotel, the finest European building in the town.

The amusements in the evening at Cairo were formerly limited to the cafés, where singing and roulette went on; but the Khédive has recently built an opera-house, a theatre, a circus, and a hippodrome, at which the French acting and dancing form the most popular attractions. The following day we devote to seeing the town, bazars, the New Mosque, Old Cairo, and the Nilometer on the Island of Roda, near which Moses is supposed to have been discovered among the bulrushes. It certainly requires two or three days simply to see the town and visit the most interesting mosques, without going in for any of the detail; then the Fossil Forest and the Tombs of the Caliphs take a day, while another day has to be devoted to the Pyramids; but as it is my present object to treat of the natural history and shooting that Egypt affords, I shall pass over the sight-seeing, as the fullest information may be obtained about them in 'Murray's Handbook' and in the countless other works which have been written upon the subject.

Leaving Cairo, let us start for the Pyramids, taking our guns with us. For some distance after crossing the Nile we ride among the native houses—dirty mud huts, and occasional palaces belonging to the Khédive or his family; for almost every respectable house on this bank belongs to the Government. We soon become well acquainted with the small white Herons (*Ardeola russata*), which are extremely abundant, and form a prominent object in every scene about Cairo and in the Delta, their clean white plumage giving them a graceful appearance on the ground; but they rise with difficulty, and are awkward in their flight. On each side of the embankment which forms the road to the Pyramids there are pools of water, the remains of the inundation which covers the country in the autumn. In these pools we find Teal very abundant, while upon the large pieces of water may be seen numbers of the common Wild Duck, Shoveller, Pintail, and Pochard, occasionally also large flocks of White-fronted and Egyptian geese. Here and there the common Heron is seen standing motionless in the mud or slowly flapping across the open country away from danger; for these cunning birds are as shy in Egypt as in Europe, and often give timely warning of danger to the other frequenters of the mudbanks. Almost every ditch or pool holds some species of wader, the commonest of which are the Greenshanks, Common Sandpiper, Green Sandpiper, Stint, Kentish Plover, Lesser Ring-Plover;

occasionally flocks of Stilts and Ruffs, and more rarely Godwits and solitary specimens of the Marsh Sandpiper, are also to be found. These and the Spur-winged Plover, which one never fails to see during the day, form the chief bulk of the birds which may be met with at all seasons on one's way to the Pyramids. A few Snipe are generally observed; but they are far more common in the Delta, near the coast, where a good shot may kill forty or fifty couple in a day in the marshes between Alexandria and Lake Menzaleh.

The plains near the Pyramids afford very good Quail-shooting in March and April; but February is too early for them, as they have not then arrived in any numbers.

The birds of prey are extremely numerous, the Egyptian Kite (*Milvus parasiticus*) being by far the most abundant in the town of Cairo itself and throughout Egypt and Nubia. Of the large Hawks, the Peregrine, Lanner, Saker, and Barbary Falcons may all be met with in the neighbourhood of Sakkarah, the Lanner being the most plentiful; this bird breeds every year on the Pyramids. The Barbary Falcon is the scarcest of the four species, and the Saker the next in rarity. Of the smaller Falcons, the Kestrel is extremely common everywhere; the Lesser Kestrel is only a spring visitant, when it becomes plentiful about Alexandria; the Merlin is very common in the spring, frequenting the Sont-woods, but it does not remain to breed; the Sparrowhawk abounds wherever trees afford it shelter. I once shot a Goshawk near Benisouef, the only specimen that I know to have been killed in the country. The Long-legged Buzzard (*Buteo ferox*) is so plentiful in some seasons, that one hardly passes a day without meeting with it. This handsome bird frequents the open fields, where it rests upon some bank or mound whilst it keeps watch over the fields for its prey, evincing a great partiality for Quail. I have here noticed some of the principal species of the birds of prey, as they cannot fail to impress the traveller at the outset with their extraordinary numbers; so that I hope what I have just written may not be thought out of place, but naturally suggested by one's first impressions of a day's sport in Egypt.

At length we arrive at the Pyramids, the wonders of the East. Their gigantic size is hard to realize when close to them, for want of smaller objects for comparison; but a climb up the rough stones to the top will best convince one of their magnitude. The view, however, from the summit is disappointing, as it does not open out a much wider prospect than one has from the base. Facing us to the east, beyond the river stands Cairo, and behind it the Mokattam Mountains, ending abruptly on the north of the range at that city, but extending southward in a flat-topped ridge as far as the eye can see. Between this range and the Pyramids lies the fertile country, the valley of the Nile and the garden of Egypt: to the north-east extends the low flat land of the Delta; and to the west lie the trackless sands of the Libyan Desert—over which the eye cannot range far, owing to the unevenness of the ground. Visiting the interior of the Pyramids is more unsatisfactory; for one climbs and slides along a narrow dark passage, to be shown a room in the very centre, where a sarcophagus was found, but which has been removed.

The next object to be seen is the Sphinx, which has sadly suffered by the hand of time, having lost its nose, which gives it an unpleasant expression. In front of the Sphinx the sand has been removed, and the ruins of a temple excavated, in which there are some huge masses of granite. These must have cost no small labour to convey to their present site, as the nearest granite-quarries are at Assouan, over six hundred miles to the south. The only birds we met with at the Pyramids were the Lanner and Kestrel Falcons, the Crag Swallow, Mourning Chat, and a stray Bifasciated Lark, which truly desert-bird is rarely seen in Egypt.

Returning to Cairo by the same way that we came, we shot a few more ducks and an occasional snipe or two. The black and white Kingfishers (*Ceryle rudis*) are very plentiful, and never fail to attract attention as they hover over the pools in search of their finny prey, which they appear rarely to drop upon directly from the bank where they have been sitting, as does our own Kingfisher, but hover like a Hawk over the water—and if unsuccessful in their dart, rise apparently unconcerned, to go through the evolution again and again until they succeed, when they retire to the bank to enjoy their meal. The next day we ride to the Fossil Forest, a part of the Arabian or Eastern Desert, where the ground is strewn with the shattered remains of fossil trees. The spot is not picturesque, but is curious on account of the quantity of silicified wood which is scattered around, and gives one a fair notion of what a desert is like. We lunch in this wild and desolate spot, where the Gazelle and Raven alone are to be found, the latter watching the stranger patiently, in anticipation of the meal which awaits him from the fragments shortly to be left by the departing visitors. It is curious that in this desert spot, where a few green weeds are the only vegetation, snails should abound, although they are not met with south of this locality in Egypt, not even along the cultivated banks of the river. On our way home we stop to examine the quarries of white limestone, and soon fill our pockets with a rich harvest of fossils: a small species of Crab (*Portunus leucodon*) is tolerably plentiful; univalves and bivalves of many kinds are abundant; and we meet with several of the saw-shaped spines of an Echinoderm (*Cidaris veronensis*), and, of course, quantities of Nummulites, which are the characteristic fossils of this formation. Yesterday we purchased of the Arabs several of the fine Miocene Echinoderms (*Clypeaster ægyptiacus*) which they always bring to the traveller at the Pyramids, and also a piece of white limestone filled with small Nummulites. Our dragoman, always anxious to explain every thing, told us that the builders of the Pyramids had been fed upon lentils, and that this was a piece of their bread made of that seed, but that time had hardened it into the stony substance which we then held in our hands. Although he tried hard to persuade us that he was right, we could not induce him to taste our specimens of nummulitic limestone.

Near the Tombs of the Caliphs, which we pass on our way to the town, we see numbers of the Egyptian Vulture (*Neophron percnopterus*), the natural scavengers of the Arabs outside the town, while the dogs perform that office within the gates. The Tombs of the Caliphs are very picturesque, each with its dome; they are built of red sandstone, which imparts to them such a sameness of colouring with the surrounding desert that it detracts somewhat from their real beauty. This want of variety in the colouring is the great drawback to Egyptian scenery.

February 10th.—Having got our supplies on board the dahabeah and laid in a good store of powder and shot, we weigh anchor and row out into the stream on our way down to Damietta. The crew sing loudly to a monotonous tune, accompanied by the darabouca, or native drum, while they keep time to the rowing of the oars, concluding each stanza or verse with a long-drawn shout; the dragoman meanwhile busies himself firing off his gun as fast as he can, which is his mode of saluting such towns or dahabeahs as we pass. Indeed a dragoman or any other native never misses an opportunity of making a noise when he has the chance. But upon this occasion our dragoman was not fortunate; for on ramming down a large piece of paper over the powder, the ramrod got fixed in the rusty barrel, which had probably not been cleaned since his last trip, and now, his native cautiousness coming to the fore, he calls up one of the servants to fire off his gun while he gets out of the way for fear of its bursting: the old weapon, however, stands the trial; and the servant, wishing to do all honour to the town, discharges the piece in that direction, and sends the ramrod flying—heaven knows where.

We have great satisfaction in feeling that we have begun the boat-trip, and that all our troubles in selecting a dragoman and bargaining are over for a time; and as our new home is clean and comfortable, with all our household gods around us and every one anxious to please, we feel how thoroughly enjoyable the life on our boat is, as we sit on deck under the cloudless heavens sparkling with innumerable stars, and watch the dark outline of the great city of the East which we are fast leaving behind us, while the crescent-shaped moon is rising over the mountains of the Mokattam. The nights, however, are chilly up to the end of February; so we do not long remain on deck, but retire to the cabin, where the dragoman is waiting to announce dinner.

Our dragoman is a native of Egypt. He wears the fez cap with the invariable yellow, red, and blue scarf tied round it in the form of a turban, a flowing black coat, in shape much resembling a dressing-gown, a long blue waistcoat, much embroidered with no end of useless little buttons, and lower down a pair of bags of the same material, through which his legs appear clothed in cotton stockings of matchless whiteness, terminating in black shoes with steel buckles. He is a fair specimen of the present god of the Nile, the dragoman, who is worshipped by the natives wherever he goes, on the chance of backsheesh, which, by the way, they seldom get for nothing. This peculiarly attired individual, owing to his long dress, curious squeaky voice, and the motherly care he takes of us, we nicknamed 'the Mother,' while Abdallah and Salem, the two trusty attendants, owing to their equally flowing robes, we called 'the Girls.' Abdallah, a Copt or Christian, is always most anxious to thrust his services upon us, and to keep Salem, whom he bullies, as much in the background as possible; and in this he is pretty successful, for he is the 'Mother's' favourite. He is not a very bright specimen, and hardly understands a word of English, while Salem speaks it tolerably fluently. The two 'Girls' differ in dress as well as in creed; for although both wear the red fez and red slippers with white socks, which never *will* keep up, Salem has a black coat and vest after the form of the 'Mother's,' with a yellow silk scarf tied round the waist, while Abdallah, over a similar long black waistcoat, wears a grey English shooting-coat. Both wear white bags, contrasting strongly with their brown legs, which are exposed from the knee downwards.

The dinners which our dragoman provided throughout the tour were excellent; indeed in this respect he exceeded the terms of the contract, which we had taken care to draw up very minutely, as this saves a great deal of trouble afterwards; for we suspect that a careless contract often leads dragomans to fancy that they can impose upon the traveller; and this is probably the reason why some parties disagree with them.

After dinner we go on deck again, where the 'Girls' bring us our long chibouques, which they have duly lighted for us, and our cups of coffee, which, after the true Turkish fashion, are extremely small, and contain the very essence of coffee, with a quarter of a cupful of dregs. This may appear unpleasant to the uninitiated; but one soon comes to appreciate the coffee in this fashion, while there is certainly none like it for flavour. A slight breeze having sprung up during dinner, the crew have laid aside their oars, and are now singing their strange wild and plaintive song, while one of them keeps time on the darabouka. This instrument consists of an earthen jar with a piece of parchment stretched over its wide mouth, The night is beautiful; the moon, which has now risen, casts its silvery light upon the rippling waters, and our white sail is filled with the soft breeze.

The 'Mother' now makes his appearance, and, after the usual salutation of the East, begins the conversation. "I hope you very good appetite," the way he always commences after dinner; "the crew play to show they much pleased." If this was a fact, I believe they were always pleased when they had nothing else to do. He then told us that we should soon have to anchor for the night, as we were approaching a bridge which is only opened at certain hours; and here the lights appear shining upon the water, and the dim outlines of several vessels are seen through the gloom. He had plenty of stories to tell us of the sport that was to be had, and drew our attention to the cry of the wildfowl, the ducks and geese, which we heard from time to time in the darkness; then he called up an Abyssinian servant, whom we christened Dango, as being something like his original name but rather more convenient. He was formerly a servant of Mr. Münzinger, the Consul at Massoua, had been through the Abyssinian campaign with our army, and was brought to Egypt, I believe, by Colonel Thesiger on his way home. He was extremely willing and obliging, and proved most useful on our shooting-expeditions; so, as I shall often have occasion to speak of him in my present narrative, I may as well take this opportunity of introducing him to the reader. To look at, one would say he is about thirty years of age—short and active, with a deep coppery complexion, a large mouth, a woolly head, and a small beard. He is dressed in a blue serge shooting-jacket and trousers with a broad white stripe down the side, a fez cap, and very dilapidated boots, which latter, by the way, were rather an encumbrance than otherwise, for he could walk better without them; he was, however, extremely proud of being their possessor, as I suppose he considered that they gave him an air of respectability, until about a week later, when they dissolved, like brown-paper, in a marsh, and left his feet bare. Thus ended these relics, which had probably been through the Abyssinian campaign.

We now come to our moorings for the night; and the

crew's work being over, they soon fall asleep, while we retire to the cabin to talk over our adventures.

February 11th.—We rise early, and after a cup of coffee start out for a couple of hours' shooting before breakfast. The cool fresh air is delicious; but the grass is very wet from the heavy dew, which glitters on the bright green herbage under the rays of the morning sun. We pass through a portion of the town on the western bank of the river, and then cross the latter by a bridge, where we soon come upon some pools and a half-dry canal, where we find wildfowl tolerably abundant. This canal being about eighty yards broad, the ducks avoid us by flying down the centre, so that we only get a few uncertain long shots at them; for they are too shy to allow us to stalk them; and, indeed, the ground throughout Egypt is very bad for that purpose, owing to the want of covert, the banks being of smooth mud from which the water has recently retired. However, we kill a few Shoveller, Pintail, and Pochard; but Teal most frequently come to the bag. Greenshanks are tolerably plentiful here, while, lower down, the Redshanks become most numerous. Whenever we find other game scarce we fall back on the Pigeons, for which Egypt is famous, as they are always welcome to the crew. The number of these birds, which live in a semidomesticated state, is quite marvellous. The natives in most of the villages build a second story to their houses, solely for the sake of these pigeons, which flock to them as soon as they are built; but they require that their houses should be kept more cleanly than the abodes of the natives; otherwise they leave for better quarters. What would an English farmer say to having these myriads of pigeons feeding on his land? Yet there is no denying that the Egyptian crops thrive well nevertheless; and their guano is there considered to more than compensate for the grain they eat, as this kind of manure is particularly valued for the cultivation of the sugar-cane.

Although the native gives himself so much trouble to keep a stock of these birds in the villages, none dispute the stranger's right to shoot as many of them as he pleases in the fields; and it certainly adds considerably to the pleasure of the Nile-trip always to feel oneself lord of the manor, with perfect liberty to shoot what we please and walk where we like, regardless of crops or boundaries. We are always welcomed by the native, who for the sake of seeing sport, which he thoroughly appreciates when he meets with a good shot, will go out of his way to point out some ducks which he has seen on a neighbouring pool, or will dash into the water after any bird that may have fallen in. I have often been much amused watching them hunt a wounded duck, which they will rarely fail to secure; for they are perfect adepts in the art of swimming.

As we were shooting round a village, the Sheik, or head man, came out to see the sport, and invited us to his house to take coffee, which is always ready, and acceptable any time of the day. Then there flocked around us all the rising generation of the village, and the women, in their long blue dresses, with their faces wrapped up in white cloths, only showing their bright black eyes, which they fix upon us—in admiration? No, rather in wonder why we have come there, and why we are dressed so differently from their own people.

On occasions like this, I have often fancied how much our position resembled that of our caged animals at home. We are the queer beasts, whose every action is watched, and who excite as much amusement out here as we feel when looking at "our poor relations," the monkeys, at the Zoological Gardens. Showing the natives the action of our breech-loaders and letting them look through our field-glasses never failed to excite the interest of the chief men of the company, who are seldom satisfied until they have had the gun in their own hands, and pinched their fingers in shutting it up. But it is time to be on the move again; so we make a rise and a salaam to the sheik, and, throwing a few coppers among the small boys, we proceed on our way, mutually pleased with our rencontre.

The Egyptian is certainly not a bad character. He may be poor and idle; but he will exert himself for the smallest coin, and is always willing to please; in fact, they are an extremely harmless people, although a dragoman never fails to impress one with the necessity of firing a shot or two on anchoring for the night, just by way of explaining to the natives, should there be any robbers among them, that the boat is armed. As an extra precaution, too, we have some of the natives from the village to guard the shore at night. This we look upon as a small tax upon travellers, rather than as a really necessary precaution; for the guards often sleep very soundly during the night, as we found on one occasion, when we went the rounds and saw the two guards fast asleep; so we took their guns away and brought them on board, as a testimony in the morning of their good behaviour.

We arrive at Beuha on the 13th, where we have to wait some hours ere they open the bridge over which the railway from Alexandria to Cairo crosses the Nile. As this proan extremely bad shooting-ground, we are not sorry when we can again get under way. The previous day, near Farshoum, I had some fair duck-shooting along a half-dry canal, which is always the best kind of place to get at the ducks; and there we saw a large flock of Avocets, the first I had met with; but they were too shy to let us approach within shot.

I shall now hurry on our journey, as the days on the Nile are spent in a very similar manner, while we float along the smooth surface of its waters. At Zitfeh I met with innumerable flocks of pigeons. With twelve cartridges I killed three dozen of them; but finding quantities of Turtle Doves, we devote our attention to them in preference, as they afford far better shots, and are excellent eating.

February 17th.—A strong northerly wind detains us at Shinibin; so we start out early, in hopes of walking to Lake Menzaleh. We first cross some flooded rice-fields, where we disturb immense flocks of Gulls and Terns, make a fair bag of Snipe and Golden Plover, and meet with vast quantities of Sandpipers of various species. Leaving the rice-fields we cross a heath, where our delighted eyes see what we imagine to be a large sheet of water in front of us, but which a ten minutes' walk proves to be nothing but a mirage. We are again de ceived in a similar manner; and this makes us somewhat doubtful when we really do see water; however, our minds are soon set at rest by a large flock of geese alighting with a splash upon what turns out to be an extensive shallow lake. Here we spend two or three hours rather unsuccessfully, as the ducks mostly keep out in the middle. Continuing a little further we find a succession of small ponds, but do not reach Menzaleh, and then return to our boat with a well-filled and varied bag.

To-day we first meet with the Ichneumon, a large species of the Polecat tribe. This beast was formerly held sacred by the Egyptians, to whom it rendered some service by devouring the eggs of the crocodile and killing snakes. It is now abundant in the Delta, but rare to the south of Cairo.

February 19th.—We arrive at a small village, about five miles by water from Damietta, where we remain for several days, as it is close to a reedy marsh, the best locality for snipe that we shot over in Egypt. Here one may kill forty or fifty couples of snipe in a day for a whole week without going over the same ground twice. However, I was not very successful the first day, owing to my having obtained a guide who told me that duck was in great abundance; consequently I reserved my fire for them, never having had a real good day's duck-shooting in Egypt. I must confess that my companion showed his sense in being contented with the snipe-shooting and in not following me on my wild-goose-chase. With my guide I plunged into the thick reeds, whence I could not see ten yards in front; here I waded, in mud up to my knees, for half an hour straight out towards the centre of the lake, and began to get very tired of seeing nothing, when up rose an old Bittern from its noonday slumbers; him I shot in hopes that the report might disturb some of the numerous waterfowl of which I had heard so much from my guide, but the existence of which I began to doubt. Save a few Marsh-Harriers, no birds were roused by the sound; consequently my temper began to fail me; so, after struggling on for some distance further and finding nothing but reeds, I turned about, and was heartily glad when I found myself once more on the snipe-ground, where I bagged ten couple in about half an hour. My spirits now rose again, so that I allowed myself once more to be beguiled into another search for duck. This time I started in a small boat made of reeds, and, passing through a narrow channel, got into the clear water in the centre of the lake. Again I was disappointed; not a bird was to be seen; but being out there, I determined to spend half an hour punting round the edge of the reeds, but all to no purpose; there were no wild-fowl, and again the serenity of my temper was disturbed. I could not, however, resist laughing at the explanation of my guide, as, laying his head upon his hand, and pointing with the other to the bottom of the lake, he told me that they were all asleep down there during the heat of the day, but that they would come up again in the evening. I heard afterwards, on good authority, that they do come to this lake in great numbers earlier in the season. Ducks are certainly extremely abundant in the neighbourhood; for that evening we saw what we at first took to be a thunder-cloud, but what proved to be an immense flock of wildfowl, and I saw similar flocks upon several occasions towards flight-time, but could never get within range.

The pretty White-tailed Plover, *Chettusia leucura*, though formerly considered rare, is abundant about this lake, as well as near Alexandria and in the Fayoom. Having beaten the greater part of the ground, we leave this place and stop at Damietta, where we dine with the Consul in the true Egyptian style. He lives in a large house surrounded by a garden fragrant with orange-blossoms and bright with gaily coloured flowers. The dinner consists of a great variety of dishes, chiefly minces, hashes, and vegetables of many kinds. Although, like a true Mahomedan, he does not drink wine himself, he does not impose the same restriction on his guest. We here meet an Italian who lives at Damietta; he is a very good sportsman, and accompanies us next day to show us the best shooting-ground.

The Consul provides us with horses equipped with velvet and gold saddle-cloths, which look rather out of character with our rough shooting-suits. We are taken to the same lake that we had been shooting around for the last week; we have, however, a pleasant day's sport, and collect a few Painted Snipe. We did not find many of these birds; but our Italian friend told us that they are often met with here, in flocks of twenty or thirty, when they are easily scattered, and will then lie close, like Jack Snipe, and are consequently easily shot; but they are very poor eating. He also told us that November and December are the best months for duck-shooting, when he has killed hundreds of them in their flight from Lake Menzaleh to this marsh.

On the 26th we leave Damietta, and return up the Nile with as little delay as possible, as the season is becoming late for ascending the river, and reach Cairo on the 1st of March. Finding that a new awning is required for the boat, we set the men to work at it, while we lay in fresh supplies and finish seeing the town. I was very fortunate in collecting birds during this three weeks' tour in the Delta, and obtained several species which we did not meet with later; so, as a guide to other ornithologists, I will give a short list of the birds which should be obtained during a similar tour, and which are not so likely to be met with higher up the Nile.

1. *Aquila imperialis*, Imperial Eagle.

2. *Circus æruginosus*, Marsh-Harrier, far more abundant in adult plumage in the Delta than elsewhere.

3. *Scops giu*, Scops Eared Owl, tolerably plentiful near Alexandria.

4. *Centropus ægyptius*, Egyptian Lark-heeled Cuckoo.

5. *Alcedo bengalensis*, Small Indian Kingfisher.

6. *Acrocephalus stentorius*, near Damietta in March and April.

7. *Calamodyta melanopogon.* In the same marsh through-the year.

8. *Chettusia leucura*, White-tailed Plover.

9. *Rhynchæa capensis*, Painted Snipe.

Bittern, Spotted Crake, many kinds of Ducks, Gulls, and Terns. Among the common English birds which are likely not to be met with south of the Delta, are the Blackbird, Robin, Stonechat, Linnet, Chaffinch, Goldfinch, Rook, Starling, Golden and Grey Plovers, and Water-Rail.

CHAPTER II.

THE GEOLOGY OF EGYPT.

I FEEL that some apology is due to the reader for the following chapter, in which I shall digress from the general purpose of this work to give a sketch of the geology of the country; for after having spent several months upon the great mudbank of Egypt, the Delta of the Nile, one may feel curious as to its formation and the aspect the country would have presented had the Nile been a clear and sparkling stream without an annual overflow. In that case how different would have been the scene! Egypt is a creation of the Nile; and not only does its trade depend in a great measure upon the river, but every cultivated spot owes its existence to the alluvium brought down by those fertilizing waters. Without this sediment in the Nile there would be an uninhabitable sandy desert where a fruitful country, teeming with trade and civilization, has now existed for thousands of years; for Egypt, as we see it, is nothing but a thin sheet of alluvium, spread by the Nile over an arid tract in the course of countless ages. This alluvial soil varies greatly in thickness in different parts of the valley; but its general appearance and chemical properties are much the same everywhere. The larger portion of this soil is derived from the great Nile-tributaries, more especially from Abyssinia, which is drained by the Atbara and Blue Nile, which join the main stream at Damer and Khartoum respectively. By far the greater mass of the soil brought down by the river is deposited towards its present mouth, and forms the Delta. Now the real Delta of the Nile is that flat triangular portion of Egypt having for its apex Memphis, more than one hundaed miles from the sea, and its base formed by a coast-line two hundred miles in length, Port Saïd being at its eastern angle; so that the real Delta contains an area of one hundred square miles, while that portion of Lower Egypt commonly known as the Delta, has Cairo at the apex of the triangle, and is bounded on the east by the Damietta and on the west by the Rosetta branches of the Nile, allowing only an extent of ninety miles for its base or coast-line; so that the portion usually spoken of as the Delta is not half the real Delta of the Nile.

The rate of deposit and the time required for the formation of the Delta must be purely hypothetical, as all the bones and shells which have been discovered are similar to those now existing in the Nile or living on its banks; and as no pit has been sunk below the sea-level, the absence of marine shells in these deposits is not surprising; and probably even if such a pit were sunk, it would pass through river-alluvium for a considerable depth below the sea-level, as has almost invariably proved to be the case when like experiments have been conducted in other Deltas. Besides, we have evidence that the Delta has been slowly sinking for a considerable time, as we already remarked when we visited "Cleopatra's Baths," which are now below the level of the sea; and beneath the waters of Lake Menzaleh may be seen the banks of some ancient arm of the Nile, as well as the ruins of a town.

The rate of yearly deposit is undoubtedly very small; and

this probably accounts for the great absence of lamination in the alluvium; for the successive deposits would naturally become mixed by cultivation, the boring of insects, and the natural cracking of the mud as it dries, together with the drifting of the particles by the wind.

We know that the sea once washed the foot of the rocks on which the Pyramids of Sakkara stand, the bases of which are now bathed by the inundations of the Nile from seventy to eighty feet above the Mediterranean; but when we attempt to carry back our ideas to such a remote period, we are lost in the contemplation of so vast an interval of time during which the Nile has deposited the hundred square miles of soil which now form its true Delta. Besides the great volume of alluvium brought down from the river-sources, there is vast degradation taking place along its course; for the atmosphere acts very considerably in crumbling the sandstone; and the wind, carrying these particles along, adds to the Nile-deposit, forming sandbanks in the river, which are now added to and then swept away again by some slight alteration in the currents; and, owing to the power of the wind to drift sand, the physical aspect of Nubia is constantly changing. This is probably the great source from which the sandy particles in the Nile-deposit are derived, while the clayey portions are mostly brought down from Abyssinia. In Nubia we can trace the effects of the tremendous scouring which the country has undergone, at one time or another, in the torrent-beds and deep valleys of denudation which are cut through the horizontal strata. The heavy storms which occasionally break over the country bear a large amount of strata into the river.

The Nile, like other rivers, has often shifted its course, as is shown by the presence of beds of alluvium many feet above the level of the present high Nile: that it has changed its bed and altered its elevation even within the historical period, is evident from marks left by the swollen river on monuments both in Egypt and Nubia. Close to the famous rock temple of Aboo Simbel is a small temple, where at the present time the Nile, when high, washes the door-sill and the legs of a seated figure. At Kom Ombo, twenty-five miles north of Assouan, the old temple is built on a heap of alluvium, which is now being rapidly undermined, while shallows and sandbanks are being formed on the opposite side of the river. At Silsilis the river has changed considerably within the historical period, and is still encroaching on the left bank. Further north, in a small grotto, the high Nile rises above the threshhold, and washes a set of river-gods up to their necks. While throughout Egypt the Nile appears to rise higher now than it did formerly, in Ethiopia it has sunk; for at Semneh, thirty-five miles south of Wady Halfeh, just beneath the eastern temple, there are some early hieroglyphic inscriptions, recording the rise of the Nile during the reign of Amun-ni-he III., about 2000 B.C., from which we learn that in those days it rose considerably higher at this spot than it does at present.

The present fall of the Nile below the First Cataract is five inches in the mile, or 300 feet from Assouan to Alexandria; but it must have been greater formerly, before the formation of the Delta, as the Mediterranean then extended inland as far as Memphis, forming a bay or gulf 100 miles in length; and the Nile must have been sixty feet lower at that point than it now is, *i.e.* at the level of the sea. The force of the Nile-current must therefore have been stronger formerly than it is at present, and would consequently have swept nearly all the silt below the first impediment in the river into the sea, so that the extension of the Delta must have been more rapid then than in the present day. As the Delta increased, the rapidity of the stream decreased, so that much of the mud, instead of being cast into the sea, would be deposited along the river-bed, the sluggish stream having lost the power to drive it forward; and in this manner the bed of the river has gradually been raised, so that at Memphis it is now sixty feet above the level of the sea. This variation in the level of the river-bed, and consequent change in the force of the stream, must have distributed the sediment very unevenly over the Delta. But there is a more powerful reason for its uneven distribution, which arises from the manner in which Deltas are formed*.

On coming into contact with the sea the running water of the river is checked, and the earthy matter it contains settles down to the bottom, the larger particles falling near the river-mouth, while the finer ones, which take longer to subside, are carried further out to sea; and thus, in course of time, a mud-bank of a certain extent is raised, until it becomes almost dry at low tide. Through this the river shapes its bed, gradually embanking itself; for, as it overflows its channel it comes into contact with the still sheet of water which covers this low alluvial flat, and the running water thus checked is forced to deposit its silt along the junction with the still water. By slowly depositing mud along its course the river gradually raises its bed, until the body of its waters is higher than the neighbouring swamp; it then bursts its banks, and flows

* See Hugh Falconer on the formation of Deltas, 'Quarterly Journal of the Geological Society,' 1865, vol. xxi. p. 372.

along the lowest level, and, repeating the same process, fills up that depression, and forms a new bed again in another part, thus continuing to raise new beds, for itself in the lowest part of the land through which it flows. After a long cycle of years it may come again to that channel which it first left, which will probably not have risen one foot, while the neighbouring country may have risen twenty or thirty feet.

Thus we see that rivers in alluvial soils, especially in Deltas, have a tendency to raise their banks and confine themselves to their beds for an indefinite time, until accident bursts their bounds; so that any chronological conclusions founded upon such data must be very fallacious, whether derived from borings into the strata or from calculations based upon mere superficial deposits.

We may sum up our knowledge relating to the alluvial deposit of the Nile, and the alterations which have taken place in the bed of the river, under the following heads:—

1. The land is slowly sinking in Lower Egypt.

2. No very marked change has taken place in the bed of the river in historical times.

3. The river is always slightly shifting its bed.

4. The Nile, within the historical period, has risen to a different height at places from that to which it rises at the present day.

5. The Nile was formerly a more rapid river.

6. All bones and shells found in the alluvium may be referred to species now inhabiting the Nile-valley.

7. No marine shells have been discovered in the alluvium of the Nile.

8. No chronological evidence can be drawn from the thickness of the beds of alluvium.

In order to give a slight idea of the geological formation of Egypt and Nubia up to the Second Cataract, and also to indicate whence the ancient Egyptians procured the granite and greenstone for their obelisks and statues, as well as to show the general distribution throughout the country of that splendid white limestone on which they executed some of their finest carving, I shall give a short sketch of the formations which contain them, with their general localities; for by understanding the geology of a country we add considerably to our knowledge of its physical geography. These rocks may be conveniently divided, for our present consideration, according to their mineralogical characters, into four distinct groups, which I shall enumerate in their order of superposition, beginning with the most recent.

1. *Alluvium of the Nile.*—This forms the entire Delta, and extends in a thin layer over all the cultivated land of Egypt and Nubia, and is generally bounded on either bank by cliffs. Large tracts towards its edges have in many places been covered over by the sand borne from the deserts, and are no longer cultivated. This alluvial soil may often be traced at a considerable distance from the river by the nodules of "natron" (a species of travertine) which are met with on the desert sand wherever it overlies an ancient deposit of the Nile. The alluvium consists of a mixture of sand and clay, and is occasionally, though rarely, intersected by thin beds of "natron," of the appearance of white limestone.

2. *Sandstone.*—This formation overlies the limestone rocks both in Egypt and Nubia. At Silsilis it shows itself in considerable thickness, and has here been largely quarried by the ancient Egyptians. It imparts at this part of the Nile-valley a wilder character to the scenery than lower down the

river. The sandstone varies considerably in itself, its lower strata often forming a coarse conglomerate, and varies in colour from deep red to green and yellow, and is generally darker than the sand upon the desert, this being probably due to the colouring-matter having been more easily decomposed and washed away than the pink and white grains of silica. This formation appears chiefly, if not entirely, to belong to the Miocene period; and the deserts on each side of the Nile are, no doubt, due solely to its decomposition. I believe it to be erroneous to suppose that the sea left the sand of the desert as we now behold it, but that it was formerly a sandstone, its particles being cemented together by the same materials as that which we now see forming the "Red Mountain," near Cairo, and the thick formation at Silsilis, and that the loose sand of the desert has been formed by its disintegration by atmospheric action; for we cannot study these strata without frequently meeting with examples of recent degradation going on upon a large scale; and when we consider the vast time during which the atmosphere has been acting upon these strata, we need not be surprised at the extent of its ravages.

3. *Limestone.*—This is throughout of an extremely pure whiteness, and is first met with in the mountains of Nummulitic limestone near Cairo, and extends throughout the whole of Egypt in remarkably flat-topped ranges, forming at places steep perpendicular cliffs down to the water's edge, as at Gebel e' Tayr and Gebel Aboofayda, but is driven back inland at Silsilis by the sandstone strata, while in Nubia, near the river, it is only met with in detached masses forming outlying hills. The desert on each side of the Nile is generally bounded by steep cliffs; for the cultivated land of Egypt

lies in the great rent in the limestone formation hollowed out by the Nile waters, and which averages, from Cairo to Assouan, five or six miles in breadth. Such is the wealthy land of Egypt; for the desert is only a home for the Gazelle and the Vulture.

4. *Crystalline rocks.*—These are not met with until we reach Assouan; but there they are seen in vast masses hemming in the river on all sides at the First Cataract. Here the scenery changes from the fruitful land of fertile Egypt into the bleak and barren realms where the huge granite rocks rise in stately grandeur around the struggling waters of the Nile as they force their way through the narrow channels of the Cataract. The granite rocks bind the river so closely on either side throughout its course between the First and Second Cataracts, that they leave but a slight margin on its banks for cultivation in Nubia, which country is almost entirely composed of these rocks, with here and there a limestone mountain, the whole surmounted by the sandstone strata, which has been much worn away, and in some parts almost entirely decomposed into loose sand, forming in many places "dunes."

The crystalline rocks are of two kinds, viz. a rich pink granite, by far the most abundant, and "greenstone," which forms dykes through it. These dykes are well exhibited at the First Cataract, and appear to run very constantly from east to west, owing to their being more easily decomposed than the surrounding granite; the water-courses of the Cataract almost invariably follow their directions. They show the line of very ancient prehistoric volcanic action in a country which appears ever since to have remained remarkably undisturbed by subterranean fires; for, except at the junction of these crystalline rocks with the superincumbent stratified formations, we find a great absence of all fissures, rents, and faults, except such as have evidently been formed by atmospheric causes; and the stratified rocks throughout Egypt and Nubia being remarkably horizontal, we are led to believe that they rose slowly without any very marked local volcanic action.

The atmospheric causes have had a far greater power in decomposing the strata than one would expect to find in such dry countries. Rain does occasionally fall, though rarely, but at such times generally in tremendous downfalls, as testified by the ravines and deep torrent-beds, which are by no means uncommon in the limestone strata, as, for instance, the valley by which we approach the "Tombs of the Kings" at Thebes.

The desert is constantly encroaching upon the cultivated land; and this is especially the case in Nubia, where the inhabitants have become scarce by emigration to the busier parts of Egypt; for arable land on the confines of the desert, if left alone for a few years, gets covered up by drift sand, and becomes barren and useless, so that it cannot again be cultivated without great labour.

Besides the formations above enumerated, there are two minor ones, parts of the great freshwater deposit of the Nile, which deserve special notice.

1. *Natron or Kunkur.*—A species of travertine, composed of lime in hard concretionary masses, or perhaps more often tufaceous and nodular. It is formed by the action of the air upon the chemical constituents of the alluvium; and its presence, as already mentioned, on many parts of the desert near the river indicates an alluvial subsoil, and testifies to the encroachment of the desert upon the cultivated land.

2. *A fine clay*, which is found chiefly in caves only accessible to the river-water at high tide. This might naturally be expected to contain bones and throw some further light upon our knowledge of the animals which inhabited the country at a former period, as it would certainly do in a damper climate; but, owing to the dryness of the atmosphere, the bones no doubt decompose before they can become buried in these beds, which must take a long time in forming, as they are not assisted by any dropping from the ceilings, but are entirely composed of the fine mud brought there during the short period of high Nile. This clay is extremely useful, being employed for the manufacture of the "goulos," or water-bottles, so much used in Egypt.

CHAPTER III.

FROM CAIRO TO ASSOUAN.

The regular tour by dahabeah up the Nile is by far the most pleasant way of seeing Egypt, as it is free from all the annoyances of waiting for trains or camels, attendant upon a tent-life in a country where there are no hotels save at Alexandria, Cairo, Suez, and Port Saïd: and it is really enjoyable; for, when once the contract has been signed, there are no further troubles in store, unless one has been exceptionally unlucky in the choice of a dragoman. All goes smoothly; the dahabeah, roomy and clean after one's own choice, is extremely comfortable, and all our requirements are at hand The progress may be slow; but, as we are constantly advancing, it conquers distance, while the panorama of Egypt unfolds itself before us, ever changing, and, throughout our course, studded with ruins of a bygone race which cannot fail to excite the admiration and interest of all who see them.

First we pass the Pyramids of Geezeh, Sakkara, and Dashoor; one of these, known as the pyramid of Myccrinus, or Menkera, is said to have been built by a woman who, on account of her great beauty, was called Rhodopis, or the rosy-cheeked one, and who became Queen of Egypt. Moore has availed himself of a legend connected with this Pyramid in his 'Melodies':—

"Fair Rhodope, as story tells,
The bright unearthly nymph who dwells
'Mid sunless gold and jewels hid,
The Lady of the Pyramid."

This legend tells of a marvellously lovely woman, who might be seen sitting naked on the summit of the pyramid; her excessive beauty was such that she drove the wanderers in the desert mad when they beheld her.

Another legend of this fair Rhodopis, as told in Strabo's time, seems like the origin of the story of Cinderella. A slave at the time, she went one morning to bathe in the Nile, leaving her slippers on the bank, when either an eagle or the wind, according to different versions, carried them away and dropped them at the feet of the king, who was at the moment on his throne of justice in the market-place at Memphis. He was so enchanted with the tiny slippers, that he would not rest until he discovered their owner, who so well pleased him that he made her his queen.

Landing at Memphis, the ancient capital of this rich and fertile country, but whose site is hardly to be traced at the present day, we ride off to the desert to visit the Serapeum, or tombs of the sacred Bulls. The massiveness of the sarcophagi in which these animals were interred with all pomp, cut out of solid granite and brought many hundred miles from the quarries of Assouan, cannot fail to impress the traveller with the durability which was the great aim of all the ancient Egyptian monuments. Near the Serapeum is a small temple, where the sculpture is admirably cut; it is more beautifully executed than any that one sees higher up the Nile, but is not so ancient as most of the temples. Hence to Golosanch the scenery presents very little variety, the western bank being highly cultivated and dotted at short intervals with mud villages, invariably surrounded by groups of palms and sont trees, while beyond lies the Libyan desert, on the borders of which stand the many pyramids which impart such a striking character to the scenery; on the eastern bank the white, flat-topped range of hills separate the cultivated land from the Arabian desert within a couple of miles from the river's bank. Though for many miles the antiquarian and sightseer will meet but little to attract his attention, the sportsman will find this by no means a bad part of the river for Ducks, Geese, and Sandgrouse or Snipe in the winter, and for Quail after the middle of March. Near Golosaneh there are some very good places for Geese and the larger birds, such as Pelicans, Cranes, &c.; while in the rough halfa grass, which covers much of the land near that town, and on the island opposite, Sandgrouse are at times extremely plentiful.

On passing Golosaneh, after a small bend in the river, we come to Gebel e' Tayr, where there is a Coptic convent, notorious in former times for the infamous trade carried on there in preparing guardians of the harems. Here the rocks rise precipitously from the water's edge, presenting a scene of wild grandeur, which, when coloured by the setting sun, and softened down by the mellow tints of the western sky, forms a most impressive landscape, while the rich verdure of the opposite bank contrasts well with the bleakness of these cliffs. The inhabitants of the convent are lithe, well-built men, and wonderfully active in the water; they swim off to the passing vessels to ask for backsheesh, making the Christian religion which they profess a plea for charity. A few days later we pass Minieh, the chief town of Middle

Egypt; it is of considerable size, possesses a large sugar-factory, and has direct communication with Cairo by rail. On the following day we reach Beni Hassan, where the small rock-temples are well worth visiting; for on their walls are depicted incidents illustrative of the people who formerly dwelt in the country; among the subjects, their games, with wrestlers in a variety of attitudes, and many of the common birds of Egypt are most faithfully delineated.

At Sioot we stop to see the "girls make dance," as our dragoman expressed it. This performance, unlike any European dance, does not consist of any peculiar step, but of a sort of shivering motion of the body from the hips upwards, which, while it hardly reaches the graceful, borders rather closely on what strict mortals might call the indecent. It is generally danced by two at a time, both women dressed in loose trousers of blue or white, or of some striped material tied round the ankles, and thin white shirts cut rather low; over this is worn a jacket, the sleeves generally tight, but cut up from the wrist to the elbow, ornamented with numerous small gold buttons; on their heads they wear a small kind of Fez cap thickly covered with strings of gold coins, and round the neck more strings of gold coins; they have numerous rings of silver or gold round their wrists and ankles, and large silver rings through their ears. Their nails are stained red with henneh, the invariable custom of women in Egypt, their eyelids are blackened, and their chins, foreheads, and cheeks, are generally marked with the "elegant tattoo" in blue. To their middle fingers and thumbs are attached small silver cymbals, or castanets, to accompany their dance. The doors being shut, we sit round on the divans to see the performance; the matron of the establishment plays or, rather, beats time on the darabouca; and some other native plays on a reed-pipe, or else sings. The girls are given tumblers of araki (a very strong liquor), to add spirit to their dance, and then they begin, walking with small steps towards each other, waving their arms over their heads, and quivering all the time. Such a dance is too simple for a description to give much idea of it; it is wild and uncivilized-looking, and, when properly danced, is not devoid of attraction. The figures of the women, which are extremely fine, show a suppleness and activity which one cannot fail to admire; and occasionally one meets with some very handsome faces among the dark-skinned professional dancers, some of whom come from Nubia and Ethiopia, and many from Abyssinia.

Setting sail again from Sioot, we find the ever tortuous course of the river delays us much; for, although we sail freely up the first reach, the wind is taken out of our sails by the next bend, up which we have to tack; thus it happens that we are rarely able to sail for many consecutive hours; and consequently the average pace is very slow, and one can generally keep up with the boat while shooting along the bank.

Near Soohag there are two large buildings in the mountains, about seven miles from the town, known as the White and Red Convents, which, though generally neglected, are worthy of a visit; and the ornithologist should make the excursion if he is desirous of obtaining *Bubo ascalaphus*, or *Corvus umbrinus*. Here, at Soohăg, begins the Bahr Yoosef, the waters of which fertilize the Fayoom some 250 miles distant. As we ascend the river, we come to the perpendicular rocks of Gebel Aboofayda, which rise precipitously out of the water: this is a good locality for meeting with the Crocodile; and here, during my last tour, Lord Ducie killed one, which, on dissection, proved to contain in its stomach all the ornaments of a native child.

At Dendera there is a large wood of dhoum palms and other trees, rendering it a good locality for the collector; in fact, the whole way from Dendera to the First Cataract I consider the best part of Egypt for collecting all kinds of birds except Gulls and Waterfowl. At Thebes we find many other dahabeahs moored in front of the ruins of Luxor. The front of the temple, with its huge columns, now forms the face of the Consul's house, a Consul of all nations, speaking good English. A few miles south of Thebes, on the west bank, towards Erment, there is a good lake for Snipe and Waders, which, however, becomes dried up by the middle of March. Near El Kab, on the shore, are plenty of water-birds; and this is the only place in Egypt at which I met with the Glossy Ibis; in the mountains I found also *Saxicola monacha*, a rather rare species of Chat, abundant. About four miles inland from Edfoo there are two or three ponds frequented by wildfowl. At Gebel Silsilis the river is hemmed in on both sides by steep sandstone-rocks; and the whole scenery becomes wilder and more rocky between this and the First Cataract. Some seven or eight miles below Kom Ombo there is a large tract covered with halfa grass, which affords good Sand-grouse- and Quail-shooting.

At Assouan we first meet with the granite rocks which extend throughout Nubia from the First to the Second Cataract, changing the scenery from the wide fertile valley, bounded by flat-topped limestone ridges, into the contracted river, hemmed in by irregular masses of granite and greenstone, scantily bordered with vegetation along its banks. The scenery of this part of the Nile is more grand and picturesque; from Assouan to Philæ it is studded with islands, which divide it into numerous channels; and its waters, which we have travelled on so smoothly for 700 miles, here become turbulent and broken as they rush through the very narrow channels, and surge over the half-sunken rocks which bar their headlong course: this is the First Cataract, a series of rapids extending over about three miles, from the south of the island of Sehayl up to within two miles of the island of Philæ. The large island of Elephantine and that of Sehayl both lie below the Cataract; a few palm and sont trees are scattered over them; and the latter island is a good locality for obtaining *Crateropus acaciæ,* which I found breeding there in the beginning of April. Near the most turbulent part of the rapids is to be procured a Black-and-White Wagtail (*Motacilla vidua*): a small colony exists here; and the species is not to be found elsewhere in Egypt. Although it has chosen so wild a scene for its habitation, it is a sociable bird, frequently flitting by the side of, or alighting on, the dahabeah during its passage up the Cataract. There are a few other species of small birds to be remarked in this neighbourhood; on the islands several kinds of Warblers are abundant, among which I found *Sylvia Rüppellii* on the one opposite Philæ, and *Sylvia melanocephala* most abundant on the island of Sehayl. On the mainland *Saxicola leucopygia* is plentiful, the black-headed specimens being the most commonly seen, while in Nubia the white-headed ones are most frequent; but I shall speak of this again in my description of the species. At Assouan the two closely allied species of Desert-Lark, *Ammomanes isabellina* and *A. fraterculus,* are almost equally common, this being, as it were, the southern limit of the former and the northern limit of the latter; or, more correctly, I should say, from my own experience, that I found the former most abundant to the north, while I met with none but *A. fraterculus* to the south. On our return journey, about the 20th of April, I found *Turtur Sharpei* breeding in great abundance on the island of Schayl, where I frequently procured its nest in the low sont bushes, generally with young birds; it is never placed on the ground, as is frequently the case with *T. senegalensis*.

I shall pass rapidly over my Nubian experiences, as I only spent a fortnight between the First and Second Cataracts, and there is no very great variety of large birds on this part of the Nile; indeed there is no big game for the sportsman. On the 6th of April I first met with the beautiful yellow-breasted Sunbird, *Nectarinia metallica*, the most thoroughly tropical form I came across during my tour; this lovely little bird is by no means uncommon here in April, when it had evidently only just arrived from its winter quarters; probably later it descends the Nile below the First Cataract, as I found it on the 14th within twenty miles of Philæ. Here, in April, I first saw the Common Swallow and House-Martin descending the Nile in abundance. Along the banks I met with *Motacilla melanocephala* and *M. flava* in numerous large flocks, never mixed; and although I shot a great number of the latter, I never came across a single specimen of the typical *M. cinereocapilla* among them, although this latter bird was also abundant in more scattered flocks. Among the other common small birds, *Saxicola leucopygia* is perhaps the most plentiful; *Ammomanes fraterculus*, *Aëdon galactodes*, *Anthus campestris*, *A. arboreus*, and *Hypolais elæica* are very abundant. Among the birds of prey we met with *Circaëtus gallicus*, *Falco lanarius*, *F. æsalon*, and *F. tinnunculus*, *Circus æruginosus*, and *C. pal-*

lidus; among the Waders, *Ciconia alba*, *C. nigra*, *Numenius arcuatus*, *Herodias garzetta*, *Himantopus candidus*, *Totanus stagnatilis*, *T. ochropus*, and *Œdicnemus crepitans*. Occasionally we saw *Crateropus acaciæ* in small parties of three or four; and at Wady Halfa is to be found *Pycnonotus arsinoë*. Among the Gulls we frequently saw flocks of a large species, probably the Mediterranean Herring-Gull, *Larus leucophæus*; and we shot the Lesser Black-headed Gull, *L. fuscus*, and the Scissor-bill, *Rhynchops flavirostris*, travelling northwards down the Nile towards the end of April. Nubia, for the ordinary Nile-tourist, has many charms: the scenery is finer, and the air purer and fresher than lower down; there is also here a marvellous absence of fleas and flies.

On our return-journey we found *Rhynchops flavirostris* evidently preparing to breed, towards the end of April, on the sandbanks near Kom Ombo and Erment. On the 20th of April we first met with the Common Turtledove (*Turtur auritus*) at Edfoo; it had just arrived in the country, and soon became extremely abundant; six days later we found the Roller and Oriole just arrived from their winter quarters, and on the same day shot the only specimen of *Botaurus minutus* which we met with in Egypt, at Esné. It is an interesting sight to watch the vast flights of certain birds wending their way north, on their annual migration. Towards the end of March and beginning of April we saw many of the sandbanks literally whitened by dense flocks of White Storks; and one evening such an immense flight of Pelicans came streaming down the river, that they must have taken nearly half an hour to pass our boat in one continued unbroken cloud, although we kept up a steady fire at them as they came over our heads about forty yards high. We noticed upon several successive evenings, towards sunset, a flock of *Larus fuscus* pass our boat: if it was the same flock on each occasion, they would appear to migrate very slowly; for we were only doing about ten miles a day at the time. At the First Cataract we met with *Glareola pratincola* on the 14th of April, likewise descending the Nile in great numbers.

This ends my journal on the Nile; and I next give a rough sketch of my excursion into the Fayoom.

CHAPTER IV.

THE FAYOOM.

I MUST now beg my readers to accompany me, under other escort, but at a similar season of the year, to the Fayoom, where I intend to make a tour under canvas, and afterwards proceed to the Delta.

My present dragoman is very different to our friend of former chapters. He is a Syrian, young, good-looking, and active, by name Henry Bousitil, British subject, and dressed in English style,—a Norfolk shirt and knickerbockers, but with a fez cap, bound round with the bright yellow silk scarf. He was with the British army throughout the Abyssinian campaign, and afterwards in the Shangallah country, with Mr. Powell, when in search of his murdered brother's remains. He is of a more warlike disposition than the dear quiet old man of my former tour, and is rarely without two revolvers stuck in his belt. Our friend Dango still accompanies us, but instead of the 'Girls,' we have got a sharp-looking Maltese servant, Luici, with a very decided squint, less bright than he looks, but honest, willing, and a good hand at pitching a tent. Having thus introduced my staff, let us proceed on our journey.

February 15th.—After an early breakfast I leave the New Oriental Hotel at Cairo, and drive off with my dragoman. We cross the river to the Geezeh station, where we find the baggage in a van, under the escort of Luici and Dango. The train, which should have started at 9 o'clock, gets off about 10, and, after going very slowly for two hours, stops at El Wasteh (Zowyeh), the junction for the Fayoom. Here we have to wait for the up-train from Minieh, which may arrive at any moment, but is, of course, late; so that we do not start again until 4.30 P.M., thus reaching Medineh el Fayoom, the capital of the district, at 6 P.M., when we pitch our camp at once close to the station.

The camp consists of a large tent for myself, and a smaller one to cook in. The baggage is certainly bulky and heavy, the canteen and stores taking up much room, while the ammunition adds considerably to the weight; but I expect to fire the latter away pretty freely during the month I purpose spending in the Fayoom. This is a strange part of Egypt, being detached from the cultivated valley of the Nile by the desert, which surrounds it on all sides. Railway communication is at times stopped by the drifting of the sand; and thus we are, as it were, on an island of fertility, of very considerable extent, surrounded by a sea of sand. In the north-west portion of this fertile tract lies the brackish lake of Birket el Korn, about five miles wide by thirty long. It has been encroaching of late years upon the fertile land to the south and upon the desert to the north; but in former times it evidently spread much further into the desert than it now does, as testified by the natron and freshwater shells which are spread over the latter close up to some ruins, which now stand about two miles from the lake. The Fayoom is supplied with water from the Bahr Yoosef, a small offshoot of the Nile, to which this large fertile tract owes its existence.

February 16th.—Being impatient to get to work, I start at an early hour, with Dango and a guide, from Medineh for the Great Lake, Birket el Korn, which is some fifteen miles distant, as the crow flies. The guide takes me to the sugar-factory of Shebooksi, at Farocha, a village some two miles from the lake; and as I soon shoot out my cartridges at Duck and Snipe, and get, without difficulty, within shot of a large flock of Geese, I am favourably impressed with my prospects. On returning to the factory, as my dragoman has not turned up, I look after quarters for myself, and meet with the greatest civility from the French engineers, who put me up for the night; and in their company I spend a very pleasant evening. They doubt my dragoman getting camels, as they are all seized by the Government for the transport of sugar-cane: and their doubts are realized; for about 9 o'clock he arrives by train with the baggage, so that the camp is pitched and ready by an early hour on the following morning. The factory is on a large scale, but cannot all be worked for want of a sufficient supply of the cane, although all the camels of the Fayoom are seized by Government to bring it in from the fields, except those belonging to the Bedouin Arabs, who resist this tax. The Government intends to construct another sugar-factory in the Fayoom, which appears premature, as they have not yet enough cane to keep one going; they are, however, preparing more ground for its cultivation. The cultivated part of the Fayoom is very flat, and has but few trees. The towns are two miles distant from the lake at this season; but the Bedouin Arabs establish colonies of reed sheds at frequent intervals near the shore, wherever the ground has dried sufficiently, and a stream of good water renders it a suitable spot.

I was decidedly late in visiting the Fayoom for sport. I believe the best season would be from October to the end of January; for in February the Snipe and Duck are leaving, while the Quail have not yet arrived; so that I was satisfied to get an average of ten head of waterfowl, chiefly Teal, in a day, with occasionally a fair bag of Snipe. The latter were uncertain, as I only found a few good places for them; but I met with a liberal supply of odd birds, such as Pelicans, Cormorants, Herons, Spoonbills, &c., and some rather good hare-shooting among the bushes in the more desert parts. My chief object being to collect the different birds of Egypt, I was not disappointed, as I got many species which I had never met with in other parts of the country.

Any one visiting this lake for sport should not fail to bring with him a small shallow boat, and be prepared for a certain amount of cold, as even up to the end of February the nights are unpleasantly chilly. The banks are mostly open and bare, even on the cultivated side, while on the opposite side the desert comes down to the water's edge; so that all the duck-shooting is to be obtained by rowing among the thick, but generally narrow, strips of reeds, which extend for some distance out into the lake. The water among these reeds is often from eight to ten feet deep; and as they rise high above the surface, it shows to what a size the reeds grow out here. On the desert side I have had some good Cormorant-shooting, killing twenty one evening in about two hours, on their flight across a narrow strip of land. The most abundant Duck on the lake is *Nyroca leucophthalma*, the Ferruginous Duck, which may be seen in immense numbers far out on the open water; but it was some time before I could obtain a specimen, as they are extremely watchful, except when they happen to come singly among the reeds to feed; when a large flock of them rises with their running kind of flight, like a Coot, the noise may be heard for miles. The Purple Gallinule, *Porphyrio hyacinthina*, is most plentiful on the desert side, where it may generally be found sitting up in the high reeds; and here, too, the Purple Heron is very common, and by no means shy, always frequenting the thick reeds, and never exposing itself on the open desert like the Common Heron. I also found the Little Cormorant abundant, as well as the fine Great Blackheaded-Gull, *Larus ichthyaëtus*, and saw the Great White Heron and Great Crested Grebe, but was unable to procure specimens. Among the small waders I found *Totanus stagnatilis*, *Ægialitis pecuarius*, *Chettusia Villotæi*, and *Limosa melanura* very abundant; and among the birds of prey, *Aquila nævia*, *Pandion haliaëtus*, and *Buteo ferox* plentiful, and less shy than on the Nile.

February 20th.—Owing to the insects being numerous and of a disagreeable kind, we move into a nice green field, where we are not destined, however, to remain long; for on the following day the embankment of the Bahr Yoosef gives way, and floods the country between the sugar-factory and the lake. The parched soil absorbs it so fast, that the inundation approaches us but slowly; and my dragoman being prompt in turning out an Arab village, we managed to get all our things in safety to an embankment on the border of the lake, while the spot where our tent had been an hour before became a sheet of water knee-deep. Darkness having set in before our move, I hastened to the embankment to select a spot and light a fire to guide the others to me. As the night was delicious, twinkling with innumerable stars, this little excitement was rather pleasant than otherwise; for although my regular dinner was swallowed up by the Bahr Yoosef, I fared pretty well upon such dishes as were brought in at odd intervals with other things, beginning with a custard-pudding, which I ate with an *impromptu* spoon made out of a reed. My only uneasiness was, when I heard the water wash against the embankment, whether it would rise high enough to disturb us again: it did not do so, however; for there being a great number of natives at the factory, they managed to repair the broken embankment in a few hours, and so stop further mischief. We decide to start early the following morning, to take up a position more to the eastward; so the dragoman goes to get the necessary order from the authorities, who promise to let us have camels whenever we wished. They do not, however, arrive till 3 P.M., although I have been waiting since 10 A.M.; consequently, owing to the crookedness of the paths, which in Egypt never go straight for twenty yards, we are only about five miles, as the crow flies, from the factory when night sets in, and compels us to stop close to an Arab village of some half-dozen mud huts, a population of a score or so of natives, and at least as many dogs. The latter, detecting the stranger through the canvas of the tent, make a raid upon me, trying hard to get through the canvas; and night is made hideous by their howls, in spite of the efforts of Dango and the dragoman, the former armed with a big stick, the latter with his revolvers, to quell the disturbance. Determined not to spend another night here, I rise with the sun, and set out to explore the country, and find a bushy spot, the best place for hares I have yet come across. They are lean, deformed-looking animals, all legs and ears; for the latter are an exaggeration of those of our own species, and are exactly represented on the ancient hieroglyphics. I have also some rather better duck-shooting to-day, with a moderate sprinkling of Snipe and Quail; so, having selected a suitable spot, I return to camp; and, although only one camel can be procured, the tents are moved, and established close to the lake, near a narrow strip of land which runs out for a considerable distance into it. I see a number of Geese; but they are extremely shy, only allowing me to get one long shot at them, which seems to have the effect of keeping them on the alert during the whole of my stay here. I also often see jackals and wolves skirting the sugar-cane or near the bushes towards sunset, and kill specimens of each with ordinary shot.

Fish abound in the lake, and run to a considerable size; but are all of a coarse description. The natives go out fishing in clumsy, heavy, high-sided rowing-boats; and in one of these I cross the lake to explore the desert side, which is certainly the best for wild-fowl shooting as well as for collecting birds. The natives are highly pleased, as I am very successful in shooting the Cormorants, which abound on this side. While lunching under a small bush by the water's edge, a Pelican and Cormorant come over at the same moment; and, thanks to my having large shot in my gun, I bring both down, right and left, the Pelican falling without a motion in the midst of the party. The wind having risen, they try to persuade me to remain here for the night; but I decline, and get them off at 4 o'clock. The boat is so badly constructed that, in spite of having three men to each oar, a captain, his scribe, and a boy to look after the nets, we are drifted considerably out of our course, land two miles from where we had started, and take three hours instead of one in crossing. But what matters? We have accomplished our purpose; and what is time in Egypt? Alas! I know too well that it does not pass currency for money out here, although it may cost the traveller dearly.

I remain in this camp till the 5th of March, spending some days paddling about, or waiting for Duck among the half-sunken bushes and reeds. This is most enjoyable, away from the natives, who, with the best intentions, often get terribly in the way, and are utterly useless in finding Quail or Snipe, though they make first-rate retrievers in open water, rarely failing to capture a wounded duck, such capital swimmers are they. Other days I spend after Duck and Snipe in the boggy ground or among the drains; or, going inland, I beat the bushes and fields for Hares, Quail, and Sandgrouse, the latter birds being very plentiful in the Fayoom. When the game-birds have begun to get shy, I make a raid upon the small birds for my collection, and recognize the well-known note of the Common Bunting. This is the first time I have met with it in Egypt, though I afterwards find it plentiful in the Delta in March. I also get several specimens of Savi's Warbler and the Aquatic Pipit, and also an *Anthus Raalteni*, a South-African Pipit, a bird which has never before been procured so far north. While passing over a desert patch of sand, four Goatsuckers, *Caprimulgus isabellinus*, rose from under my feet, uttering a little snapping note, and three took refuge in the bushes; but after an hour's search I procured them. All four proved to be males, from which I conclude they had only just arrived.

March 5th.—Cross the lake with all my camp, and remain on the desert side until the 11th, passing the whole of the day upon the water among the reeds. Unfortunately a strong wind continues so steadily during the whole time of my stay, that in my frail india-rubber canoe I am often unable to follow up the sport as I could have wished; however, I get a few Pelicans, a fair amount of Ducks, and plenty of Cormorants. I tried the latter for dinner one day, and found them not very bad, though I preferred the Pelicans; both are far better than the Wild Geese, which, after one trial, were ever after excluded from the bill of fare. The Purple Gallinule is tolerably abundant, but I more frequently heard than saw it; its note, by no means musical, resembles the noise one might expect a donkey to make if it had a sore throat. I was very glad to meet with the Lesser Cormorant, as at the time I was not aware that it occurred in Egypt.

I saw numerous tracks of Wolves and Jackals, and also the footprints of the Wild Boar, but am at a loss to know what the latter animal can find to feed upon, as this side appears entirely barren; so much so, that on my way to some Roman ruins, about two miles inland, I did not meet with a single bird.

March 10th.—I was to have returned to the other side of the lake to-day; but the boatmen go off early in the morning to pick up their nets on the other side; so that when ready to start I find no boat to take me, which causes me to vent my displeasure in a few words to the dragoman, and settle to remain here another day. This I know he does not like, as he considers this side unsafe, on account of the wandering Arabs, who are said occasionally to attack the stranger who takes the liberty of pitching his tent upon their desert soil; so that my dragoman has had to mount guard every night himself, as our native guard would be sure to run away if a wandering party of Bedouins made their appearance. Such are the guards the stranger employs in Egypt to protect him against the phantom of their own creation, the Arab bandit; for if he exists anywhere but in their own imagination, he is extremely rare, probably not from any innate notion of right or wrong, but simply from fear of the consequences; for the natives are rarely above laying their hands upon any thing they can take with safety, but have a great regard for their own skins. Another of their weaknesses is never to tell the truth at first; so invariable is this rule, that one may safely disbelieve their first statement, and if they adhere to it, abandon all hope of getting at the truth; but if they afterwards reverse their previous statement, what they have last said may be believed.

The day being calm, I am able to go where I like in my canoe, and pick up a very varied bag. I get some fine old specimens of the Purple Heron, my previous ones having been in immature plumage. I also meet with a large flock of Bitterns perched up in the thick reeds, which they leave unwillingly, waiting almost for my boat to shake the reeds they are sitting on. There are only six species of Duck plentiful here, the Mallard, Ferruginous Duck, Teal, Pintail, Shoveller, and Gadwall; of each of them I obtain specimens to-day, which shows what a varied bag one is likely to make out here; and this to the ornithologist gives additional charms to this wild, rough kind of shooting, where one never knows what the next shot will produce, whether Pelican or Snipe. A breech-loader is consequently most serviceable, as one can change the charge to suit the occasion. A few Eley's wire cartridges with No. 1 shot, which I had with me, proved extremely effective with the larger birds and the immense flocks of

Ducks, which rarely allow one to approach within ordinary range.

March 11th.—The boat is ready when I want it this morning, the dragoman having probably passed on a few of my remarks to the crew, who are all activity, for fear of diminishing the much-coveted backsheesh, the only great motive power in Egypt. We return to nearly the old camping-ground opposite the sugar-factory, and I find the Snipe-shooting much improved by the few days' rest it has had; and the Ducks, too, have returned to their old quarters. I discover that I have brought from the other side more than I intended; for on sitting down a scorpion bites me: at the moment I thought it was a needle in my chair; nor was it painful until the following day, when there was a good deal of inflammation, which lasted for about three days, when it quickly subsided, and was never more than simply unpleasant, possibly owing to my applying "eau de luce" at once, and being in capital training.

March 12th.—The day is beautiful, not a ripple on the water, not a cloud in the sky, intensely hot in the sunshine; but the air feels pure and light, and as I paddle over the smooth water I admire the loveliness of the climate, and feel how enjoyable this life is away from all native interference. I have left them tending their flocks by the water's edge, or gathering in their luxuriant crops of clover, whilst I am paddling among the water-plants and half-sunken bushes. At intervals I land on some small island for Snipe and Waders, while Ducks come flying over my head either singly or in small flocks.

The level of the lake has much sunk since I was here

before, and many sand-banks have appeared, which form favourable resorts for the Godwits and Ruffs; numbers of Spotted Eagles and Ospreys sit lazily upon the sand, or upon the matted bushes and reeds. I recognize three specimens of *Turtur Sharpei* by their more sandy colouring than *T. senegalensis*, the ordinary Egyptian Dove, and by their more active flight; while pursuing them, I get a varied bag of Waders, including half a dozen Snipe. Throughout the Fayoom snakes abound: but one island literally swarmed with them; for in merely walking round it, though only 100 yards in length, I killed three, one about 7 feet long; and while washing my hands I almost touched a villainous-looking little rascal, which I stoned to death. I believe, however, in general they are not very poisonous.

March 13th.—Having now collected most of the birds which I expected to find in the Fayoom, I decide to return to Cairo, as I propose spending a month in the Delta before leaving for England; so I rise early, and get all my baggage up to Shebooksi, the sugar-factory, by 10 A.M., to be ready for the train to Medineh, whenever it may start; for no one knows even the probable hour of its departure, as it has to come from Medineh, picking up sugar-cane by the way. It arrives at about 1 o'clock, and, after several hour's work shunting carriages, it starts with us at 4 P.M. On reaching the first station, it is found that about a dozen carriages are required there to be filled with sugar-cane, so the train returns to the factory to fetch them. At length, after having done its work in true Egyptian fashion, we arrive at Medineh about 6 P.M., where we pitch our camp for the night. Next morning we go on by train to Icadwa, some five miles distant, and stop there for two days' shooting round some pieces of water: one, a small lake surrounded by rushes, abounds with Snipe; but the Ducks are impossible to be got at, as the banks are flat, and there is no covert to hide a person; while at the other lake, or rather reservoir, for it is walled half way round, there is a capital embankment, admirably suited for concealment, with water on both sides; and there fair sport may be had at flight-time, or by driving the birds over by a boat on the lake. Being alone, I have to content myself by getting Dango to drive the Ducks off the smaller piece of water, and then pursuing them on the large reservoir, in my canoe,—not very satisfactory work, as a strong wind makes the lake very rough, and on the open water it is impossible to approach the large flocks of Ducks and Geese that one sees. I only get ten Ducks in the day; but probably a party of four or five guns would have got a much larger proportion, as they could have worked properly. Earlier in the season I expect these lakes, and another which I did not visit, would prove better for sport than the large lake of Birket el Korn.

March 16th.—Leave Icadwa by train at 10 A.M., and arrive at the junction Zowyeh at 11.30; hearing that I shall have to wait a couple of hours, I go after Quail, and have some very fair sport close to the station. I return needlessly early; for my train does not arrive till 4 P.M., so that I only get to Imbaba station at Cairo at 6.30.

Among the birds which the ornithologist should not neglect to get from the Fayoom are:—*Herodias alba*, *Ardea purpurea*, *Phalacrocorax pygmæus*, *Porphyrio hyacinthina*, *Podiceps cristatus*, and *Nyroca leucophthalma*, all most abundant on the desert side; and *Pandion haliaëtus*, *Caprimulgus isabellinus*, *Chettusia Villotæi*, *Ægialitis pecuarius*, *Pelecanus crispus*, and *Larus ichthyaëtus*, equally distributed, or most plentiful on the cultivated side of Birket el Korn; and among the commoner birds, to complete a collection, the Curlew, Black-tailed Godwit, Moor-Hen, Spotted Crake, Water-Rail, Little Grebe, Cormorant, Tufted Duck, Gadwall, and Spoonbill, may be all easily obtained in the Fayoom.

I had intended to spend a month in the Delta; but this tour was cut short by my getting a slight attack of marsh-fever near Damietta, where, however, I was long enough to see that the reedy lake close by should not be visited later than February for Snipe-shooting; for, although I did one day get twenty couple, and found Ruffs and Redshanks very plentiful, still it was far inferior to what I had known it earlier in the season. However, the ornithologist will find a greater variety of birds; and I was very glad to meet with a small and rare Warbler, *Calamodyta melanopogon*, extremely abundant in the thick sedge, also plenty of *Acrocephalus stentorius*, although by the end of March it had not begun to utter its loud love-notes, from which it derives its name.

I shall now end my journal, which I have purposely confined within narrow limits, as my sole object in publishing it is to give a general notion of the ornithological sport to be obtained during the ordinary traveller's visit to the magnificent country of Egypt, which yearly attracts more visitors, most of whom become interested in the rich variety of birds which may there be collected. I have likewise given a slight sketch of the geology, as the Nile-tour allows so much time for reflection, and the geology of a country teaches one more of its general appearance than an ordinary and more lengthened description of the scenery alone would afford; while, for my special purpose, it may be said that the difference of soil will often account for the difference of the avifauna: thus, in a sandy, rocky district we should not look for Snipe, nor in the marshy localities should we seek for the Sand-Grouse and the numerous desert forms which abound in Egypt.

BIRDS OF EGYPT.

Family TURDIDÆ.

1. Turdus viscivorus, L. *Missel-Thrush.*

Rüppell mentions having once observed it in the neighbourhood of Suez in April. This is the only evidence I can find of the occurrence of this bird in Egypt; and it is far from conclusive. I therefore give no description of this well-known species.

Fig. Sharpe and Dresser, B. of Eur. part vi.

2. Turdus pilaris, L. *Fieldfare.*

The Fieldfare is a winter visitant in Egypt. I saw a specimen in a bird-stuffer's shop at Alexandria, which had been killed in the man's garden that winter (1871); and he told me that it was common there during the colder months.

Head, nape, and rump grey; centre of the back, scapulars, and wing-coverts brownish chestnut; wings and tail black, the feathers of the former edged with very pale brown; under surface, throat, and crop buff, spotted with black, the remainder white, with the centres of the feathers on the flanks marked with rich dark brown; legs and beak pale brown; irides brown.

Entire length 11 inches; culmen 0·7; wing, carpus to tip, 5·5; tarsus 1·3.

Fig. Sharpe and Dresser, B. of Eur. part ix.

3. TURDUS MUSICUS, Linn. *Song-Thrush.*

The Song-Thrush is tolerably abundant in Egypt, especially in the Delta, and, according to Hemprich and Ehrenberg, is met with in Nubia, where, however, it is of rare occurrence. I believe that it occasionally remains in the country to breed; for I have shot it twice near Benisooef at the end of March.

Upper parts dark olive-brown, the head slightly shaded with golden brown; wings dark brown, the feathers washed with golden brown on the outer webs, the median and greater wing-coverts tipped with buff; tail similar in colour to the top of the head; lores, eyebrow, throat, crop, and sides of the throat and chest buff; centre of the chest and abdomen white; sides of the throat and chest and sides of the body spotted with dark brown; under wing-coverts ochre; beak brown, shaded with yellow towards the base of the lower mandible; legs brownish flesh-colour; irides brown.

Entire length 8·8 inches; culmen 0·7; wing, carpus to tip, 4·7; tarsus 1·3.

Fig. Sharpe and Dresser, B. of Eur. part v.

4. TURDUS MERULA, L. *Blackbird.*

The Blackbird comes to Egypt in the winter, but is not common in the country. I have met with it on two occasions

—once in the Delta, and once near Benisooef at the end of March, when I saw a pair together.

Male. Entire plumage black; beak yellow; legs and irides dark brown.

Female. Upper parts brown; chin greyish white, passing into deep ferruginous brown on the upper part of the breast; remainder of the underparts dusky brown. Beak dark brown, with yellowish-brown edges.

Entire length 10 inches; culmen 1; wing, carpus to tip, 5; tarsus 1·3.

Fig. Sharpe & Dresser, B. of Eur. part x.

5. Turdus torquatus, L. *Ring-Ouzel.*

Keyserling and Blasius state that this bird comes into Egypt in the winter; and von Heuglin (Orn. N. O. Afr. p. 387) says that a naturalist in Cairo informed him that he had often killed it in Lower Egypt.

A broad white gorget on the breast; remainder of the plumage dull black with brown edges to the feathers; plumage darkest on the back of the neck and chest, and lightest about the quills. Legs brown; beak yellowish brown; irides dark brown.

Entire length 12 inches; culmen 1; wing, carpus to tip, 5·5; tarsus 1·5.

Fig. Sharpe & Dresser, B. of Eur. part x.

6. Pycnonotus arsinoë (Licht.). White-vented Bulbul.

Von Heuglin observes (Orn. N. O. Afr. p. 379) that this bird has been met with as far down the Nile as Central Egypt. It appears, however, to be of rare occurrence within our limits, while in some parts of Nubia it is very plentiful, especially near Wady-Halfeh, where it may be seen usually in pairs or families, hopping about on the roofs of the houses or flitting among the trees which are interspersed in that village. The Rev. A. C. Smith, in his 'Attractions of the Nile' (vol. ii. p. 222), gives a very good description of the habits of this species, which he calls *Ixos obscurus*.

Head brownish black, shading off gradually on the throat; the latter, as well as the crop, remainder of the upper parts and wings, uniform medium brown; tail rather darker; chest, abdomen, and *under tail-coverts white*. Beak brownish black; legs and irides dark brown.

Entire length 7·2 inches; culmen 0·6; wing, carpus to tip, 3·4; tarsus 0·8.

7. PYCNONOTUS XANTHOPYGIUS (Licht.). *Yellow-vented Bulbul.*

Von Heuglin mentions (Syst. Ueb. p. 30) that *P. levaillantii*, Temm., is found in the Fayoom and Middle Egypt, and in his large work (Orn. N. O. Afr. p. 399) reiterates the statement, calling the bird *P. nigricans*, Vieill. Mr. Sharpe (Ibis, 1870, p. 432), in referring to this last work, writes:—"I rather doubt if a comparison of the true *Ixus nigricans*, from South Africa, with Abyssinian specimens would confirm the identity of the two species." It appears far more probable that *P. xanthopygius*, a Palestine bird, should be met with in Egypt than *P. nigricans*, the South-African form; and as the two differ but very slightly, the South-African bird being distinguishable by a red eyelid, it appears highly probable that Von Heuglin has confounded the two species; so I have regarded the names *P. nigricans* and *P. levail-*

CRATEROPUS ACACIÆ.

lantii in the above-mentioned references as synonymous with *P. xanthopygius*, and therefore give a description of the last-named bird from a specimen collected by Canon Tristram in Palestine.

Head and throat black, the latter shading into dark brown on the lower part; back and scapulars mouse-colour; wings browner; tail brownish-black; chest and flanks stone-grey, shading almost into white on the lower part of the abdomen; *vent and under tail-coverts bright yellow*; beak black; legs brownish-black; irides brown.

Entire length 8 inches; culmen 0·7; wing, carpus to tip, 3·7; tarsus 0·85.

8. Crateropus acaciæ (Licht.). *Egyptian Bush-Babbler.*

(Plate I.)

This species, though not uncommon in any part of Nubia, rarely descends the Nile below Assouan. I met with it on several occasions on a small bushy island immediately below the First Cataract, where I obtained four specimens, and on the same island in April found two nests of this species, in construction and size closely resembling that of our Common Blackbird. They were built entirely of a coarse grass which grows abundantly in Egypt, and were on each occasion placed in a thick sont bush, about five feet from the ground. This bird is lively and cheerful in its habits, and appears to keep exclusively to the sont bushes, where it creeps among the thorny and tangled boughs, incessantly uttering its babbling song, which is rather pleasing and, when once heard, cannot be mistaken. On the approach of danger it immediately ceases its note, and creeps off at the further side of the bush.

Entire plumage sandy colour, shading off into white on the chin; top of the head, ear-coverts, and back of the neck shaded with ashy, and with narrow stripes of dark brown down the centre of the feathers; beak yellowish flesh-colour, darkest on the culmen; legs pale brown; irides hazel.

Entire length 10 inches; culmen 0·7; wing, carpus to tip, 3·8; tarsus 1·3.

9. MONTICOLA SAXATILIS (L.) *Rock-Thrush.*

The Rock-Thrush is a winter visitant to Egypt and Nubia, arriving there about September, and leaving again in April, at which seasons it is tolerably plentiful in the Delta in the neighbourhood of burial-grounds and the less-frequented embankments.

Entire head and neck blue-grey, almost shading off into black on the upper part of the back and scapulars, where the feathers are tipped with buff; remainder of the back white, with the feathers more or less broadly edged with slaty grey; tail-coverts yellowish rufous; tail deep rufous, the two centre feathers strongly shaded with dusky; wings brown; under surface of the body bright rufous, with white edgings to some of the feathers; beak black; legs and irides dark brown.

Entire length 7·5 inches; culmen 0·8; wing, carpus to tip, 4·8; tarsus 1·1.

Fig. Sharpe & Dresser, B. of Eur. part x.

10. MONTICOLA CYANA, L. *Blue Rock-Thrush.*

According to Von Heuglin (Orn. N. O. Afr. p. 372), the

Blue Rock-Thrush is only a visitor in Egypt and Nubia during the spring and autumn months; and he considers it less abundant than the Rock-Thrush, whereas from my own observations it appears to be the commoner bird of the two. I have frequently met with it among the rocks in Upper Egypt in April, where I think that it probably breeds.

Entire plumage indigo, with cobalt reflections on the head and throat; wings brown; tail black; legs and beak black; irides dark brown.

The immature birds differ in their prevailing tint being ash-brown, with more or less blue on the back, while the under surface of the throat and body is mottled, owing to the centres of the feathers being generally very pale brown, barred on the chest and abdomen with dusky.

Entire length 9 inches; culmen 0·9; wing, carpus to tip, 5; tarsus 1·2.

Fig. Sharpe and Dresser, B. of Eur. part viii.

Fam. SYLVIIDÆ.

11. Saxicola œnanthe (Linn.). *Common Wheatear.*

This well-known Chat is a very regular visitant to Egypt and Nubia in the spring and autumn, when it is abundant throughout the country.

Male in breeding-plumage.—Forehead and eyebrows white; lores, cheeks, and ear-coverts black; top of the head, hind part of the neck, back and scapulars grey; rump and upper tail-coverts white; wings brown, with a pale edging to some of the feathers; tail white, with the two centre feathers and the apical third of the remainder dark brown; underparts creamy white, shaded with ferruginous buff, especially on the throat; beak and legs black; irides brown.

Female.—The upper parts are brown instead of grey; forehead and eyebrow buff, and the coloration of the underparts not so clear.

In autumn and winter the plumage of the male resembles that of the female.

Entire length 6 inches; culmen 0·5; wing, carpus to tip, 3·6; tarsus 1·1.

Fig. Gould, B. of Eur. pl. 90.

12. Saxicola saltatrix, Ménétr. *Ménétriés's Wheatear.*

This Chat is an abundant resident throughout Egypt and Nubia. It has frequently been mistaken for *S. œnanthe*, owing to its plumage and habits being very similar. It is, however, a larger bird, and the beak is stouter in proportion to its size. Many ornithologists imagine this species to be the *S. isabellina* of Rüppell (Atl. p. 52, t. 34 *b*); but that plate seems to represent the female of *S. monacha*.

Male and female alike in plumage throughout the year, and differing only from the female of *S. œnanthe* in being slightly more robust, in having the brown end to the tail rather broader, and a little less white on the rump.

Entire length 6·5 inches; culmen 0·5; wing, carpus to tip, 3·7; tarsus 1·15.

13. Saxicola amphileuca, Hempr. & Ehr. *Eastern Black-eared Wheatear.*

This Chat is not a resident in Egypt and Nubia, but

arrives in March, and soon becomes abundant, usually frequenting the more cultivated portions of the country, where it may often be seen in the neighbourhood of villages, perched upon some low bush or reed fence.

Breeding-plumage.—Forehead, lores, cheeks and ear-coverts black; wings black, secondaries occasionally slightly edged with very pale buff; tail white, except the greater part of the two centre feathers and a broad end to the remainder, which are black; the rest of the plumage glossy white, tinted with pale dusky on the back of the head, and with buff on the upper parts of the back and chest; beak and legs black; irides brown. In winter the wings and tail are brown and the back is darker.

The sexes are similar in plumage.

Entire length 5·8 inches; culmen 0·5; wing, carpus to tip, 3·5; tarsus 0·9.

14. Saxicola eurymelæna, Hempr. & Ehr.

This is the common Egyptian form of the Black-throated Wheatear. It does not winter in Egypt and Nubia, but is most abundant in those countries in the spring and autumn. Like the last species, it prefers the more cultivated parts, especially the neighbourhood of cotton-plantations, which offer it a favourable retreat when pursued.

Male. Only differs from *S. amphileuca* in having the *entire throat black.*

Female. Top of the head, ear-coverts, back and scapulars brown; eyebrow not very distinct, and of a sandy colour; throat pale dusky brown; remainder of the plumage similar to the adult male in summer, excepting that the wings and tail are browner.

Entire length 5·7 inches; culmen 0·5; wing, carpus to tip, 3·5; tarsus 0·9.

15. Saxicola xanthomelæna, Hempr. & Ehr.

This species is very closely allied to *S. eurymelæna*, but is of rare occurrence in Egypt and Nubia. Mr. E. C. Taylor obtained the only specimen I know of from Egypt, and has kindly lent it to me for my description.

Very similar to *S. eurymelæna*. The beak and legs are rather stouter, and its plumage differs in the following manner: *no black feathers in front of the forehead*; top of the head and nape clear ferruginous buff; back white; a broad uninterrupted brown end to the tail; the black on the throat extends on each side and joins the scapulars.

Entire length 6 inches; culmen 0·55; wing, carpus to tip, 3·3; tarsus 1.

Dr. Otto Finsch says (Tr. Z. S. vii. p. 323) that *Saxicola finschi*, von Heugl., from Egypt, is nothing but the present species, as he has been informed by Herr von Pelzeln, who has examined the typical specimens from the desert of Sakkara in the Vienna Museum.

16. Saxicola deserti, Rüpp. *Desert Chat.*

This Chat is abundant in Egypt and Nubia, where it remains throughout the year, and may usually be met with along the embankments or on the confines of the desert.

Male in breeding-plumage.—Forehead and eyebrows white; top of the head, nape and back of the neck pale brown, inclining to sandy on the back and scapulars; rump, tail-coverts and base of the tail white, remainder of the tail dark brown; wings dark brown; secondaries and some of the wing-coverts edged with white. Throat and sides of the neck black, remainder of the underparts cream-colour, faintly shaded with rufous on the chest; beak and legs black; irides brown.

Winter plumage.—Feathers of the throat broadly edged with white, and pale edgings to all the feathers on the wing.

Entire length 6 inches; culmen 0·5; wing, carpus to tip, 3·5; tarsus 1.

Fig. Temm. P. C. 359.

17. Saxicola homochroa, Trist.

I have a female specimen, shot by myself at Assouan on the 15th of April, which I have compared with a bird in Mr. E. C. Taylor's collection, killed by him near Cairo in January, and determined for him by Canon Tristram, the original describer of the species (Ibis, 1859, p. 59).

These specimens only differ from *S. deserti* in the same points as some females of *S. stapazina* differ from the males of that species, and are similar to them in their habits and in being residents in Egypt and Nubia. In my opinion the absence of a black throat simply arises from the age or sex of the specimen, and not from any specific difference. I have, however, separated this form from *S. deserti* in deference to Canon Tristram's opinion.

Similar in plumage to *S. deserti*, except that it has *no black on the throat.*

Entire length 6 inches; culmen 0·5; wing, carpus to tip, 3·4; tarsus 0·95.

18. Saxicola mœsta, Licht. *Saxicola erythropygia*, Taylor, Ibis, 1867, p. 60.

This species of Chat is of rather rare occurrence in Egypt, where, according to Heuglin (Orn. N. O. Afr. p. 356), it remains throughout the year on the confines of the desert and among the rocks. Mr. E. C. Taylor has procured it in Egypt; but it has never fallen under my notice.

Forehead and sides of the crown whitish; head and back ashy-brown; lower part of the back, rump and upper tail-coverts rich tawny; wings blackish brown, the primaries edged with fulvous, and some of the greater coverts tipped with the same colour; tail blackish-brown, all the feathers white at the base for half their length, and some of them narrowly tipped with white; sides of the face and throat black, as well as the under wing-coverts; rest of the under surface of the body dull cream-colour, gradually shading into tawny on the lower flanks; vent and under tail-coverts bright tawny like the rump; bill and feet black.

Entire length 6·2 inches; culmen 0·65; wing 3·7; tail 2·6; tarsus 1·0.

Mr. E. C. Taylor has been so kind as to lend me the original specimen of his *Saxicola erythropygia*, which I consider to be the present species. It has been erroneously confounded with *S. philothamna* of Tristram by Dr. von Heuglin (Orn. N. O. Afr. p. 355); but it is certainly distinct from that species, as the following tabular comparison will testify :—

S. philothamna.	*S. erythropygia.*
Top of the head and nape white, shaded on the crown with dusky.	Top of the head and nape the same colour as the back.
Back dusky black, shaded with grey.	Back ashy-brown.
Rump and upper tail-coverts white shaded with pale rufous.	Rump and upper tail-coverts bright rufous.
Basal half of the tail bright rufous.	Basal two thirds of the tail white, tinted with rufous at its junction with the brown end.
Under tail-coverts buff.	Under tail-coverts bright rufous, paler than those above the tail.

The specimen described is ticketed by Mr. J. K. Lord, who procured it at Hor Tamanib, in Nubia, a female; but I think it is really a male; and Mr. Taylor's specimen is possibly an adult female about to lose its winter plumage.

19. Saxicola lugens, Licht. *Mourning Chat.*

This Chat is a resident in Egypt and Nubia throughout the year; but its numbers are increased during the winter months. Mr. E. C. Taylor writes (Ibis, 1867, p. 60), "This is the most abundant of all the Chats near Cairo in the winter."

Top of the head and nape pale dusky, inclining more or less to white towards the beak, on the eyebrows, and on the nape; rump, upper tail-coverts, chest and abdomen white; vent and under tail-coverts buff; tail white, except a broad band at the tip and the greater part of the two centre feathers, which are dark brown; remainder of the plumage black, shading into brown on the quills; beak and legs black; irides brown.

Entire length 6·5 inches; culmen 0·55; wing, carpus to tip, 3·8; tarsus 1.

The sexes are similar in plumage.

Fig. Temm. Pl. Col. 257, fig. 3.

20. SAXICOLA LEUCOMELA (Pall.).

According to Von Heuglin (Orn. N. O. Afr. p. 351) this species comes during the spring and autumn migrations into Egypt and Nubia.

I think it possible that *S. lugens* will be found inseparable from the present bird.

21. SAXICOLA MONACHA, Rüpp. *Hooded Chat.*

(Plate II.)

This species appears to be nowhere common, although it ranges throughout Egypt and Nubia, and is a resident, frequenting the desert and rocky districts. I only met with a small colony of these Chats at El Kab, where I obtained a male and female in full breeding-plumage on the 26th of February.

Male in breeding-plumage.—Top of the head and nape, *lower part of the back*, upper and under tail-coverts, and *abdomen white*; tail white, with obsolete brown marks near the tip of some of the feathers and at the apex, three quarters of the two centre ones brown, with pale edgings; rest of the

plumage black, with the feathers on the pinion narrowly edged with white; beak and legs black; irides brown.

Entire length 6·8 inches; culmen 0·6; wing, carpus to tip, 4·3; tarsus 0·9.

Female in breeding-plumage.—Upper parts hair-brown, shading off to cream-colour on the rump and upper tail-coverts; tail cream-colour shaded with rufous, excepting three quarters of the two centre feathers as well as half the exterior web of the outer rectrices, and the ends of all of them brown; underparts dull white, shaded with hair-brown on the sides of the crop; legs black; beak and irides dark brown.

Entire length 6·8 inches; culmen 0·6; wing, carpus to tip, 4; tarsus 0·9.

As will be seen by the plate, the sexes are very different in colour; and I have placed the hen bird in the foreground for the sake of comparison with *S. isabellina* of Rüppell, which is supposed by some naturalists to have been founded on a female of the present species.

22. Saxicola leucopygia, Brehm. *White-rumped Chat.*

This Chat remains throughout the year in Egypt and Nubia. It is generally first met with by the Nile-tourist at Assouan, and on entering Nubia becomes extremely abundant. Brehm separated this species into two, under the names *S. leucocephala* and *S. leucopygia*, the former being distinguished by a white head; this, however, is only a mark of age; so, as Brehm is the author of both names, I have selected the latter as most appropriate for this species. For proof of the identity of *S. leucocephala* and *S. leucopygia*, see my paper (Ibis, 1871, p. 53). They appear to breed very early; for in

April I saw many young birds just able to fly. In Nubia they are daily to be seen hopping among the rocks or perched upon the mud walls of the native houses.

Very old birds.—Top of the head, rump, vent and tail-coverts white; tail white, except the apical half of the two centre feathers, which is black; remainder of the plumage deep black with steel-blue reflections; beak and legs black; irides brown.

Breeding-plumage of the first year.—Top of the head blck; tail-feathers with occasional dark spots near their tips; the black of the plumage has no blue gloss; and the wings incline to brown.

Immature birds.—Beak shaded with yellow towards the tip and on the lower mandible; legs dark brown; the white feathers of the tail with brown spots near their tips.

Less-adult birds have black feathers mixed with the white crown.

Entire length 6·5 to 7 inches; culmen 0·6; wing, carpus to tip, 3·7 to 4·3; tarsus 1·0.

The sexes are similar in plumage.

23. Saxicola syenitica, Heugl.

Von Heuglin (Orn. N. O. Afr. p. 359) mentions a specimen of this Chat killed at El Kab in June 1852. This is another of Heuglin's species of *Saxicola* the distinctness of which I am inclined to doubt. I expect that it will be discovered to be founded upon a variety of plumage of *S. leucopygia*, depending on the age of the specimen.

24. Pratincola rubetra (Linn.). *Whin-Chat.*

This species is not so abundant as the Stone-Chat, but is more evenly distributed throughout the country. According to Von Heuglin (Orn. N. O. Afr. p. 338) it comes to Egypt in August, and is certainly found in the late spring, for I have shot it in Nubia on the 11th of April.

Male in breeding-plumage.—Upper part of the head and neck, back, scapulars, and tail-coverts dark brown, with broad sandy-coloured edgings to the feathers; wing dark brown, with pale narrow edgings; inner wing-coverts white, and a small patch of white on the primary coverts; *basal half of all but the two central tail-feathers white,* remainder of the tail dark brown; a white eyebrow extending from the beak to the nape, and a band of the same colour from the chin under the ear-coverts to the sides of the neck; lores, cheeks, and ear-coverts dark brown; throat, crop, and sides of the chest ferruginous buff, shading into cream-colour on the abdomen and under tail-coverts; back and legs brownish black; irides dark brown.

Entire length 5·2 inches; culmen 0·4; wing, carpus to tip, 3; tarsus 0·9.

Fig. Gould, B. of Eur. pl. 93.

25. Pratincola rubicola (Linn.). *Stone-Chat.*

This bird is very plentiful in Lower Egypt, though comparatively scarce in other parts of the country. According to Von Heuglin (Orn. N. O. Afr. p. 339) it arrives in August and leaves again in April.

Male in breeding-plumage.—Upper part of the head and neck, back, scapulars, and *tail black*, with brown edgings to the feathers; *rump and tail-coverts white*; the inner greater wing-coverts pure white, the remainder of the wing dark brown with pale edges to the feathers; throat and ear-coverts black; a large white patch on each side of the neck; breast rust-colour, fading into white on the abdomen and under tail-coverts; beak and legs black; irides brown.

Entire length 5 inches; culmen 0·4; wing, carpus to tip, 2·5; tarsus 0·9.

Fig. Gould, B. of Eur. pl. 94.

26. Pratincola Hemprichii (Hempr. & Ehr.). *Hemprich's Stone-Chat.*

Von Heuglin (Orn. N. O. Afr. p. 339) mentions this species as a probable resident in Egypt, but of rather rare occurrence.

This bird may be briefly described as follows:—Very like the English Stone-Chat, but always to be distinguished by the *basal half of the tail being white.*

27. Ruticilla phœnicura (Linn.). *Redstart.*

This bird arrives about the middle of March, when it becomes plentiful both in Egypt and Nubia. A few individuals possibly winter in the country, for I once obtained a specimen in the beginning of February. It may generally be found frequenting rows of sont trees, where it chooses some prominent bough; but if alarmed, it takes refuge at once among the foliage, or flits on before the intruder from tree to tree, resting on some shady bough a few feet from the ground. The Redstart passes southward again about September.

Male.—Throat, a band across the lower part of the forehead, extending to the eyes, and ear-coverts black, the feathers on the throat more or less edged with dirty white; forehead white; top of the head, back, and scapulars grey, more or less tinted with brown; rump and tail bright rufous, except the two centre feathers, which are almost entirely brown; wings brown, with pale edgings to the feathers; chest and flanks rufous; abdomen white; legs, beak, and irides dark brown.

Entire length 5·5 inches; culmen 0·4; wing, carpus to tip, 3; tarsus 0·9.

Female.—Plumage much duller than the male, with no black on the throat or head, and no white forehead.

Fig. Gould, B. of Eur. pl. 95.

28. Ruticilla tithys (Scop.). *Black Redstart.*

I cannot speak of this bird from personal observation, as I never met with it in the country. It is rather more partial to buildings than the last species. According to Von Heuglin (Orn. N. O. Afr. p. 334), it is not very common in North-eastern Africa in the winter, and does not travel so far southward as *R. phœnicura,* but is plentiful in Southern Nubia in September. Mr. S. Stafford Allen (Ibis, 1864, p. 237) observes that it arrives from its southern winter quarters in April; while Mr. E. C. Taylor (Ibis, 1867, p. 61) says that it is "resident in small numbers throughout the winter, frequenting ruined buildings." From the above evidence we may conclude that the present species is a resident, but that its numbers are recruited by additional birds migrating in the spring.

Male.—Top of the head, nape, back, scapulars, and abdomen pale slaty grey; sides of the face, neck, throat, and breast black; primaries and secondaries dusky, the latter with broad white outer edges; wing-coverts dusky, bordered with ashy; some of the feathers on the rump white; tail-coverts and tail bright rufous tipped with brown, and the two centre feathers dusky; the centre of the abdomen white; vent and under tail-coverts rufous; legs and beak dusky; irides brown.

Entire length 6·3 inches; culmen 0·5; wing, carpus to tip, 3·5; tarsus 1.

Female.—Above dirty ash-colour, beneath brown tinged with rufous; tail paler than in the male.

Fig. Gould, B. of Eur. pl. 96.

29. Ruticilla semirufa (Hempr. & Ehr.). *Palestine Redstart.*

Hemprich and Ehrenberg collected this species in Egypt; but it appears to be of very rare occurrence there, for I know of no other instance of its having been observed in the country.

Male.—Forehead, sides of the head, back, scapulars, wing-coverts, throat, and breast glossy black, with an iron-grey cap; wings brown; remainder of the plumage bright rust-colour, except the two centre tail-feathers, which are brown. *There is no trace of white on any part of the plumage.*

Female.—Very similar to that of *R. phœnicura.*

Entire length 5·6 inches; culmen 0·45; wing, carpus to tip, 3; tarsus 0·9.

This description is taken from two specimens kindly lent to me by the Rev. Canon Tristram.

30. Aëdon galactodes (Temm.). *Rufous Warbler.*

This species arrives in Egypt towards the end of March, and leaves again in September, during which time it may be frequently met with wherever low thick covert affords a suitable shelter. It is essentially a creeping bird, rarely showing itself in the open, and when disturbed always flying to the nearest coverts; and is very partial to banks, where the rich and prickly herbage affords it a safe retreat. I never observed it perch more than a few feet from the ground, generally on the latter, where it loves to strut with tail erect, basking its plumage in the sunshine. It is most abundant in Nubia, where it may frequently be seen on the ground searching for food at the foot of some stout young date-palm. It builds a thin nest of grass, similar to that of the Black-cap Warbler.

Upper plumage rufous, brightest on the rump and tail-feathers; wings brown, the feathers broadly edged with rufous; tail bright rufous, each feather, with the exception of the two central ones, marked with a large distinct brown spot, which in the four outer feathers on each side is followed by a clear white ending to the feathers; under parts buffish white; it has a white eyebrow; beak pale brown, lighter towards the base of the lower mandible; legs pale brown; irides hazel.

Entire length 6·5 inches; culmen 0·55; wing, carpus to tip, 3·4; tarsus 1.

Fig. Gould, B. of Eur. pl. 112.

31. Cyanecula suecica (Linn.). *Blue-throated Warbler.*

This is an extremely abundant species in some parts of the Delta, and is very generally distributed throughout Egypt and Nubia, especially in the damper localities, or where the vegetation grows to the height of several feet. Although it frequents reedy marshes and mustard-fields, or wherever the vegetation is luxuriant, it rarely alights upon the plants, but almost invariably keeps to the ground, where it runs with tail upraised, stopping every now and then to pick up an insect or to watch the intruder from the edge of its retreat. Specimens differ considerably in the colour of the spot on the throat, which may be met with in all stages from pure white to rufous. It is by no means a shy bird, and when disturbed flies but a short distance. It may be easily recognized by the rufous on the tail, which is very distinct.

Male.—Entire upper plumage brown, with a darker centre to some of the feathers on the head, the wing-feathers having a pale edging; tail, two centre feathers and the apical half of the others dark brown, remainder bright rufous; a buff eyebrow extending forward to the nostrils; a large spot varying from pure white to rufous on the throat, which is blue, bordered by a black collar, sometimes slightly edged with white, and followed by a broader rufous collar across the chest; remainder of the underparts dull white, shaded with brown on the flanks; legs, beak, and irides brown.

Entire length 5·5 inches; culmen 0·45; wing, carpus to tip, 2·8; tarsus 1.

Female.—Throat buff, shaded slightly towards its base with rufous, and bordered on the sides and crop with black mixed with a few blue feathers.

Fig. Gould, B. of Eur. pl. 97.

32. Erithacus rubecula (Linn.). *Robin.*

The Robin is confined to Lower Egypt, where it is only a winter visitant. It is as tame and familiar in the sunny climate of Egypt as it is in England, and appears to welcome the stranger, as he sits in the shade of the sont tree, by hopping from bough to bough, and peering inquisitively at him, as though it expected to recognize a friend in the traveller.

Front of the head, region of the eyes, part of the ear-coverts, throat, and fore part of the chest bright rust-colour, with a border of grey all round except on the chest; remainder of the upper parts olive; underparts white, shaded on the flanks with olive; beak and irides brown; legs pale brown.

Entire length 5·7 inches; culmen 0·4; wing, carpus to tip, 3·8; tarsus 1·1.

Fig. Gould, B. of Eur. pl. 98.

33. Accentor modularis (Linn.). *Hedge Accentor.*

Dr. von Heuglin (Orn. N. O. Afr. p. 332) mentions having seen this bird himself on one occasion in Egypt.

Head, neck, and breast, pale slate-colour, tinged with brown on the top of the head and nape; upper part of the back and shoulders reddish brown, with dusky centres to the feathers; rump and upper tail-coverts pale brown; the throat is of a paler grey than the head, and the centre of the abdomen dingy white; wing-feathers dusky, edged with reddish brown, the larger wing-coverts tipped with white; tail greyish brown, with pale edges to the feathers; flanks yellowish grey with long brown streaks; legs pale brown; beak dusky brown; irides hazel.

Entire length 5·7 inches; culmen 0·5; wing, carpus to tip, 2·8; tarsus 0·95.

Fig. Gould, B. of Eur. pl. 110.

34. Philomela luscinia (Linn.). *Nightingale.*

Although the Nightingale ranges throughout Egypt and Nubia during the winter, it is far from being common. I only once saw a pair, and heard their well-known notes, while reposing, during the heat of the day, in a small wood near Bedreshayn, in the latter end of March.

Entire upper plumage russet-brown, rather more rufous on the rump and upper tail-coverts; *tail uniform rufous brown*; underparts dull white, shaded on the sides of the neck and crop with pale brown; under tail-coverts buff; beak brown, inclining to flesh-colour at the base of the lower mandible; legs brownish flesh-colour; irides brown.

Entire length 6·4 inches; culmen 0·5; wing, carpus to tip, 3·3; tarsus 1.

Fig. Gould, B. of Eur. pl. 116.

35. Philomela major (Brehm). *Thrush Nightingale.*

This species ranges throughout Egypt and Nubia during its spring and autumn migrations, but is very scarce. Von Heuglin (Orn. N. O. Afr. p. 338) mentions having seen it in Lower Egypt between the 10th and 25th of March; and Keyserling and Blasius also remark that it occurs in Egypt.

Very similar in plumage to the last species, but slightly larger. It may be most readily recognized by the two centre tail-feathers being darker, and not so rufous as the others, and in the spurious primary being nearly obsolete.

Entire length 7 inches; culmen 0·6; wing, carpus to tip, 3·5; tarsus 1·1.

Fig. Gould, B. of Eur. pl. 117.

36. Bradypterus Cettii (Marm.). *Cetti's Warbler.*

Keyserling and Blasius mention this Warbler as occurring in Egypt; and Von Heuglin (Orn. N. O. Afr. p. 274) states that he has seen it there in the corn-fields.

Entire upper plumage russet-brown, with a rather clear white eyebrow; throat, centre of the chest, and abdomen white, inclining to brown on the flanks and under tail-coverts; beak brown, shading to flesh-colour on the lower mandible; legs pale brown; irides brown.

Wing—first or spurious primary very large; second one equal to the tenth; fourth, fifth, and sixth nearly equal and the longest.

Entire length 5·5 inches; culmen 0·45; wing, carpus to tip, 2·4; tarsus 0·85.

Fig. Gould, B. of Eur. pls. 114, 115.

37. Pseudoluscinia luscinioides (Savi). *Savi's Warbler.*

This Warbler is resident in Egypt, tolerably abundant, and generally distributed. It usually frequents the corn-fields, selecting the spots where the crop grows most luxuriantly; and it may also be found in the reedy marshes of the Delta and Fayoom, where I have frequently seen it, and occasionally procured specimens. When disturbed it leaves its shelter very reluctantly, and flits away hurriedly, flying close to the top of the herbage for a short distance, and then it suddenly dips down and is immediately hidden. Nor will it allow itself to be driven far from the place whence it originally started; but if pursued, prefers to seek shelter by creeping among the stalks of the plants rather than expose itself again by taking wing. On this account the bird is difficult to procure, and is consequently rare in collections.

Entire plumage glossy; wing pointed, first primary longest, remainder decreasing in regular order up to the ninth; tail wedge-shaped; upper parts uniform olivaceous brown. On the tail, under certain lights, can be seen numerous obsolete bars; throat and centre of the body white, remainder of the underparts soft creamy brown; beak dark brown, shading into yellowish flesh-colour towards the base of the lower mandible; legs brownish flesh-colour; irides pale brown.

Entire length 5·7 inches; culmen 0·5; wing, carpus to tip, 2·7; tarsus 0·85.

Fig. Gould, B. of Eur. pl. 104.

38. PSEUDOLUSCINIA FLUVIATILIS (Meyer and Wolf). *River Warbler.*

Dr. von Heuglin (Orn. N. O. Afr. p. 293) only quotes Temminck and Bonaparte as his authorities for the occurrence of this Warbler in Egypt. I have never found it, but consider it not an unlikely bird to be met with in the Delta.

Very similar to *Pseudoluscinia luscinioides.* Entire upper parts olive-brown; wings and tail rather less inclining to olive, the latter marked in certain lights with numerous obsolete bars;

underparts white, *shaded on the crop and flanks with olive-brown, and spotted with that colour on the throat and crop*; beak brown, shading into yellowish flesh-colour on the lower mandible; legs and irides brown.

Entire length 5·6 inches; culmen 0·4; wing, carpus to tip, 2·8; tarsus 0·8.

Fig. Gould, B. of Eur. pl. 102.

39. Calamodyta schœnobænus (Linn.). *Sedge Warbler.*

This species is plentiful throughout Egypt and Nubia. I have shot it among the sedge in the Delta and the Fayoom, in the corn-fields in Upper Egypt, and on the banks of the river in Nubia. When disturbed it flies to the stem of some plant, whence it watches the intruder for a few moments before it disappears amongst the thick herbage. Although it belongs to the group of aquatic Warblers, it often frequents the dry corn-fields, which in Egypt are never at any great distance from the water.

Upper plumage olive-brown, strongly marked with brownish black on the head; the centres of the feathers on the upper part of the back slightly shaded with dark brown; the rump and tail-coverts inclining to yellowish rufous; wings and tail brown, with pale edgings to the feathers; it has a distinct eyebrow; underparts creamy white, shaded on the sides, flanks, and under tail-coverts with yellowish brown; beak, legs, and irides brown, the former shading into flesh-colour at the base of the lower mandible.

Entire length 5 inches; culmen 0·45; wing, carpus to tip, 2·6; tarsus 0·9.

Fig. Gould, B. of Eur. pl. 110.

40. Calamodyta aquatica (Lath.). *Aquatic Warbler.*

According to Von Heuglin (Orn. N. O. Afr. p. 292) this species is sometimes common, in company with the Sedge Warbler, in Lower Egypt. I myself have never observed it, but have constantly shot *C. melanopogon*, a bird of which Von Heuglin makes no mention as being found in North-east Africa, from which circumstance I conclude that he has confounded it with some other species, possibly the present one, for no collector could have failed to meet with that bird. I brought home from my last tour no less than fourteen specimens of *C. melanopogon*, shot near Damietta during the last week in March, but never met with the present species, although I see no reason why it should not be found there.

Top of the head deep brown, with broad distinct buff-coloured eyebrows and a band of the same colour down the centre of the crown; back and scapulars ashy, shaded with yellowish brown on the centre of the back and rump, and mottled with dark brown on the centres of the feathers; wings and tail dark brown, with paler edges; underparts creamy white, shaded with brownish yellow on the crop and flanks, where there are a few narrow dark brown streaks down the centres of some of the feathers; beak brown, shading into yellowish flesh-colour on the lower mandible; legs yellowish flesh-colour; irides brown.

Entire length 4·8 inches; culmen 0·4; wing, carpus to tip, 2·5; tarsus 0·8.

Fig. Gould, B. of Eur. pl. 111.

CALAMODYTA MELANOPOGON.
EMBERIZA INTERMEDIA.

41. CALAMODYTA MELANOPOGON (Temm.). *Moustached Warbler.*

(Plate III. fig. 1.)

This Warbler, which is very rare in collections, I found in great abundance among the thick sedge of a lake near Damietta. They keep exclusively to the thick masses of reeds in very marshy districts, and may be seen clinging on to the stems as they take a last peep at the intruder before hiding themselves. They rarely show themselves boldly, but may be watched as they chase each other through the thick and matted sedge, which is seen to move as though a mouse was disturbing it. They creep and flutter along in pursuit of each other, occasionally uttering a little jarring note, and at intervals popping their heads out from among the thick covert to glance at the stranger. They have rather a pretty song, and in disposition are not shy. They may be best obtained in the Damietta marsh by walking steadily through the sedge, as they almost invariably, when first disturbed, fly to a prominent stem before hiding themselves. Though in form, size, and general appearance they much resemble the Common Sedge Warbler, they may be readily recognized, even in a wild state, by their blacker back, whiter chest, and by the absence of the yellow tints, which are so conspicuous in the latter bird.

I am surprised not to find this species mentioned by Von Heuglin in his great work on the birds of North-eastern Africa, as it is very abundant in some of the reedy lakes of the Delta, and remains in the country throughout the year.

Crown of the head black, more or less shaded with rufous; upper surface of the body olive-brown, with a chestnut shade on the rump; centres of the feathers of the upper part of the back and scapulars dark brown; wings and tail dark brown, with paler edgings to the feathers; a broad and distinct white eyebrow, and a dark streak from the lores through the eye, shading off on the ear-coverts; underparts white, shaded with brownish buff on the flanks and vent; beak dark brown; legs black; irides brown.

Entire length 5 inches; culmen 0·5; wing, carpus to tip, 2·2; tarsus 0·85.

42. Calamoherpe arundinacea (Gm.). *Reed Warbler.*

The Reed Warbler, according to Von Heuglin (Orn. N. O. Afr. p. 291), is a bird of passage in Egypt and Nubia, and is sometimes tolerably abundant in the swamps of the Delta.

The entire upper plumage uniform greyish olive; wings and tail brown, with pale edges to the feathers; it has a pale yellowish eyebrow; under surface white, washed with brownish buff on the sides of the neck, chest, and flanks; legs dark brown; beak pale brown, lightest on the lower mandible; irides hazel.

Entire length 5·5 inches; culmen 0·4; wing, carpus to tip, 2·5; tarsus 0·9.

Fig. Gould, B. of Eur. pl. 108.

43. Calamoherpe palustris (Bechst.). *Marsh Warbler.*

I cannot find any very positive evidence for including the present species in the Egyptian lists. Von Heuglin (Orn. N. O. Afr. p. 290) only quotes Rüppell as his authority for its being found in Egypt, and Lichtenstein for its occurrence in Nubia.

The differences between this species and the preceding

have never been satisfactorily defined by ornithologists; and I cannot myself find any character by which they may always be unerringly distinguished in the skin. In the freshly killed bird the legs are paler and the general colour more rufous than the Reed Warbler.

44. Acrocephalus stentorius (Hempr. & Ehr.). *Clamorous Sedge Warbler.*

This large Warbler is probably a resident in Egypt, for it certainly breeds there, and I have met with a specimen in the Fayoom as early as the 7th of March. Towards the latter end of that month I frequently saw it near Damietta, while hunting for *C. melanopogon* in the forests of thick sedge and reeds which surround some of the lakes. It generally keeps low down in the sedge, but will occasionally rise to the top of a tall reed to survey the district. Its plain colouring renders it very difficult to detect; but one is frequently made aware of its presence, either by its call, which in March consists of a single peculiarly loud note, repeated two or three times without variation, or from the movement of the sedge caused by its continual motion. In April it begins its love-song, and may then be much more easily procured. Although it frequents the thick sedge, it appears to prefer the proximity of some slight opening, such as is made by a ditch running through the swamp, in the centre of which the reeds do not grow. In such spots it may be watched with ease as it hops from reed to reed, keeping generally within a foot from the surface of the water, busily intent upon capturing the small aquatic insects and shells on which it subsists, and perfectly heedless of observation.

Upper plumage olive-brown, lightest on the rump and upper tail-coverts; wings and tail brown, with pale edges to the feathers; in some specimens there is a more or less distinct buff-coloured eyebrow extending to the beak; underparts white, shaded with buff on the vent and under tail-coverts, and with yellowish brown on the sides of the chest and flanks; the upper part of the chest has a few obsolete brown streaks; beak dark brown, shading into orange-yellow on the edges of the upper and basal half of the lower mandible; legs slaty brown; irides pale brown; *second primary considerably shorter than the third.*

Entire length 7 inches; culmen 0·8; wing, carpus to tip, 3·1; tarsus 1·05.

Fig. Allen, Ibis, 1864, pl. 1, p. 97.

45. Acrocephalus turdoides (Meyer). *Great Sedge Warbler.*

Von Heuglin (Orn. N. O. Afr. p. 289) considers this bird to be an accidental winter visitor to Lower Egypt. I have never seen a specimen from that country.

Very similar to *A. stentorius.* Underparts more inclining to buff, and without any indication of stripes; beak shorter and stouter; upper mandible distinctly notched; *second and third primaries equal and longest.*

Entire length 7 inches; culmen 0·65; wing, carpus to tip, 3·6; tarsus 1·1.

Fig. Gould, B. of Eur. pl. 106.

46. Acrocephalus arabicus, Heugl. *Arabian Sedge Warbler.*

This species is mentioned by Von Heuglin (Orn. N. O. Afr. p. 289) as occurring in Egypt near Suez. I do not know the bird; but it appears to be distinct from the last two species in the size and colouring of the beak; the other parts are described too vaguely to found any opinion upon; I therefore simply translate his Latin description.

Similar to *A. turdoides*; beak stouter, more obtuse, and higher at the base; feet longer, and superciliary streak more conspicuous and of a whiter colour; outer web of all the primaries with a narrow and conspicuous pale margin, the spurious primary whitish; breast, under wing-coverts, sides of the body, and under tail-coverts for the most part bright rufous ochre; the under mandible waxy, the whole of the upper one blackish horn-colour.

47. Cisticola schœnicola, Bp. *Fan-tail Warbler.*

This tiny but cheerful little Warbler is one of the most abundant birds in Egypt and Nubia, where it is met with in every green field, either watching our approach from some tall plant, or pouring forth its notes as it hovers over the surrounding herbage. It never frequents trees, but is equally abundant both in the dry fields and in marshes. It breeds in March, forming a charming little deep purse-shaped nest, open at the top, which I have found in clover, corn, and sedge, at a height of from a few inches to a foot from the ground. The nest is constructed of dried grass and cotton, and often thickly lined with the soft downy seeds of the reed or thistle, and is firmly secured by the interweaving of the surrounding herbage, which assists to hide it: in general appearance it looks very like the cocoon of a large caterpillar.

Upper plumage pale yellowish brown; centre of the feathers on the head dark brown, forming three more or less distinct longitudinal bands; centre of the feathers of the upper part of the back, wings, and tail dark brown; rump more or less ferruginous; tail fan-shaped, and of moderate length, with a dark spot near the tip of each feather, most visible from underneath; underparts white, inclining to pale yellowish brown towards the flanks; upper mandible brown; lower mandible and legs flesh-brown; irides brownish yellow.

Entire length 4 inches; culmen 0·4; wing, carpus to tip, 1·9; tarsus 0·8.

Fig. Gould, B. of Eur. pl. 113.

48. Drymœca gracilis (Rüpp.). *Graceful Warbler.*

This little Warbler is abundant both in the fields and marshes of Egypt and Nubia, where it remains throughout the year. Its song is powerful and melodious, and is frequently to be heard amongst the reeds. There are apparently two constant forms of this bird, but they hardly differ sufficiently to be separated as distinct species. I only brought home one specimen that exactly agreed with the plate in Rüppell's 'Atlas,' while all those that I have seen from Lower Egypt belong to the other form; that is to say, they are darker in colour, have the whole of the shaft-markings more strongly pronounced, are rather larger, and have darker bills.

In habits the former appears to be the common species in Upper Egypt and Nubia, and frequents the fields, while the latter is most abundant in the Delta, and usually to be met with in marshes or damp localities.

Tail long; upper plumage pale brown, with the centre of the feathers on the head, back, and wings rather darker; the tail has numerous narrow obsolete bars, with distinct brown spots at the end of the feathers, which are narrowly tipped with dirty white; underparts creamy white; legs brownish flesh-colour; beak brown; irides brownish yellow.

Entire length 4·3 inches; culmen 0·35; wing, carpus to tip, 1·7; tarsus 0·65.

Fig. Rüppell, Atlas, t. 2.

49. Hypolais olivetorum (Strickl.). *Olive-tree Warbler.*

Von Heuglin does not mention that this species occurs in Egypt; I have, however, a well-authenticated specimen collected by Mr. Rogers near Alexandria, and presented to me by my friends Messrs. Sharpe and Dresser. It is probably of only rare occurrence in that country; for I know of no other instance of its capture there.

Upper plumage uniform pale dusky, tinted with olive, and slightly paler on the upper tail-coverts; wings and tail brown, with pale edgings to the feathers; outer tail-feathers bordered with white, the next two on each side narrowly tipped with that colour; a faint streak in front of the eye dull white; underparts white, tinted with yellow, and slightly shaded on the sides with pale stone-grey; *beak very broad at the base, and surrounded by stout bristles*, brown above, shading into deep orange-yellow on the lower mandible; legs pale brown; irides brown.

Entire length 6·3 inches; culmen 0·6; wing, carpus to tip, 3·6; tarsus 0·9.

Fig. Gould, B. of Eur. pl. 107.

50. HYPOLAIS ELÆICA (Lind.)*. *Olivaceous Warbler.*

This is the most abundant Warbler in Nubia, and is not unfrequent in Egypt; but I have not met with it north of Dendera, although it must be found over the whole country, as it is not very uncommon in south-eastern Europe. In Nubia it takes the place of the Willow Warbler and Chiff-Chaff, but prefers to live among the higher boughs of the sont trees instead of the low thick herbage. Owing to its dull coloration it may easily be overlooked; but, if procured, may at once be recognized by the breadth of its bill.

H. languida (Hempr. & Ehr.). Under this name Von Heuglin (Orn. N. O. Afr. p. 296) has made five races or subspecies, the second of which, *H. elæica*, is the only form I think should be included within the limits of the present work.

Upper parts pale hair-brown; primaries and tail darker, with a pale narrow edging to all the feathers; underparts dirty white, the whole of the plumage faintly tinted with yellow; beak yellowish brown, darkest above; legs and irides brown.

* *Acrocephalus pallidus* (Hempr. & Ehr.), "nec Gerbe" of Heuglin (Orn. N. O. Afr. p. 294), I consider to be synonymous with *H. elæica* (Lind.).

Entire length 5·1 inches; culmen 0·45; wing, carpus to tip, 2·5; tarsus 0·8.

Fig. Bree, B. of Eur. ii. p. 54.

51. Phyllopneuste sylvicola (Lath.). *Wood Warbler.*

This species is to be met with throughout Egypt and Nubia, but is not plentiful there at any season. Von Heuglin (Orn. N. O. Afr. p. 298) considers it a not uncommon winter visitor in North-eastern Africa. I am, however, inclined to believe that it occasionally remains in Egypt throughout the year; for I have obtained a specimen near Assouan as late as the end of April.

Upper plumage bright yellowish green; wings and tail brown, the feathers distinctly edged with bright yellowish green; underparts pure white, shading into yellow under the wings and towards the throat, and becoming bright sulphur-yellow under the chin; a dusky streak passes from the bill through the eye, and directly above it a well-defined bright yellow eyebrow; beak pale brown, darkest above; legs pale brown; irides brown.

Entire length 4·8 inches; culmen 0·4; wing, carpus to tip, 3·1; tarsus 0·7.

Fig. Gould, B. of Eur. pl. 131.

52. Phyllopneuste Bonellii (Vieill.). *Bonelli's Warbler.*

Very abundant, especially in Upper Egypt, during the spring and autumn, where it takes the place of *P. trochilus* and *P. rufa* of Lower Egypt and *H. elæica* of Nubia. It is a lively cheerful bird, in habits and appearance very closely resembling the Willow Warbler.

Upper plumage ashy brown, inclining to bright yellow on the rump; wings and tail brown, edged with pale hair-brown and greenish yellow; underparts white, faintly shaded with paler brown; sides of the breast and under the wing tinted with sulphur-yellow; *a rather distinct white streak runs from the beak through the eye*; beak fleshy brown, darker above; legs pale brown; irides brown.

Entire length 4·5 inches; culmen 0·35; wing, carpus to tip, 2·5; tarsus 0·8.

Fig. Gould, B. of Eur. pl. 134.

53. PHYLLOPNEUSTE RUFA (Gm.). *Chiff-Chaff Warbler.*

The Chiff-Chaff is a winter visitant to Egypt and Nubia, and at this season is extremely abundant, especially in the Delta.

Head, back, scapulars, and upper tail-coverts olive; wings and tail pale dusky, with olive-green borders to the feathers; edge of the wing and under wing-coverts sulphur-yellow; a faint yellowish eyebrow; lores grey; underparts white, tinted on the throat, breast, and flanks with pale brownish yellow; legs dark brown; beak brown, shading off into flesh-colour at the base of the lower mandible; irides brown.

Entire length 4·5 inches; culmen 0·3; wing, carpus to tip, 2·3; tarsus 0·8.

Fig. Gould, B. of Eur. pl. 131.

54. PHYLLOPNEUSTE TROCHILUS (Linn.). *Willow Warbler.*

The Willow Warbler arrives with the Chiff-Chaff in September and leaves in March. During its stay it is very abundant both in Egypt and Nubia, especially so in the Delta, where great numbers may be seen flitting about among the prickly herbage by the sides of the embankments.

Very similar in plumage to *P. rufa*; it is a little larger, and the colours rather clearer, especially on the under surface of the body, and the legs are paler.

Entire length 4·8 inches; culmen 0·35; wing, carpus to tip, 2·7; tarsus 0·8.

Fig. Gould, B. of Eur. pl. 131.

55. PHYLLOPNEUSTE HIPPOLAIS (Linn.). *Melodious Willow Warbler.*

Von Heuglin (Orn. N. O. Afr. p. 296) mentions having observed this Warbler in Egypt singly in fig-gardens and clumps of sont trees.

The whole of the upper parts greenish ash-colour; in front of the eye is a small patch of yellow; throat and underparts pale yellow; wings and tail brown, the edges of the feathers being lighter; beak and legs fleshy brown; irides dark brown.

Entire length 5·1 inches; culmen 0·55; wing, carpus to tip, 3·15; tarsus 0·8.

Fig. Gould, B. of Eur. pl. 133.

56. PHYLLOPNEUSTE EVERSMANNI (Bp.). *Vieillot's Willow Warbler.*

I find the present species, in Mr. G. R. Gray's 'Hand-list of Birds,' vol. i. p. 215, with the locality Egypt assigned to it. This, however, is the only evidence I have for including it in the present work; for Von Heuglin does not mention it as occurring in any part of North-eastern Africa.

Very similar to *P. trochilus*; beak stronger; a distinct yellowish-white eyebrow and a dusky streak from the lores through the eye. There is no yellow shade on the rump, as in *P. Bonellii*. Legs pale brown; beak brown, inclining to yellowish flesh-colour on the lower mandible.

Entire length 5 inches; culmen 0·45; wing, carpus to tip, 2·7; tarsus 0·8.

57. Curruca hortensis (Gm.). *Garden Warbler.*

This Warbler is a spring visitant in Egypt, and is probably never very plentiful there. Von Heuglin (Orn. N. O. Afr. p. 310) mentions having obtained a specimen on the island of Roda, near Cairo, in the beginning of May. I know of no other instance of its capture in that country.

Entire upper plumage ashy brown, tinted with olive; wings and tail rather darker; an indistinct pale eyebrow; under-parts white, tinted with brown on the lower part of the throat and flanks; beak brown, much paler on the lower mandible; legs slaty brown; irides pale brown.

Entire length 6 inches; culmen 0·45; wing, carpus to tip, 3·1; tarsus 0·85.

Fig. Gould, B. of Eur. pl. 121.

58. Curruca orphea (Temm.). *Orphean Warbler.*

This Warbler, though an undoubted Egyptian species,

appears to be of very rare occurrence in that country. The only Egyptian specimen I have seen is in the collection of Messrs. Sharpe and Dresser. According to Von Heuglin (Orn. N. O. Afr. p. 310) it visits Egypt and Nubia in the autumn; and he mentions that he procured a specimen near the Pyramids.

Male.—Top of the head and ear-coverts dusky black; upper surface of the body slaty ash-colour; quills and tail brown, with broad ash-coloured edgings; the exterior feathers on each side of the latter have the outer webs and a broad apical tip white, and the next two feathers on each side are narrowly tipped with the same colour; underparts white, shaded with ashy on the flanks and under tail-coverts.

Female.—Resembles the male, except that the head is ashy grey, and the rest of the upper parts are shaded with brown; beak black, shading into yellowish at the base of the lower mandible; legs slaty brown; irides hazel.

Entire length 5·7 inches; culmen 0·55; wing, carpus to tip, 3; tarsus 0·9.

Fig. Gould, B. of Eur. pl. 119.

59. Curruca atricapilla (Linn.). *Black-cap Warbler.*

This is only a bird of passage in Egypt and Nubia, arriving on its way northwards in February and March, and passing through the country again in the autumn.

Male.—Top and back of the head black; nape and sides of the neck grey; back, shoulders, scapulars, and upper tail-coverts olive-grey; wings and tail dusky brown; throat and underparts greyish white, with a slight pink blush on the breast and flanks; beak brown; legs slate-colour; irides hazel.

Female.—Only differs from the male in having the top of the head rufous instead of black.

Entire length 5·8 inches; culmen 0·4; wing, carpus to tip, 2·8; tarsus 0·8.

Fig. Gould, B. of Eur. pl. 120.

60. Curruca Rueppellii (Temm.). *Rüppell's Warbler.*

This Warbler is moderately abundant throughout Egypt and Nubia. Its habits are not so lively as those of many of its congeners, and it may frequently be seen sitting still on the topmost bough of some low tree or cotton-plant. Von Heuglin (Orn. N. O. Afr. p. 315) calls it a bird of passage, and observes that it is not plentiful in Lower Egypt until the middle of March, when it may be met with in pairs, sometimes in company with *Sylvia subalpina.*

Male in breeding-plumage.—Head and throat black, with a white moustache; remainder of the upper parts slaty grey; wings dark brown, the feathers edged with brownish-buff colour; tail black, with the outer feather and tip of the second one white; underparts of the body white, shaded on the sides with grey, and with a rosy blush on the chest when in life.

The female is rather duller in plumage.

Entire length 5·5 inches; culmen 0·5; wing, carpus to tip, 2·7; tarsus 0·8.

Fig. Gould, B. of Eur. pl. 122.

61. CURRUCA MELANOCEPHALA (Gm.). *Black-headed Warbler.*

The present species is abundant throughout Egypt and Nubia, more especially so on the islands of the First Cataract. It is a lively bird, somewhat resembling the Lesser Whitethroat in habits.

Von Heuglin (Orn. N. O. Afr. p. 303) separates a small race of this bird under the name *Sylvia melanocephala minor*, to which he refers all the Egyptian specimens, but does not appear to place much faith in this separation, for he has not bestowed a number on the species in his book. I have not examined his type specimens; but I cannot allow that the slight difference in the measurements between the Egyptian and Piedmontese specimens in my collection justifies their separation as distinct species; I therefore give measurements of both forms, the smaller bird being an Egyptian specimen, the larger one from the Continent of Europe.

Top of the head, region of the eye, and ear-coverts black; back and scapulars slaty grey; wings dusky, with pale edges to the feathers; tail slaty black, except the exterior web of the outermost feather and the ends of the three outer ones, which are white; underparts white, shading into grey on the sides of the body; eyelids scarlet; beak black, shading off into yellow at the base of the lower mandible; legs and irides brown.

The female has a slate-coloured head, and the plumage is generally browner.

Entire length 4·5–5 inches; culmen 0·35–0·4; wing, carpus to tip, 2·1–2·2; tarsus 0·75–0·85.

Fig. Gould, B. of Eur. pl. 129.

62. Melizophilus sardus (Marm.). *Sardinian Warbler.*

According to Von Heuglin (Orn. N. O. Afr. p. 303) this rare Warbler is often to be met with in Egypt in the spring, and he mentions having killed it himself in the country.

Head, throat, and all the upper parts deep blackish grey, darkest on the forehead and round the eyes; on the chin there are a few white feathers; centre of the belly greyish white, tinged with vinous; wings and tail black, the exterior feathers of the latter edged with white; eyelids vermilion; base of the lower mandible yellow, the remainder of the beak horn-colour; legs yellowish brown; irides pale brown.

Entire length 5·2 inches; culmen 0·4; wing, carpus to tip, 2·2; tarsus 0·8.

Fig. Gould, B. of Eur. pl. 127.

63. Melizophilus provincialis (Gm.). *Dartford Warbler.*

According to Von Heuglin (Orn. N. O. Afr. p. 302) the Dartford Warbler, though rare in Egypt, has been observed by him in the Delta towards the end of March in company with *Sylvia subalpina* and *Curruca Rueppellii.*

Entire upper plumage dark slaty grey, deepest on the head and ear-coverts, and strongly tinted with olive-brown on the back; wings dusky, the feathers edged with brown; throat and underparts deep ferruginous brown, except the centre of the abdomen, which is white; beak dusky, inclining to yellow at the base of the lower mandible; legs and eyelids yellow; irides pale yellowish brown.

Entire length 5·3 inches; culmen 0·5; wing, carpus to tip, 2; tarsus 0·6.

Fig. Gould, B. of Eur. pl. 129.

64. Sylvia subalpina, Bon. *Subalpine Warbler.*

I first met this bird towards the end of March near Damietta, where I found it abundant, from which I conclude that it does not winter in Egypt. The low bushes and herbage along the sides of the embankments are the favourite resorts of this lively little Warbler; and there it may be seen constantly on the move, creeping and flitting about amongst the thick shelter, and may be easily recognized at such times by its white outer tail-feathers and diminutive size; for the Black-headed Warbler and the Lesser Whitethroat are not nearly so abundant in the Delta in March as the present bird. Von Heuglin (Orn. N. O. Afr. p. 305) considers that this species is a spring visitant to Lower Egypt.

Male in breeding-plumage.—Upper parts ashy grey; wings and tail brown, with pale edgings to the feathers; apical half of the outer feathers on each side of the tail white, the next tipped with that colour; a white moustache running down the sides of the neck; throat, crop, and flanks brick-red, of a greater or less intensity, shading into creamy white on the remainder of the body; beak brown, inclining to flesh-colour at the base; legs pale brown; irides brownish yellow; eyelids red.

Female.—Upper parts shaded with hair-brown; underparts creamy white, faintly shaded with brick-red.

Entire length 5 inches; culmen 0·4; wing, carpus to tip, 2·4; tarsus 0·75.

Fig. Gould, B. of Eur. pl. 124.

65. Sylvia conspicillata, Marm. *Spectacled Warbler.*

Canon Tristram tells me that this species is certainly met

with in Egypt, but does not remain there throughout the winter. I myself never found it; and as Von Heuglin does not include it among the birds of North-east Africa, I insert it here with some hesitation, although one might well expect to meet with it in the country.

Male.—Top of the head, cheeks, and lower part of the throat fine ash-colour; space between the eye and the beak black, whence a circle of the same colour surrounds the white of the eyes; back and scapulars vinous ash-colour; the wings blackish, broadly edged with rufous; throat white; under surface of the body white, tinged with vinous, which passes into reddish on the flanks; tail brownish black, except the outer feathers, which are nearly white, while the second and third are also tipped with that colour; beak brown, shading into yellowish flesh-colour on the basal half of the lower mandible; legs yellowish flesh-colour; irides pale brown.

Female.—Similar to the male, but paler, and the circle round the eye hardly apparent, if, indeed, at all distinguishable.

Entire length 5 inches; culmen 0·4; wing, carpus to tip, 1·3; tarsus 0·7.

Fig. Gould, B. of Eur. pl. 126.

66. Sylvia curruca (Linn.). *Lesser Whitethroat.*

This is a very abundant Warbler throughout Egypt and Nubia, frequenting the low sont and tamarisk bushes, where it may be seen flitting in and out among the thick covert, actively pursuing the small insects upon which it feeds.

Winter plumage.—Upper parts ashy brown, inclining to grey on the head and ear-coverts; underparts white, tinged with very pale brown; wings and tail dark brown, the feathers narrowly edged with ashy brown; the outer feathers on each side of the tail nearly white.

In summer the head and ear-coverts are slaty grey; beak nearly black, inclining to lead-colour at the base of the lower mandible; legs dark slate-colour; irides hazel.

Entire length 5·3 inches; culmen 0·35; wing, carpus to tip, 2·7; spurious primary 0·6; tarsus 0·8.

Fig. Gould, B. of Eur. pl. 125.

67. SYLVIA CINEREA, Bechst. *Whitethroat.*

I have shot this species both in Egypt and Nubia, but it is by no means common in either country. It frequents the young sont and other trees which afford thick covert near the ground, especially where they grow in rows along the embankments.

In breeding-plumage the upper part of the head, nape, and ear-coverts are slate-coloured, tinged with brown, while in winter the whole of the upper parts are cindery brown, tinted with rufous on the forehead and back; wings and tail-feathers dusky, edged with pale brown; secondaries more broadly edged with rufous; the underparts, in winter, are white, tinted with pale yellowish brown, especially on the flanks; while in summer plumage there is a delicate pink blush on the chest, which soon fades after death; beak brown above, changing to yellow at the base of the lower mandible; legs pale brown; irides hazel.

Entire length 5·5 inches; culmen 0·35; wing, carpus to tip, 2·8; spurious primary 0·4; tarsus 0·8.

Fig. Gould, B. of Eur. pl. 125.

Fam. NECTARINIIDÆ.

68. NECTARINIA METALLICA, Licht. *Yellow-breasted Sun-bird.*

(Plate IV.)

This beautiful little Sun-bird is the only one of the family which comes within the limits of my present work. I first met with it near Kalabshee, in Nubia, where it was tolerably plentiful in the beginning of April; and I have no doubt that it occasionally descends below the First Cataract; for on the 14th of April I noticed several specimens within twenty miles of Philæ. It is a lively bird, rarely sitting still for long together, now fluttering over a flower, now darting off to some neighbouring sont tree. The female is a dull-coloured but graceful little bird, generally in close company with her partner; and I have often watched them on some prominent twig sunning themselves, and keeping up an animated conversation in a pleasing little twittering note, evidently in full enjoyment of each other's company.

Male.—Head, throat, upper half of the back, scapulars, lesser wing-coverts, and outer web of the larger coverts bronzy green; remainder of the back metallic purple, shading into steel-blue on the rump and upper tail-coverts; tail black, shaded with steel-blue on the edges of the two long centre feathers; remainder of the wing dark brown, with a narrow paler edging to the primaries; a steel-blue collar separates the green throat from the bright yellow of the chest and abdomen; thighs black; beak black; legs and irides dark brown.

Entire length 6·2 inches; culmen 0·45; wing, carpus to tip, 2·2; tarsus 0·6.

Female.—Upper parts stone-grey, shaded with green on the rump; a creamy-white eyebrow; wings and tail nearly black;

NECTARINIA METALLICA

the edges of the feathers of the same colour as the back; underparts white, shaded with sulphur-yellow on the chest and centre of the abdomen; beak black; legs and irides dark brown.

Entire length 2·7 inches; culmen 0·45; wing, carpus to tip, 2; tarsus 0·6.

Fam. CERTHIIDÆ.

69. TICHODROMA MURARIA (Linn.). *Wall-creeper.*

According to Rüppell this species comes into Egypt; but Von Heuglin (Orn. N. O. Afr. p. 236) observes that he never met with it in any part of North-east Africa, so that I think we may fairly doubt its occurrence in the country.

Winter plumage.—Upper parts clear grey, faintly shaded with brown on the head, and inclining to slaty black on the upper tail-coverts; wings blackish; the smaller coverts bright crimson, the larger ones edged with the same colour; the basal portion of the outer web of most of the quills crimson; the outer primaries have two white spots on the inner web of each feather, the lesser ones have paler tips; tail black, with dusky ends approaching to white on the outer feathers on each side; underparts slate-colour, shading into white on the throat; beak and legs black; irides dark brown.

Summer plumage.—Darker grey, and the entire throat and upper breast black.

Entire length 6·3 inches; culmen 1; wing, carpus to tip, 3·9; tarsus 0·9.

Fig. Sharpe and Dresser, B. of Eur. part vii.

Fam. LANIIDÆ.

70. Lanius excubitor, Linn. *Great Grey Shrike.*

Dr. von Heuglin (Orn. N. O. Afr. p. 478) mentions having shot this bird himself in Egypt in the winter. This is the only evidence we have of its occurrence in that country. Messrs. Dresser and Sharpe, in an able notice on *L. excubitor* and its allies (P. Z. S. 1870, p. 591), observe, in reference to the above statement of Von Heuglin, "We are, however, sceptical enough to be very anxious to see a *specimen* of true *L. excubitor* from the shores of the Mediterranean or North-eastern Africa."

Hemprich and Ehrenberg mention it as found throughout Egypt and Nubia; and Rüppell calls it plentiful in Egypt. These latter observations, no doubt, refer to some of the allied species, as Von Heuglin and Messrs. Dresser and Sharpe are all inclined to believe.

Above pearl-grey; forehead and over the eye white; lores, under the eye, and ear-coverts black; scapulars grey, edged with white; wings black, primaries and outermost secondaries white at the base, thus forming a double bar on the wing; primaries and secondaries tipped with white; tail black, with the exception of the whole of the two outer feathers and the ends of all but the two centre ones, which are white; under surface of the body white, with occasionally a pink blush; legs and beak black; irides brown.

The sexes are alike in plumage.

Entire length 9·5 inches; culmen 0·7; wing, carpus to tip, 4·4; tarsus 1·0.

Fig. Sharpe and Dresser, B. of Eur. part ii.

71. Lanius lahtora, Sykes. *Pallid Shrike.*

This Shrike is not uncommon in Egypt and Nubia, where it remains throughout the year. Mr. E. C. Taylor mentions it (Ibis, 1867, p. 57) under the name *L. dealbatus.* Von Heuglin (Orn. N. O. Afr. pp. 480 and 483) divides it into two species, *L. leucopygus* and *L. lahtora.* All these names are synonymous with *L. lahtora*, Sykes, which has been shown by Messrs. Dresser and Sharpe (*l. c.*) to be the correct title for this species.

Upper parts grey; a line across the forehead, lores, in front and under the eye, and ear-coverts black; lower part of the scapulars white; wing black, except the basal half of the primaries and end of the secondaries, which are white, thus forming a single band on the wing; tail black, except the two outer feathers on each side, which are white with black shafts; outer web of the next and end of the next three white; under surface of the body white; beak and legs black; tarsi very stout; irides brown.

Entire length 9·5 inches; culmen 0·7; wing, carpus to tip, 4·2; tarsus 1·2.

Fig. Sharpe and Dresser, B. of Eur. part xi.

72. Lanius minor, Gm. *Lesser Grey Shrike.*

This Shrike evidently ranges throughout Egypt and Nubia, and appears to remain in the country throughout the year; for Von Heuglin (Orn. N. O. Afr. p. 477) calls it a resident in North-eastern Africa; yet I am unacquainted with any authenticated instance of its capture in Egypt.

Upper parts grey; forehead, feathers round the eye, and

ear-coverts black; wings black, secondaries narrowly tipped with white; basal portion of the primaries white, forming a broad bar on the wing; tail, four centre feathers black, two outer ones on each side white, third and fourth white, with an irregular patch of black; underparts white, shaded with pink on the flanks; beak and legs black; irides brown.

Entire length 8·5 inches; culmen 0·6; wing, carpus to tip, 4·5; tarsus 1.

Fig. Sharpe and Dresser, B. of Eur. part xiii.

73. Lanius nubicus, Licht. *Masked Shrike.*

This species is migratory, arriving in Egypt from the south towards the end of February. At Dendera, on the 25th of March, it was so plentiful that I could have counted a hundred of these birds in a day, generally in pairs. In Nubia it was extremely abundant, pairs of them flying and chattering together in every clump of trees I passed through. Its habits are very similar to those of the Wood-Chat, but it is rather more partial to groves of trees, where its well-marked plumage renders it very conspicuous.

Male in breeding-plumage.—Forehead and eyebrows creamy white; upper parts of the body blue-black; scapulars and base of the primaries white, remainder of the wing brownish black; the smaller wing-coverts edged with grey, the secondaries narrowly edged with cream-colour; tail black, except the two outer feathers and the tip of the third, which are white; underparts white, shaded with rich rufous on the sides of the neck, breast, and flanks; beak and legs black; irides brown.

Entire length 7 inches; culmen 0·55; wing, carpus to tip, 3·5; tarsus 0·9.

The female is similar, but rather paler on the back, and has the scapulars tinted with buff. The immature birds have the upper parts of the body dusky ash-colour.

Fig. Sharpe and Dresser, B. of Eur. part ii.

74. Lanius auriculatus, Müll. *Wood-Chat Shrike.*

The Wood-Chat is plentiful and evenly distributed throughout Egypt and Nubia. It does not remain in the Delta during the winter months, but appears there about the middle of March. It is rather lonely in habits, but attracts notice by the prominent position it takes up on the top of some bush or hedge.

Male.—Forehead, sides of the head and neck, and between the shoulders black; a white loral spot above the nostril on each side; top of the head and back of the neck bright chestnut; centre of the back grey; rump, tail-coverts, scapulars, and base of the primaries white; remainder of the wing black, some of the feathers narrowly edged with white; tail white at the base, remainder black, except the exterior web of the outer feather and the tips of all but the four centre ones, which are white; underparts creamy white; beak and legs black; irides brown.

Entire length 7 inches; culmen 0·6; wing, carpus to tip, 4; tarsus 0·9.

Fig. Sharpe and Dresser, B. of Eur. part i.

75. Lanius collurio, Linn. *Red-backed Shrike.*

This Shrike comes to Egypt early in August, on its way

south, and returns again in March and April; but is never plentiful, although, according to Von Heuglin, it ranges throughout North-eastern Africa.

Male.—Lower part of the forehead, lores, feathers around the eye, and ear-coverts black; upper part of the head and neck grey; upper part of the back and scapulars chestnut; rump and tail-coverts grey; tail, two centre feathers, the inner web of the next on each side, shafts, and a band at the end dark brown, remainder white; wings brown, primaries with very narrow pale edgings, inner secondaries and wing-coverts broadly edged with chestnut; underparts white, strongly shaded with rufous on the chest and flanks; beak black; legs and irides brown.

Entire length 7·2 inches; culmen 0·6; wing, carpus to tip, 3·7; tarsus 1.

Fig. Sharpe and Dresser, B. of Eur. part iv.

Fam. MUSCICAPIDÆ.

76. Muscicapa grisola, Linn. *Spotted Flycatcher.*

The Spotted Flycatcher ranges throughout Egypt and Nubia, but appears to be of rather rare occurrence in those countries; for I have only observed it myself on a single occasion near Alexandria in April. Von Heuglin says (Orn. N. O. Afr. p. 439) that this species occasionally breeds in Lower Egypt, but is more generally to be met with during its migrations in the autumn and spring.

Male.—Upper plumage hair-brown, with the centre of the feathers on the crown dark brown; wings and tail rather deeper in colour, with pale borders to the secondaries and greater wing-coverts; underparts white, shaded with hair-brown on the upper part of the chest and flanks, and spotted with that colour on the sides of the throat and crop; beak and legs brownish black; irides brown.

Entire length 5·5 inches; culmen 0·45; wing, carpus to tip, 3·3; tarsus 0·6.

Fig. Gould, B. of Eur. pl. 65.

77. Muscicapa atricapilla, Linn. *Pied Flycatcher.*

Von Heuglin (Orn. N. O. Afr. p. 438) mentions that the Pied Flycatcher is met with in Lower Egypt during its migration towards the end of March and in April. It is not, however, so plentiful as the next species.

Male in spring plumage.—A white spot on each lore, connected on the forehead; top of the head, back, shoulders, and upper tail-coverts black; nape and rump dusky; quills and scapulars dusky, with some white on the secondaries and scapulars; the greater wing-coverts broadly tipped with white; tail black, excepting the external web of the outer feather on each side and the basal portion of the inner web of all but the two centre feathers, which are white; the entire under surface white, this colour extending for three-quarters of the way round the neck; beak and legs black; irides dark brown.

The plumage of the female is duller, and she has no white spots on the forehead.

Entire length 5·5 inches; culmen 0·4; wing, carpus to tip, 3·5; tarsus 0·8.

Fig. Gould, B. of Eur. pl. 63.

78. Muscicapa collaris, Bechst. *White-collared Flycatcher.*

This species is a spring and autumn visitant, of apparently rather uncertain occurrence; for while in 1868 I frequently met with it in pairs in April between Cairo and Benisouef, in 1870, although I was in the country until the 10th of May, we never once saw it; nor did I meet with it in the Fayoom or Delta in 1871 up to the end of March. Its white and black plumage renders it very conspicuous, as it chiefly frequents the outermost boughs of the sont trees and the leaves of the date-palms, where it is ever actively engaged in the pursuit of its insect food.

Spring plumage.—Forehead and neck white; top of the head, lores, cheeks, and ear-coverts black; upper part of the back, scapulars, tail-coverts, and tail black; rump white, shaded with dusky; base of the quills, outer web of the three inner ones, and greater portion of some of the larger coverts white, remainder of the wing black; the entire under surface of the body white; beak and legs black; irides dark brown.

Entire length 5·4 inches; culmen 0·4; wing, carpus to tip, 3·4; tarsus 0·7.

Fig. Gould, B. of Eur. pl. 62.

Fam. HIRUNDINIDÆ.

79. Hirundo rustica, Linn. *Chimney-Swallow.*

This bird is properly only a spring and autumn visitant in Egypt, arriving there on its way north about the middle of April; but a few possibly remain in the country throughout the year, for we once obtained an immature specimen in the Delta on the 25th of February. In Nubia it appears to be the only Swallow, there replacing *H. Riocourii*; for on our return journey in 1870 we did not meet with a single specimen of the latter bird south of Girgeh, where in the beginning of May these two species were equally abundant.

Forehead and throat deep rufous-brown, remainder of the upper parts steel-blue; quills almost black; tail black, with large white spots on the inner web of all but the two centre feathers; a steel-blue collar at the base of the throat; remainder of the underparts cream-colour; beak black; legs and irides dark brown.

Entire length 8 inches; culmen 0·3; wing, carpus to tip, 5; tarsus 0·4.

Fig. Gould, B. of Eur. pl. 64.

80. Hirundo Riocourii, Audouin. *Oriental Chimney-Swallow.*

This species is resident in Egypt, and very abundant. It differs from the last species in not being migratory, and it keeps more exclusively to the neighbourhood of houses, usually selecting the inside of some native mud-hut for its nest, which it begins to construct in February.

Upper plumage and collar round the throat steel-blue; forehead and throat chocolate-brown; under surface of the body ferruginous brown; all the tail-feathers, except the two centre ones, having a large rufous-white spot on their inner web.

Entire length 7 inches; culmen 0·3; wing, carpus to tip, 4·8; tarsus 0·45.

Fig. Bree, B. of Eur. iii. p. 178.

81. Hirundo rufula, Temm. *Rufous Swallow.*

This species ranges throughout Egypt and Nubia, but is of rare occurrence. Towards the end of March I constantly saw a pair flying over a marsh near Damietta, and on the 30th of that month obtained one of them. Von Heuglin (Orn. N. O. Afr. p. 158) mentions that Brehm met with a specimen in Egypt in company with *H. rustica,* and that he himself observed it at Derr, in Nubia.

Top of the head, back, and scapulars steel-blue; back of the neck and rump chestnut; tail-coverts creamy white, tipped with steel-blue; wings and tail brownish black, without a spot, and slightly shaded with a green reflection; underparts cream-colour, with dark brown streaks on the shafts of the feathers, more distinct on the throat; under tail-coverts tipped with black; beak black; legs and irides dark brown.

Entire length 7 inches; culmen 0·3; wing, carpus to tip, 4·7; tarsus 0·55.

Fig. Gould, B. of Asia, part xx.

82. Cotyle rupestris (Scop.). *Crag-Swallow.*

I have never seen an Egyptian specimen of this Swallow; and Von Heuglin observes that he never found it in any part of North-eastern Africa; yet he includes it (Orn. N. O. Afr. p. 163), upon the authority of Brehm, who says that it is, though rarely, to be met with in Egypt. I am, however, very sceptical as to its ever having been found in that country.

Similar in plumage to *C. obsoleta,* but *considerably larger* than that bird, and darker and browner on the flanks, abdomen, and under tail-coverts.

Entire length 5·3 inches; culmen 0·3; wing, carpus to tip, 5·2; tarsus 0·45.

Fig. Gould, B. of Eur. pl. 56.

83. Cotyle obsoleta, Cab. *Pale Crag-Swallow.*

This species of Crag-Swallow is very plentifully distributed throughout Egypt and Nubia, where it is a resident. It only frequents the rocky districts, and is therefore of rare occurrence in the Delta, although at Cairo and the Pyramids it is abundant. It may be easily recognized by the paleness of the colouring of its back. It begins to breed about the middle of February, placing its nest under the shelter of an overhanging rock, or attaching it to the ceiling of some of the less-frequented passages of the ruined temples, or even occasionally in the native dwellings. The eggs of this species are white, spotted with rufous brown, and are very like those of *Hirundo rustica.*

Upper plumage very pale brown, darkest on the head, and especially in front of the eyes, and palest on the rump; wings rather darker than the back, except on the outer web of the feathers; the tail with a large white spot on all but the two centre and two outer feathers; underparts creamy white, shaded with hair-brown on the flanks and under tail-coverts; tarsi unfeathered; legs brown; beak black; irides dark brown.

Entire length 4·7 inches; culmen 0·3; wing, carpus to tip, 4·5; tarsus 0·4.

84. Cotyle riparia (Linn.). *Sand-Martin.*

This bird arrives in Egypt in great abundance in March, and towards the end of April commences breeding in colonies in the banks by the river side. It is extremely partial to the neighbourhood of water, and may be constantly seen skimming over the surface in its graceful flight, at times just touching the surface sufficiently to raise a slight ripple, or dashing rapidly after its mate in the exuberance of its spirits.

Upper parts and a broad collar on the chest mouse-colour, palest towards the tail; remainder of the underparts white; beak black; legs brown; irides dark brown.

Entire length 4·6 inches; culmen 0·2; wing, carpus to tip, 3·7; tarsus 0·45.

Fig. Gould, B. of Eur. pl. 58.

85. Cotyle minor, Cab.

According to Von Heuglin (Orn. N. O. Afr. p. 167) this bird inhabits Egypt and Nubia, and breeds in colonies in the river banks, like *C. riparia*, between the months of February and May.

I have never seen this species myself; and Mr. Sharpe, who has written a complete Monograph of the African Swallows (P. Z. S. 1870, p. 303), has not been able to make it out satisfactorily. For the better elucidation of the species, I quote his remarks as follows:—"According to Dr. Cabanis this Martin approaches *C. riparia* and *C. palustris* in form and colour, but is larger than the former and smaller than the latter, and differs from both in the form of the tail, and also in the colour of the underside, as in this species both the grey breast-band and white throat are wanting. The chin and throat down to below the breast are yellowish grey.

"I have now a specimen lying before me of what I take to be this species, brought from Abyssinia by Mr. Blanford, and I cannot see that it is really distinct from *Cotyle paludicola*. It appears to be identical with a Natal specimen of the latter in my own collection, with the exception of the length of the wing, which is longer in my Natal bird. I cannot perceive, even in the rather unsatisfactory diagnosis of Dr. Cabanis, any real characters whereby the species may be distinguished from *C. palustris*."

86. Chelidon urbica (Linn.). *House-Martin.*

Our Common Martin may occasionally be met with both in Egypt and Nubia, but does not appear to make its home in those countries; for on each occasion when I observed it during the months of April and May it seemed to have no fixed abode, but to be on its way northward. This may possibly be accounted for by the general absence of large houses, against which we know this bird usually likes to place its nest.

Rump and underparts white; wings and tail dark brown; remainder of the plumage steel-blue; beak black; irides dark brown; *tarsi and feet covered with little white plumes.*

Entire length 5·5 inches; culmen 0·3; wing, carpus to tip, 4·2; tarsus 0·4.

Fig. Gould, B. of Eur. pl. 57.

Fam. MOTACILLIDÆ.

87. Motacilla alba, Linn. *White Wagtail.*

This is one of the most abundant birds in Egypt and Nubia during the winter; but its numbers diminish considerably as spring advances, and in Nubia I found it comparatively rare in April.

Winter plumage.—Crown of the head and nape black, or inclining to black; remainder of the upper plumage slaty grey; wings dark brown, most of the feathers broadly edged with dirty white; tail dark brown, with the exception of the two outer feathers on each side, which are white; forehead and underparts white, with a black crescent-shaped collar; legs and bill black; irides dark brown.

In summer plumage the throat is black.

Entire length 7 inches; culmen 0·4; wing, carpus to tip, 3·4; tarsus 0·9.

Fig. Gould, B. of Eur. pl. 143.

88. Motacilla vidua, Sund. *White-winged Wagtail.*

This species, although I believe it to be a resident in Upper Egypt and Nubia, is most abundant at the First Cataract, the only place where I myself have met with it. Although it has selected this barren and rocky district, where the Nile dashes over the rough granite rocks in a turmoil of waters, it is by no means an unsociable bird, but appears to welcome the stranger as it flits from rock to rock along the shore or alights upon his "dahabeah." It is ever active in the pursuit of food, which consists chiefly of a small green beetle, and is perfectly heedless of intrusion. Its sociability was the chief cause of its safety; for the banks being crowded with natives hauling at the boat prevented the possibility of my shooting it on several occasions. It is a beautifully marked species, the pure black and white of its plumage rendering it very easy to distinguish from *M. alba*. In April I found it beginning to breed. Much confusion has been created in the nomenclature of this species, which is usually called *M. lugubris*, and is thus designated by me in one of my papers to 'The Ibis.' Having compared my Egyptian specimens with examples of *M. vidua* in Mr. Sharpe's collection from all parts of Africa, I cannot see any specific distinctions.

A very plain white band passes from the beak over the eye to behind the ear-coverts. The following portions of the plumage are black:—lores, cheeks, ear-coverts, a band down the side of the neck joining a crescent-shaped patch on the front of the chest; top of the head, back of the neck, back, scapulars, tail, except the two outer feathers on each side; wing, except the basal portion of all the quills but the two outer ones, the edges of the secondaries, and the greater portion of the larger wing-coverts, which are white; remainder of the plumage white; beak and legs black; irides dark brown.

Entire length 7 inches; culmen 0·6; wing, carpus to tip, 3·5; tarsus 0·9.

89. MOTACILLA SULPHUREA, Bechst. *Grey Wagtail.*

I was never fortunate enough to meet with this species myself in Egypt, although it is undoubtedly to be found there, probably as a winter visitor. Mr. E. C. Taylor (Ibis, 1867, p. 63) says that he saw it at Cairo in January; and Dr. A. Leith Adams (Ibis, 1864, p. 22) mentions that it was met with in its usual retreats as far south as Nubia.

Upper plumage slaty grey, shading off on the rump and upper tail-coverts into bright greenish yellow; wings dark brown, the secondaries broadly edged with yellowish white; tail dark brown, the three outer feathers on each side white; underparts white, usually strongly tinted with sulphur-yellow from the chest downwards, and always brightest on the under tail-coverts; a distinct white eyebrow; beak pale brown, darkest towards the tip; legs flesh-brown; irides brown.

In summer plumage both sexes assume a black throat.

The tail is longer than in any of the Yellow Wagtails.

Entire length 7·5 inches; culmen 0·45; wing, carpus to tip, 3·3; tarsus 0·8.

Fig. Gould, B. of Eur. pl. 147.

90. Budytes flava (Linn.). *Grey-headed Yellow Wagtail.*

This and the next two species are generally considered to be mere varieties of the same bird; and in large series of specimens it is difficult, if not impossible, to draw the line between them. However this may be with birds from other localities, in Egypt and Nubia they appear to keep perfectly separate. I only met with the true *B. flava* of Linnæus about the middle of *April* in Nubia, travelling northward in large flocks, out of which I killed more than twenty specimens without finding the least variation in plumage; while I had already found *B. cinereocapilla*, one of the most abundant birds in Egypt, in *March*. The true *B. flava* may be most readily distinguished by a well-defined white eyebrow, which is absent in the next two species or subspecies. I would also draw attention to the slight, but constant, difference in the measurements of my Egyptian specimens of *B. flava* and *B. cinereocapilla*.

Top of the head and nape grey, remainder of the upper parts greenish yellow; wings dark brown, most of the feathers broadly edged with pale brownish yellow; tail dark brown, the two outer feathers on each side white; underparts bright yellow, shading off to white at the chin; a *distinct white eye-brow*; bill and legs dark brown; irides brown.

Entire length 6·5 inches; culmen 0·5; wing, carpus to tip, 3·2; tarsus 0·9.

Fig. Gould, B. of Eur. pl. 146.

91. Budytes cinereocapilla (Savi). *Grey-headed Yellow Wagtail.*

This is the most abundant form of Yellow Wagtail in Egypt, where it appears to remain throughout the year. It is very Pipit-like in its habits, and is more frequently met with in pairs and flocks in the fields than by the water's edge. I have before me six Egyptian specimens of this species, shot between the 1st of March and 5th of May. They differ from the two specimens from which I described the last species in the *entire absence of a white eyebrow*, and in the rather darker colour of the cheeks and ear-coverts. These six specimens do not vary one tenth of an inch in any of the following dimensions.

Entire length 6 inches; culmen 0·5; wing, carpus to tip, 2·9; tarsus 0·9.

Fig. Bree, B. of Eur. p. 143.

K

92. BUDYTES MELANOCEPHALA, Savi. *Black-headed Yellow Wagtail.*

In Nubia I frequently met with this bird in April, in flocks among the herbage by the river-side. Although I shot many specimens out of these flocks, I never came across a grey-headed bird among them. They were evidently migrating northward at that season. In the Fayoom in March I shot the only pair of these birds which I saw there. Specimens from Egypt appear to have the black head remarkably well defined.

Top and sides of the head, ear-coverts and nape jet-black; remainder of the plumage similar to that of *B. flava*, except that it has no white eyebrow and no white on the chin.

Entire length 6·7 inches; culmen 0·5; wing, carpus to tip, 3·3; tarsus 1.

Fig. Demidoff, Voy. Russ. Merid. tab. 2.

93. ANTHUS PLUMATUS (Müll.). *Tree-Pipit.*

This bird arrives about March, when it becomes plentiful throughout Egypt and Nubia.

Upper plumage olive-brown, with the centre of most of the feathers dark brown; wings and tail dark brown, the feathers edged with pale olivaceous brown, outer feathers of the tail nearly white; underparts white, tinted with pale brownish yellow on the sides of the throat and chest; chest, and occasionally the flanks, distinctly marked with longitudinal dark brown spots; beak brown, paler at the base of the lower mandible; legs pale fleshy brown; irides brown.

Entire length 6·2 inches; culmen 0·45; wing, carpus to tip, 3·5; tarsus 0·8.

Fig. Gould, B. of Eur. pl. 139

94. Anthus pratensis (Linn.). *Meadow-Pipit.*

The Meadow-Pipit is of rare occurrence in Egypt and Nubia, where it is a winter visitor. I have only one Egyptian specimen, which was killed near Alexandria in April.

Entire upper plumage olive-brown, with the centre of the feathers dusky, the edgings to the quills being narrow; of the tail, the outer feather has the exterior web dull white, and a large wedge-shaped white spot at the tip; the next feather has a similar but smaller spot; the two centre feathers are dusky; and the others are brown, with narrow edgings of olive-colour; the entire under plumage is buff, richest on the breast and flanks, with an oval dusky spot along the shafts of the feathers on the breast and flanks, and a line of dusky spots from the base of the lower mandible down the side of the neck; beak dusky, shading into deep yellow towards the base of the lower mandible; legs fleshy brown; irides brown.

Entire length 5·8 inches; culmen 0·4; wing, carpus to tip, 3·1; tarsus 0·9.

Fig. Gould, B. of Eur. pl. 136.

95. Anthus cervinus, Pall. *Red-throated Pipit.*

This species is one of the most abundant birds throughout Egypt and Nubia. Its numbers are somewhat decreased by the month of April; but I believe it remains there throughout the year.

Upper plumage olive-brown, with the centre of the feathers dark brown; wings and tail dark brown, the feathers edged with pale brown, the outer feather on each side of the tail nearly white; underparts buff, with large longitudinal dark brown spots on the chest and flanks; throat and feathers round the eye more or less rusty-red, occasionally with a violet tinge on the former; beak brown, inclining to pale yellowish brown towards the base of the lower mandible; legs pale brown; irides brown.

Entire length 6·2 inches; culmen 0·45; wing, carpus to tip, 3·5; tarsus 0·8.

Fig. Gould, B. of Eur. pl. 140.

96. Anthus spinolettus (Linn.) *Water-Pipit.*

This species is a winter visitor to Egypt, when it probably ranges throughout the country, but has not, to my knowledge, been met with in Nubia. It is most plentiful in the Fayoom and Delta, where I found it very abundant in the marshes in February and March. Owing to its simple colouring it may be easily overlooked; but if sought for, it may be recognized from *A. cervinus* (the only Pipit it is likely to be confounded with) by its rather larger size and darker coloration.

Upper parts and ear-coverts olive-brown, shading into umber-brown on the rump; feathers on the head, upper part of the back, and scapulars with dark centres; wings and tail dark brown, with pale edges to the feathers; exterior web and end of the outer tail-feather and tip of the next one white; eyebrow buff, underparts creamy white, strongly shaded on the throat, crop, and flanks with pinkish brown, and with a few longitudinal brown spots on the flanks; beak, legs, and irides brown, the former shading into pale brownish yellow towards the base of the lower mandible.

Entire length 6·3 inches; culmen 0·5; wing, carpus to tip, 3·5; tarsus 0·9.

The description is taken from a specimen shot in the Fayoom on the 4th of March.

Fig. Bree, B. of Eur. ii. p. 164.

97. ANTHUS RAALTENI, Temm. *African Tawny Pipit.*

I shot a Pipit in the Fayoom on the 3d of March, 1871, which I refer with some hesitation to this species, inasmuch as the bird was moulting at the time I procured it, and looks very ragged. It is, however, undoubtedly a new bird to Egypt. I met with a pair on a broad sandy ridge close to the great lake of Birket el Korn, and observed them in the same spot on several occasions. They frequented the desert sand, over which they ran swiftly, and never left it for the cultivated fields, which were close by; and in habits they appeared very similar to *A. campestris,* for which I at first mistook them. The following description is taken from my Egyptian specimen.

Upper plumage rather pale ashy brown, faintly tinted with rufous on the crown of the head; feathers on the top of the head and upper part of the back with darker brown centres; wings brown, the coverts shaded with chestnut, very strongly on the shoulders; the inner feathers of the median and greater coverts and the inner secondaries nearly black, with very broad sandy edges, remainder of the feathers on the wing very narrowly edged with pale sandy, almost approaching to white on the wing-coverts; tail-feathers rather narrow and pointed, the two outer ones on each side white, the exterior one having about half the inner web brown, the next with the shaft and two-thirds of the inner web of that colour, remainder of the tail brown, with paler edges to the feathers; lores white; eyebrow cream-colour; underparts white, shaded with sandy yellow on the front of the chest, where there are a few brown spots; the sides of the throat are also slightly spotted; beak and legs yellowish flesh-colour, the former inclining to brown on the upper mandible; irides brown.

Entire length 5·9 inches; culmen 0·6; wing, carpus to tip, 3·1; tarsus 1.

98. Anthus campestris, Bechst. *Tawny Pipit.*

This species is abundantly distributed throughout Egypt and Nubia. It is an early spring visitant, arriving about the middle of February. It chiefly frequents the confines of the desert, where its plumage harmonizes with the colour of the sand, and renders it difficult to be seen.

Entire upper plumage pale sandy-brown, the centre of the feathers inclining to dark brown, which gives it a somewhat mottled appearance, especially on the head; wings dark brown, the feathers edged with pale sandy-brown; tail dark brown, the two outer feathers broadly edged with dull white, the two centre ones with pale sandy-brown; underparts buff, inclining to very pale russet-brown on the chest and flanks, the former occasionally marked with small longitudinal brown spots; beak fleshy brown, inclining to dark brown on the upper mandible; legs pale fleshy-brown; irides hazel.

Entire length 7 inches; culmen 0·6; wing, carpus to tip, 3·5; tarsus 1.

Fig. Gould, B. of Eur. pl. 137.

Fam. ALAUDIDÆ.

99. CERTHILAUDA DESERTORUM (Stanley). *Bifasciated Lark.*

I have occasionally, though rarely, met with this bird in Egypt, and always singly; yet Dr. A. Leith Adams (Ibis, 1864, p. 24) says that it is not uncommon in small flocks along the edge of the desert from the Pyramids to Nubia. It is essentially a desert bird, so that it is only upon journeys which take us into those sandy wastes that we are likely to meet with it. It runs with great swiftness, and when flying may easily be recognized by the distinct black and white markings on the wings.

Upper plumage sandy colour, usually slightly tinted with grey towards the nape; primaries dark brown, secondaries white, with dark brown blotches about the centre; tail dark brown, with the two centre feathers approaching to sandy colour, and the exterior web of the outer feathers on each side white; it has a white eyebrow; underparts white, tinted occasionally with pale buff on the crop, and more or less spotted with dark brown on the lower part of the throat and crop; beak horn-brown; legs pale fleshy-brown; irides brown.

Entire length 8 inches; culmen 1; wing, carpus to tip, 5; tarsus 1·3.

Fig. Gould, B. of Eur. pl. 168.

100. Ammomanes lusitana (Gm.). *Desert-Lark.*

The present species and its closely allied form *A. fraterculus*, Trist., are abundant throughout Nubia, frequenting the confines of the desert.

I have before me a series of twenty-four specimens of *Ammomanes* from Egypt, Nubia, Palestine, and Abyssinia, apprently, at first sight, including three races:—1st, the paler one, the true *A. lusitana*, ranging throughout Egypt as far as Assouan; 2nd, *A. fraterculus*, Trist., very abundant in Nubia and Upper Egypt, and agreeing precisely with typical specimens from Palestine in Canon Tristram's collection; 3rd, a race from Abyssinia, collected by Mr. Jesse, which is much darker and smaller than *A. fraterculus* from Palestine. Of these three races, the first and second, *i. e. A. lusitana* and *A. fraterculus* (the only two which I have to consider in the present work), appear to me to be simply subspecies or races, and exhibit scarcely sufficient distinction to warrant their separation into different species; for when we examine a series collected between Cairo and Assouan, these two races merge imperceptibly into each other. Yet in the present work I have separated them under their distinctive names, *A. lusitana* being described from one of my paler specimens collected at El Kab, and *A. fraterculus* from a type specimen in Canon Tristram's collection from Palestine, which agrees perfectly with most of my Nubian birds.

Upper plumage pale sandy colour, inclining to cinnamon on the rump and base of the tail; wings and tail pale brown, with sandy edgings to the feathers; underparts cream-colour; beak flesh-colour, darkest towards the culmen; legs pale brown; irides brown.

Entire length 6·4 inches; culmen 0·6; wing, carpus to tip, 3·8; tarsus 0·85.

Fig. Temm. Pl. Col. 244. fig. 2.

101. Ammomanes fraterculus, Trist. *Tristram's Desert-Lark.*

Very closely allied to the last species. Abundant in Upper Egypt and Nubia.

Very similar to *A. lusitana, but of a generally darker hue*; upper plumage tinted with ash-colour; *throat rather faintly spotted with brown.*

Entire length 6 inches; culmen 0·5; wing, carpus to tip, 3·6; tarsus 0·8.

102. Ammomanes arenicolor (Sundev.). *Sandy-coloured Desert-Lark.*

Mr. G. R. Gray (Hand-list of B. vol. ii. p. 122) gives the locality "Lower Egypt" for the present species. Dr. von Heuglin (Orn. N. O. Afr. p. 685) considers *A. arenicolor*, Sundev., to be synonymous with *A. cinctura*, Gould, but does not mention it as observed in Egypt. Professor Sundevall, however, in his original description (Öfv. Kongl. Vet. Akad. Förh. 1850, p. 128), says that it is found in Lower Egypt and Arabia Petræa, having often been confounded with *A. lusitana.*

Somewhat similar to *A. lusitana*, but a little smaller, and having not so large a bill, the colour of the tail different, and also the relations of the quills.

103. Galerita cristata (Linn.). *Crested Lark.*

This is one of the most abundant birds in Egypt. It is very similar to the Skylark in general appearance; but it never soars very high, and has but an indifferent song.

I have before me for comparison one hundred specimens of the present species from S. Europe, N. Africa, Abyssinia, the River Gambia, and China; from among this series the Egyptian specimens may be easily picked out by their generally darker coloration, while some of those from Algeria and Palestine are the lightest in the series. Above the First Cataract I observed that the Crested Lark appeared lighter in colour than those in Egypt.

The following description of the plumage is taken from five specimens shot by myself in Egypt:—

Upper plumage very similar to that of *Alauda arvensis*, but darker; wings brown, feathers paler towards their edges, inner web of the quills marked with cinnamon-brown; tail dark brown, outer feathers edged with buff: a crest on the head of narrow dark brown feathers, edged with sandy; underparts creamy-white, shading off darker on the sides of the chest and flanks, and spotted with dark brown on the sides of the throat and crop; two thirds of the under surface of the wing pale cinnamon-brown; beak yellowish-brown, darkest on the culmen; legs pale brown; irides brown.

Entire length 6·7 inches; culmen 0·6; wing, carpus to tip, 4; tarsus 1.

Fig. Sharpe & Dresser, B. of Eur. part xiii.

G. rutila (Müll.) of Mr. G. R. Gray's 'Hand-list of Birds' (vol. ii. p. 119) has the locality Egypt attached to it. As I cannot detect any specific difference in the Crested

Larks from Egypt, I have followed Von Heuglin (Orn. N. O. Afr. p. 681) in considering this name a synonym of *G. cristata* (L.).

104. Alauda arborea, Linn. *Wood-Lark.*

Brehm mentions having met with the Wood-Lark once in Lower Egypt in the winter. As I know of no other instance of its occurrence in the country, it may, doubtless, be considered a rare straggler.

Plumage similar to that of *A. arvensis,* with the following distinctive characters:—a clear sandy-coloured eyebrow, separating the top of the head from the ear-coverts; the wing-coverts tipped with white; outer web of the second tail-feather only bordered with white, and all but the two centre ones tipped with that colour; spots on the throat richer in colour and more distinct.

Entire length 7 inches; culmen 0·5; wing, carpus to tip, 4; tarsus 0·9.

Fig. Gould, B. of Eur. pl. 167.

105. Alauda arvensis, Linn. *Sky-Lark.*

In writing upon *A. arvensis* I include the subspecies *A. intermedia,* as determined by Messrs. Sharpe and Dresser (B. of Eur. part vi.). Von Heuglin (Orn. N. O. Afr. p. 679) regards the Sky-Lark as an occasional and not very regular visitor to Lower Egypt. From my own observations I cannot altogether agree with him, as on two occasions when I visited the Delta in February, and during my stay in the Fayoom in that same month, I found it plentiful in flocks; so that I consider it regular in its visits and abundant in Lower Egypt during the early spring. I have a specimen collected at Alexandria in March which corresponds in every respect with *A. arvensis* from England; the other specimens, four in number, which I collected in the Delta and Fayoom, are the true *A. intermedia* of Swinhoe.

Upper plumage brown, with pale edgings to the feathers, more especially on the back of the neck; rump inclining to grey; upper tail-coverts strongly tinted with rufous; quills brown, narrowly edged with dull white; wing-coverts paler than the back, and more sandy in colour; tail brown, the two centre feathers lighter and washed with grey towards the tip; outer feather on each side white, the inner web edged with dusky; the second feather has the outer web white; cheeks and eyebrows sandy colour; under surface of the body creamy-white, with the lower part of the throat and crop washed with yellowish brown and streaked with dark brown; beak flesh-colour, shading into brown on the culmen; legs flesh-colour; irides brown.

Entire length 7·7 inches; culmen 0·6; wing, carpus to tip, 4·4; tarsus 0·9.

A. intermedia, Swinhoe. P. Z. S. 1863, p. 89.

I only separate the present form as a subspecies of *A. arvensis*, a mere climatic variety, similar in measurements to that bird but differing in plumage, yet so slightly that a description almost fails to point out any true distinction, though in a series of Larks the eye will enable one readily to distinguish the bird. Von Heuglin (Orn. N. O. Afr. p. 679) has included this subspecies under *A. arvensis* without remark. It is the *A. cantarella* of authors, but not of Bonaparte, who appears to have applied that name to the true *A. arvensis* of Italy. In keeping the name *A. intermedia* of Swinhoe for this subspecies, I have followed Messrs. Sharpe and Dresser in their admirable work on the birds of Europe (part vi. *Alauda arvensis*, p. 6), in which they specially notice this Sky-Lark from Egypt.

It differs from the typical *A. arvensis* in being slightly smaller, and in the plumage being rather lighter in colour and more grey, especially on the upper part of the back; the markings are more pronounced, the spots on the chest slightly more distinct; and it has a more clearly defined eyebrow.

Fig. Sharpe and Dresser, B. of Eur. part vi.

106. Calandrella brachydactyla (Leisler). *Short-toed Lark.*

This Lark arrives in March, when it may be met with abundantly throughout Egypt in large flocks.

Upper plumage very similar to that of *Alauda arvensis*; wings brown, the feathers edged with sandy colour; tail dark brown, the two outer feathers on each side strongly marked with cream-colour, and the two centre ones broadly edged with pale russet; *underparts dull white without spots*, and with a more or less distinct brown shade on the crop, and occasionally marked with a brown blotch on each side of the crop; beak pale whitish brown, darkest on the culmen; legs pale yellowish brown; irides brown.

Entire length 5·5 inches; culmen 0·4; wing, carpus to tip, 3·5; tarsus 0·8.

Fig. Gould, B. of Eur. pl. 163.

107. Calandrella reboudia, Trist. *Algerian Short-toed Lark.*

This species is very closely allied to *C. brachydactyla*, and appears to be a resident in Egypt; for Mr. E. C. Taylor killed some specimens in the month of January near Cairo, out of a flock which he found on the desert. It is, however, of very rare occurrence in the country; and I not aware of its ever having been met with in Upper Egypt or Nubia.

Upper plumage, wings, and tail similar to those of *C. brachydactyla*; *under plumage of a purer white, and distinctly spotted with brown* on the centre of the feathers of the crop and flanks.

Entire length 5·3 inches; culmen 0·35; wing, carpus to tip, 3·3; tarsus 0·8.

108. Calandrella minor, Cab.

Von Heuglin (Orn. N. O. Afr. p. 697) mentions the present Lark as a bird of passage in the spring and autumn in both Egypt and Nubia.

Of this species we have examined two specimens lent by Dr. Peters, of Berlin, to Messrs. Sharpe and Dresser, for the purposes of their work on the birds of Europe. They were sent from Egypt by Ehrenberg; and although closely allied to both the foregoing species, they seem to differ from *C. brachydactyla* by being much smaller, and from both in their pale coloration and yellow bill.

Total length 5·3 inches; culmen 0·4; wing, carpus to tip, 3·7; tail 2·5; tarsus 0·85.

109. Melanocorypha calandra (Linn.). *Calandra Lark.*

The Calandra Lark occasionally passes the winter months in Lower Egypt; but its appearance is of uncertain occurrence, and its numbers limited. Rüppell mentions it as a plentiful winter visitor to Egypt and Nubia; but as I can find no evidence of its capture above Cairo, I am inclined to consider its range on the Nile to be limited to Lower Egypt.

It must be observed that the Calandra Lark of Egypt may, after all, not be the true *M. calandra* (Linn.); for Messrs. Sharpe and Dresser (B. of Eur. part viii.) have shown that an allied species, *M. bimaculata* (Ménétr.), is the Calandra of Abyssinia; and as this bird extends through Palestine and South-Eastern Europe to North-Western India, it is quite possible that it passes through Egypt on its migration. In the work above mentioned a good figure will be seen of this bird, which differs from the ordinary Calandra in having no white on the wings, but has white spots on the end of the tail-feathers, instead of the outer feathers being for the most part white.

Upper plumage similar to that of the Sky-Lark; primaries edged with white, secondaries tipped with that colour; outer feathers of the tail pure white, second feather edged and tipped with white; underparts white, with a very distinct black patch on each side of the upper part of the chest; crop spotted with brown on the tips of the feathers; flanks shaded with brown; beak pale yellowish-brown, darker above; legs pale brown; irides brown.

Entire length 7·2 inches; culmen 0·7; wing, carpus to tip, 5·2; tarsus 1·2.

Fig. Sharpe and Dresser, B. of Eur. part v.

110. RHAMPHOCORIS CLOT-BEY (Temm.). *Thick-billed Calandra.*

The typical specimen of this Lark came from Egypt; yet it appears to be extremely rare in the country; for I know of no other specimen having been procured in that locality.

Upper plumage sandy colour, slightly tinted with ashy towards the head; centres of the feathers on the head occasionally marked with dark brown; primaries brown, edged on their outer webs with buff, secondaries broadly edged with white; tail white, inclining to sandy colour towards the centre feathers, and broadly tipped with dark brown, forming a triangle with its apex about the centre of the tail; two centre tail-feathers sandy colour, darkest towards the apical half; feathers round the eye white; cheeks, ear-coverts, and sides of the throat black; underparts white, tinted with sandy colour on the sides of the breast and flanks, and spotted wth brown, mostly towards the centre of the abdomen; *beak very stout and notched*, of a pale buffish colour; legs pale buff, claws short and thick; irides brown.

Entire length 6·3 inches; culmen 0·7; wing, carpus to tip, 4·9; tarsus 0·9.

Fam. EMBERIZIDÆ.

111. EMBERIZA MILIARIA, Linn. *Common Bunting.*

According to Von Heuglin (Orn. N. O. Afr. p. 658) this species is a winter visitor to Egypt, but is rarely observed in Nubia. I first met with it on the 4th of March, in the Fayoom, and afterwards found it abundant near Damietta, towards the end of that month, when I generally met with it in small flocks.

Upper parts and ear-coverts pale brown, with a greyish shade on the back, the centres of the feathers being dark brown except on the rump; wings and tail dark brown, with pale edgings to the feathers; feathers round the eye, and underparts, cream-colour, spotted with brown on the throat, chest, and flanks, mostly so on the sides of the throat and crop; beak brownish flesh-colour, shading into dark brown on the culmen; legs flesh-colour; irides brown.

Entire length 6·5 inches; culmen 0·5; wing, carpus to tip, 3·6; tarsus 0·95.

Fig. Sharpe and Dresser, B. of Eur. part viii.

112. Emberiza hortulana, Linn. *Ortolan Bunting.*

The Ortolan is only a bird of passage in Egypt, and I am not aware of its having been captured in Nubia, although according to Von Heuglin (Orn. N. O. Afr. p. 662) it is very plentiful in Abyssinia from September to April, and occasionally breeds there.

I have shot it on several occasions in Middle Egypt in April. It arrives on its northward migration about the end of March, and returns through the country in the autumn.

Male.—Head and neck yellowish grey; throat, feathers round the eyes, and under the ear-coverts pale yellow; back, scapulars, and wing-coverts pale chestnut, with the centre of the feathers dark brown; primaries dusky brown, narrowly edged with pale yellowish brown; tail, two exterior feathers on each side having the apical half white, with a streak of brown along the quills, remainder of the feathers dark brown, bordered with pale brown; underparts pale rufous, shaded with yellow; legs and beak flesh-colour; irides brown.

Entire length 6 inches; culmen 0·4; wing, carpus to tip, 3·6; tarsus 0·75.

Fig. Sharpe and Dresser, B. of Eur. part vii.

113. Emberiza cæsia, Cretzsch. *Cretzschmar's Bunting.*

This is a spring visitant, arriving in Egypt about the end of March, and does not appear to be abundant at any season. I only shot it once, near Cairo, in the beginning of April. The Rev. A. C. Smith ('Attractions of the Nile,' vol. ii. p. 232) mentions seeing it at Alexandria. According to Von Heuglin (Orn. N. O. Afr. p. 663) it is most plentiful in the spring, during March and April, and in the autumn, when it may often be found in company with *E. hortulana.* It breeds occasionally in the Delta and near Cairo.

Head, nape, and crop slaty grey; upper plumage chestnut, with the centres of the feathers on the back dark brown; wings brown, the feathers edged with pale chestnut; tail brown, the feathers edged with chestnut, the end-third of the two outer feathers on each side white on the inner web; in front of the eye, *throat, under the ear-coverts, and abdomen chestnut*; beak, reddish brown above; legs brown; irides brown.

Entire length 6·2 inches; culmen 0·4; wing, carpus to tip, 3·3; tarsus 0·7.

Fig. Sharpe and Dresser, B. of Eur. part ii.

114. EMBERIZA INTERMEDIA, Michah. *Smaller Reed-Bunting.*

(Plate III. fig. 2.)

I met with a single specimen of this Bunting (a female) in the reedy marsh near Damietta on the 22nd of March, and brought home the skin.

Von Heuglin never observed this species himself in North-eastern Africa (Orn. N. O. Afr. p. 668), but includes it on the authority of De Selys-Longchamps, who says that it is found at Damietta; so that it is evidently of rare occurrence in Egypt, and, as far as we know, confined to a very limited portion of the Delta.

Female.—Top of the head and ear-coverts mixed rufous and sandy brown, the centres of the feathers black; nape blacker; back of the neck ashy brown; back and wing-feathers dark brown, broadly edged with rufous and pale brown; rump ashy brown; upper tail-coverts rufous brown; tail, outer feather, and apical third of the next one white, with some brown along the shaft, remainder of the tail dark brown with pale edgings; throat and feathers round the ear-coverts yellowish white, with two broad brown stripes on each side of the throat; remainder of the underparts creamy-white, with rufous-brown streaks on the centres of the feathers of the chest and flanks; beak and legs dark brown; irides brown; *diameter of the beak* 0·3.

Entire length 5·8 inches; culmen 0·4; wing, carpus to tip, 3; tarsus 0·8.

Male.—Top of the head, nape, cheeks, ear-coverts, and throat black; under the ear-coverts, sides and back of the neck, and under surface of the body white.

The figure is taken from my Damietta specimen, which is still in my collection.

Fam. FRINGILLIDÆ.

115. PASSER DOMESTICUS (Linn.). *Common Sparrow.*

The Sparrow is as abundant in Egypt and Nubia as in Europe, and remains there throughout the year.

Male.—Top of the head, nape, and sides of the breast slate-colour; chin, throat, and region of the eyes black; behind the eye a small white spot; ear-coverts greyish-white, and behind them a broad band of chestnut extending over the eye; back and scapulars chestnut, with black centres to the feathers; rump and upper tail-coverts greenish grey; quills black, edged with chestnut; lesser wing-coverts chestnut, the lower row broadly tipped with white, forming an alar bar; tail dark brown, the feathers edged with yellowish brown; under-parts pale dusky grey; legs and beak pale brown; irides hazel.

Entire length 5·5 inches; culmen 0·5; wing, carpus to tip, 3·1; tarsus 0·6.

Fig. Gould, B. of Eur. pl. 184.

116. PASSER ITALIÆ (Vieill.). *Italian Sparrow.*

According to Von Heuglin (Orn. N. O. Afr. p. 630), this bird is to be met with in Egypt and Nubia, and extends its range as far south as the Blue Nile. I have never, to my knowledge, seen an Egyptian specimen of this Sparrow.

Male.—Top of the head and back of the neck chestnut;

cheeks pure white; a white eyebrow; remainder of the plumage similar to that of *P. domesticus*.

Female.—Resembles that of *P. domesticus*.

Entire length 5·5 inches; culmen 0·5; wing, carpus to tip, 3; tarsus 0·6.

Fig. Gould, B. of Eur. pl. 185.

117. PASSER SALICICOLA (Vieill.). *Spanish Sparrow*.

Abundant during the winter in Egypt, rarely, however, remaining late enough to breed. Dr. A. L. Adams (Ibis, 1864, p. 23) says that in November and December, during the ripening of the dhurra, Spanish Sparrows assemble in enormous numbers, and do great damage to the crops; and Mr. E. C. Taylor (*op. cit.* 1867, p. 65) says that this species is more abundant even than *P. domesticus*. This can only hold good in speaking of the winter months, as during three tours in Egypt I never met with this species later than the beginning of February. Von Heuglin (Orn. N. O. Afr. p. 632) declares that it breeds in Egypt in March, and in Nubia in August and September—a statement which I am inclined to doubt,

Male.—Top of the head and nape chestnut, the feathers slightly edged with pale brown; remainder of the upper plumage similar to that of the Common Sparrow, but rather darker on the back; cheeks, ear-coverts, and sides of the throat white; feathers in front of and under the eye, throat, and crop black, those on the latter part edged with white; abdomen white; the centre of the feathers on the flanks black; beak brown, paler towards the base of the lower mandible; legs pale brown; irides brown.

Female.—Very like that of the Common Sparrow.

Entire length 6 inches; culmen 0·45; wing, carpus to tip, 3; tarsus 0·8.

Fig. Gould, B. of Eur. pl. 185.

118. PASSER MONTANUS (Linn.). *Tree-Sparrow.*

Von Heuglin (Orn. N. O. Afr. p. 633) states that this species comes into Egypt probably as a winter visitant.

Both sexes are alike in plumage, and closely resemble the male of *P. domesticus*, but are smaller, and differ in having the top of the head chocolate, a black patch on the ear-coverts, and some of the wing-coverts tipped with buff, forming two bars on the shoulders.

Entire length 5·3 inches; culmen 0·4; wing, carpus to tip, 2·8; tarsus 0·5.

Fig. Gould, B. of Eur. pl. 184.

119. COCCOTHRAUSTES VULGARIS, Pall. *Hawfinch.*

Dr. Cavafy has kindly written to me, informing me that he received a specimen of this bird from Alexandria in 1859. This is the only instance of its occurrence in Egypt that I know of.

A narrow edging of feathers round the beak and a large patch on the throat black; top of the head, cheeks, and rump chestnut-brown; back and sides of the neck ash-colour; back and scapulars deep brown; most of the greater and the last row of the smaller wing-coverts white, forming a large central mark; remainder of the wing-feathers black, with green and violet reflections; *the secondaries are square at the ends, and the smaller primaries end in abrupt wavy lines*; centre feathers of the tail brownish white, the outer ones black, and the intermediate ones have more or less broad white ends; beak and legs fleshy brown; irides white.

Entire length 7 inches; culmen 0·8; wing, carpus to tip, 4; tarsus 0·85.

Fig. Gould, B. of Eur. pl. 199.

120. Fringilla cœlebs, Linn. *Chaffinch.*

I met with several specimens of this bird near Damietta in March; and on the 28th of that month I shot one, in order to verify the species. It is only a winter visitant to Egypt, and appears to be rarely seen above Cairo, and probably never ranges above the First Cataract.

Von Heuglin (Orn. N. O. Afr. p. 640) observes that Dr. Hartmann met with it at Thebes in February. This is the most southern point on the Nile that we have any positive record of its occurrence.

Male.—Top of the head and back of the neck grey; upper part of the back and scapulars chestnut; rump yellowish green; lesser wing-coverts white, the greater ones tipped with yellowish white; outer web of the quills narrowly edged with yellow, with some white at the base of all but the three outer ones; remainder of the wing brownish black; tail with some white on the two outer feathers, the remainder dark brown; cheeks, throat, and underparts ferruginous; beak and legs fleshy brown; irides brown.

Entire length 6 inches; culmen 0·45; wing, carpus to tip, 3·4; tarsus 0·7.

Female.—Upper plumage olive, inclining to yellowish green on the rump; wings dusky brown, the feathers edged with yellowish white; three white bands are formed on the wing by some of the primaries being marked with white, and the greater and lesser wing-coverts being edged with the same colour; underparts dusky white.

Fig. Gould, B. of Eur. pl. 187.

121. Carduelis elegans, Steph. *Goldfinch.*

Abundant in the Delta in winter, but I am not aware of its having been met with south of Cairo. I shot a specimen out of some large flocks that I fell in with near Damietta in March.

Male.—Feathers round the beak and region of the eye black; forehead, and a broad patch beneath the chin, crimson, a black patch covering the top of the head and half encircling the ear-coverts, the latter being nearly white; back and sides of the chest pale olive-brown; wings black, with a large golden-yellow patch crossing their centres; quills tipped with white; tail-feathers black tipped with white; under surface of the body white, tinted on the breast and flanks with pale brown; legs and beak flesh-brown; irides brown.

Entire length 5 inches; culmen 0·4; wing, carpus to tip, 3; tarsus 0·5.

Fig. Gould, B. of Eur. pl. 196.

122. Estrelda melanorhyncha, Antin. *Black-billed Finch.*

This bird was discovered by Antinori near Alexandria in 1861. Von Heuglin (Orn. N. O. Afr. p. 577) has not, apparently, been able to identify the species, which he fancies must belong to the genus *Euplectes*, as Antinori has heard that it is found in spring near Jaffa in bright plumage. If it should be a Weaver bird, this will be, as Von Heuglin justly remarks, a curious circumstance, as extending the range of the genus *Euplectes* into the Palæarctic region.

The following is Antinori's description:—"Very small the whole of the upper surface of the body chestnut-olive, underneath of an ochreous-isabelline colour; wings dusky; tail-feathers blackish, the side ones terminating in a yellowish-grey spot; bill black; feet horn-colour. Size of *Amadina ultramarina*."

123. ÆGIOTHUS RUFESCENS (Vieill.). *Lesser Redpole.*

I include this species on the authority of Rüppell, but I think it is highly probable that it is not met with in Egypt; for Von Heuglin observes that he never found it in any part of North-eastern Africa, and I myself know of no instance of its capture there.

I have not given a detailed description of this well-known bird. It may briefly be said that it is like the Common Linnet, but is much smaller, with brighter crimson on the forehead and breast, and having a white belly, with stripes on the flanks and no white on the tail. This diagnosis will serve for the recognition of the species should any one meet with the bird in Egypt.

Fig. Gould, B. of Eur. pl. 194.

124. Serinus hortulanus, Koch. *Serin Finch.*

Von Heuglin (Orn. N. O. Afr. p. 647) mentions that he met with the Serin Finch in the Delta and in the neighbourhood of Cairo in pairs and small flocks during the month of March.

Male.—Forehead, breast, and rump bright lemon-yellow, the lower abdomen and vent white; cheeks yellow, tinged with greenish; upper surface of the body olive-green, with central streaks of dark brown to each feather, the flanks also streaked with dark brown; bill brownish white, the lower mandible paler; feet fleshy brown; iris dark brown.

Total length 4·5 inches; culmen 0·35; wing, carpus to tip, 2·8; tarsus 0·5.

Female.—Much duller than the male, and having no yellow forehead; breast not so bright, and streaked all over with brown markings.

Fig. Gould, B. of Eur. pl. 195.

125. Linota cannabina (Linn.). *Linnet.*

This is a common winter visitant to Lower Egypt, where it remains until the end of February. I have never met with it above Cairo; but it probably ranges into Nubia, as it is mentioned by Blasius as occurring in Abyssinia.

My description is taken from a female specimen, which I shot in the middle of February in the Delta.

Top of the head, nape, and ear-coverts ashy grey; centre of the feathers on the top of the head dark brown; forehead marked with cherry-coloured reflections; back, scapulars, and wing-coverts chestnut; primaries black, edged with white;

ERYTHROSPIZA GITHAGINEA.

upper tail-coverts white, with black centres to the feathers; tail-feathers pointed and black, with white edges; underparts white; throat marked with longitudinal dusky spots; sides of the chest rose-colour, inclining to cherry-red; flanks chestnut; beak dark brown, inclining to flesh-colour towards the base of the lower mandible; legs and irides brown.

Entire length 5·5 inches; culmen 0·4; wing, carpus to tip, 3·2; tarsus 0.6.

Fig. Gould, B. of Eur. pl. 191.

126. ERYTHROSPIZA GITHAGINEA (Licht.) *Desert-Bullfinch.*

(Plate V.)

This pretty little bird, rendered so conspicuous by its bright red bill, is very plentiful in Upper Egypt and Nubia, where it may be met with in pairs and flocks along the confines of the desert. It invades the cultivated land for its food, which consists entirely of small seeds, and at such times may be seen clustered in groups upon the mustard- and other plants, which wave to and fro under the weight of the birds as they busily peck away at the seeds. In flight it closely resembles the Linnet; but its pale roseate tints easily distinguish it from any other Egyptian Finch.

Male in breeding-plumage.—The feathers round the beak are brightly tinted with rosy red; top of the head, ear-coverts, and sides of the neck delicate ashy grey, shading on the nape and back into soft pinkish brown; rump and upper tail-coverts pink, the feathers edged with carmine; wings brown, with broad pink borders to the secondaries and wing-coverts, all being narrowly edged with carmine; tail brown, with similar edging towards the base of the feathers; underparts pink, with the ends of the feathers carmine; beak bright orange-red; legs brownish flesh-colour; irides brown.

In winter plumage, pink takes the place of the carmine.

Entire length 5 inches; culmen 0·4; wing, carpus to tip, 3·3; tarsus 0·7.

The immature bird is of a general sandy colour, with the centre of the feathers of the wing and tail dark brown; beak pale yellowish brown.

The figures are taken from an adult male and an immature bird, both shot by myself on the 7th of May.

Fam. ORIOLIDÆ.

127. ORIOLUS GALBULA, Linn. *Golden Oriole.*

This bird passes through Egypt and Nubia on its spring and autumn migrations, but does not remain to breed in the country. In spring it arrives about the middle of April, when it is rather plentiful among the thicker-foliaged trees.

Male.—Brilliant golden yellow, with the exception of the lores, which are black; wings black; most of the quills tipped with pale yellow, and a yellow spot about the middle of the wing; tail black, with the end bright yellow; beak red; legs brown; irides crimson.

Female.—Colours duller, top of the head, back, and scapulars greenish yellow, bright on the rump; wings brown, feathers edged with white; a less amount of yellow on the tail; throat and centre of the body stone grey, more or less shaded with yellow; flanks and under tail-coverts yellow, with occasional stripes of pale dusky or brown down the centres of the feathers.

Entire length 9·5 inches; culmen 1; wing, carpus to tip, 6; tarsus 0·9.

Fig. Gould, B. of Eur. pl. 71.

Fam. STURNIDÆ.

128. STURNUS VULGARIS, Linn. *Starling.*

This bird is a winter visitant, and may be found plentifully in the Delta up to the end of March; it may also occasionally be met with in Middle and, possibly, Upper Egypt.

General plumage deep metallic green, with purple reflections on the throat and back; more or less of the feathers on the upper surface tipped with buff, and those on the under surface with white, according to the age of the bird; wings and tail brown, with pale edging to the feathers. Legs pale brown; beak brown, except in breeding-plumage, when it is bright yellow; irides dark brown.

Entire length 8·3 inches; culmen 1; wing, carpus to tip, 4·8; tarsus 1·2.

Fig. Gould, B. of Eur. pl. 210.

129. PASTOR ROSEUS (Linn.). *Rose-coloured Pastor.*

Von Heuglin (Orn. N. O. Afr. p. 531) says that he only knows of a single instance of this bird's capture in Egypt, when a young bird was killed in a field near Cairo, on the 25th of August, 1864.

Entire head and neck purplish black; wings and tail black, with green and purple reflections; remainder of the plumage pale pink; basal half of the beak black, remainder yellowish brown; legs pale brown; irides dark brown.

Entire length 8·5 inches; culmen 0·8; wing, carpus to tip, 5·1; tarsus 1·2.

Fig. Gould, B. of Eur. pl. 212.

Fam. CORVIDÆ.

130. CORVUS UMBRINUS, Hedenborg. *Brown-necked Raven.*

This Raven is very plentiful throughout Egypt and Nubia. It prefers desert and rocky districts to the more cultivated parts, and may frequently be seen near the Pyramids, on which it yearly builds. Like the Common Raven it nests both on rocks and trees, in the latter instance usually selecting the crown of some lofty date-palm. It is essentially a desert-bird, and therefore not to be met with in the Delta.

Entire plumage blue-black, except the feathers of the head and neck, which are brown almost approaching to black. Legs and beak black; irides very dark brown.

Entire length 22·5 inches; culmen 2·6; wing, carpus to tip, 15·8; tarsus 2·6.

131. CORVUS AFFINIS, Rüpp. *Abyssinian Raven.*

This small species of Raven is a resident in Egypt and Nubia, but is rather uncommon. I have seen a specimen from Egypt in Mr. E. C. Taylor's collection, obtained by Mr. Clark Kennedy during his visit to that country.

Entire plumage black, slightly shaded with brown on the throat. The hairy coverts to the nostrils are very stiff and fully developed, and directed forwards and upwards in a fan-shape on the sides of the beak. Beak and legs black, the former very stout and short; irides brownish black.

Entire length 19·5 to 20·5 inches; culmen 2·2 to 2·5, diameter of the beak 1·1; wing, carpus to tip, 15 to 15·5; tarsus 2·5 to 2·7.

Fig. (head only) Schl. Bijdr. Dierk. Afl. pl. vii. 1 *b*. fig. 26.

132. Corvus cornix, Linn. *Hooded Crow.*

This is the common Crow of Egypt, but in Nubia it is less plentiful. It begins breeding towards the end of February, when its nest may be procured in almost every clump of sont trees.

Head, throat, wings, and tail blue-black, remainder of the plumage stone-grey. Legs and beak black, irides very dark brown.

Entire length 18 inches; culmen 2; wing, carpus to tip, 12; tarsus 2·2.

Fig. Gould, B. of Eur. pl. 222.

133. Corvus frugilegus, Linn. *Rook.*

Large flocks of the Common Rook may be met with in the Delta up to the end of March, but it does not remain to breed in the country. It is rarely seen south of Cairo, although upon one occasion I observed a few at Memphis; this may be owing to the fact that snails and slugs, delicacies on which this bird delights to feed, are entirely absent from Upper Egypt.

Entire plumage blue-black. Legs and beak black, irides dark brown.

Entire length 18·5 inches; culmen 2·3; wing, carpus to tip, 11·5; tarsus 2·1.

Fig. Gould, B. of Eur. pl. 224.

134. Corvus monedula, Linn. *Jackdaw.*

Von Heuglin (Orn. N. O. Afr. p. 498) observes that Rüppell mentions the Jackdaw as plentiful in Lower Egypt. I consider this evidence insufficient, and therefore give no description of this well-known bird.

135. Pica caudata, Keys. & Bl. *Magpie.*

According to Bonaparte the Magpie is to be met with in Egypt and Nubia, and Rüppell states that it is tolerably plentiful in Lower Egypt during the winter. Von Heuglin, on the other hand (Orn. N. O. Afr. p. 497), affirms that it was never seen by Hemprich and Ehrenberg, Brehm, or himself in the course of all their travels in North-Eastern Africa. There is a Magpie in the Frankfort Museum labelled "from Egypt;" but as this may have been a tame bird, and as the statements of Bonaparte and Rüppell are not always to be relied upon, I feel that I should not be justified in including the Magpie among the true Egyptian birds, and therefore do not describe it.

136. PYRRHOCORAX ALPINUS, Vieill. *Alpine Chough.*

I consider the occurrence of this species in Egypt very doubtful; for it is included solely upon the authority of Hasselquist.

Entire plumage uniform black; beak yellow; legs vermilion, with the soles of the feet and claws black; irides dark brown.

Entire length 15·5 inches; culmen 1; wing, carpus to tip, 10·2; tarsus 1·7.

Fig. Gould, B. of Eur. pl. 218.

Order PICARIÆ.

Fam. YUNGIDÆ.

137. YUNX TORQUILLA, Linn. *Wryneck.*

The Wryneck is not uncommon as a spring and autumn visitant, but is much less plentiful in Upper Egypt and Nubia than lower down the Nile, where it is usually to be met with singly, perched upon some low hedge.

Upper plumage grey mingled with rufous, and the whole delicately pencilled with dusky; a patch of mottled black and rufous runs from the back of the head to the centre of the back; on the scapulars there is a band of black and buff spots; wings brown, the quills barred with rufous; tail ashy brown, beautifully pencilled and irregularly barred with black; chin white, throat buff, the whole evenly barred with pure black; under surface of the body white shaded with yellow on the flanks and under tail-coverts, and with brown barbed spots on the centres of the feathers. Legs and beak fleshy brown; irides pale brown.

Entire length 7 inches; culmen 0·4; wing, carpus to tip, 3·5; tarsus 0·8.

Fig. Gould, B. of Eur. pl. 233.

Fam. CUCULIDÆ.

138. Cuculus canorus, Linn. *Cuckoo.*

The Cuckoo arrives from the south in March, and is gone again by May, returning once more in August. I have shot it on several occasions; but it does not appear to be very abundant in the country at any season.

Upper plumage slaty grey, wings browner; inner web of the quill-feathers banded with white; tail black tipped with white, and with white spots along the shafts of the feathers; throat slaty grey; remainder of the under plumage white, barred, with dusky on the body. Base of the bill, legs, and irides yellow, remainder of the beak black.

Entire length 14 inches; culmen 0·9; wing, carpus to tip, 9; tarsus 0·9.

Fig. Gould, B. of Eur. pl. 240.

139. Coccystes glandarius (Linn.). *Great Spotted Cuckoo.*

This graceful bird is a resident in Egypt and Nubia, and may be met with abundantly in the clumps of sont trees, usually in pairs or small family parties. They are by no means shy, and will often sit motionless on a bough while one walks beneath the tree. In Egypt they breed at the same time as the Hooded Crow, and invariably select a nest of that species in which to deposit their eggs.

Von Heuglin (Orn. N. O. Afr. p. 787) is of opinion that they first lay their eggs on the ground and then carry them in their beaks to the nest they have selected, in the same manner as the Common Cuckoo does. About half of those that I saw even as late as May were in immature plumage.

Top of the head crested, and of a pale slaty-grey with fine dusky streaks along the shafts of the feathers; remainder of the upper plumage olivaceous brown, all the feathers of the wing and upper tail-coverts tipped with white; tail bronzy black tipped with white; throat buff; under surface of the body creamy white. Legs slate-colour; beak dark brown, inclining to yellow at the base of the lower mandible; irides brown.

Entire length 17 inches; culmen 1; wing, carpus to tip, 8; tarsus 1·3.

The females have the primaries more or less strongly marked with rufous. The immature birds have the top of the head black, primaries more rufous, and the throat yellow.

Fig. Gould, B. of Eur. pl. 241.

140. Chrysococcyx cupreus (Bodd.). *Bronzy-green Cuckoo.*

Herr F. Heine (J. f. O. 1863, p. 350) states that this bird, which he calls *Lamprococcyx chrysochlorus*, comes into Egypt. This Von Heuglin (Orn. N. O. Afr. p. 777) disbelieves; for, as he observes, it is a truly tropical species, never occurring in Nubia or in northern Senaar and Kordofan, and consequently still less likely to be met with in Egypt. I perfectly agree with him in considering that the present species does not come into Egypt, and have in consequence not described its plumage.

141. Centropus ægyptius (Gm.). *Lark-heeled Cuckoo.*

(Plate VI.)

Von Heuglin (Orn. N. O. Afr. p. 796) considers *C. ægyptius*, Gm., to be synonymous with *C. senegalensis* (Briss.); but this latter name cannot hold good, as it has been given by Linnæus to the West-African form. I have in my collection four skins of *C. ægyptius* from Egypt, and one of *C. senegalensis* from West Africa, and they certainly are distinct species. *C. ægyptius* is, I believe, confined to North-eastern Africa, and is most abundant in Lower Egypt.

In habits it is lazy, and prefers creeping among the thick beds of cane and the upper branches of the more densely foliaged trees to showing itself in the open, and is consequently not very common in collections.

Top of the head, ear-coverts, and nape brownish-black with an oily green reflection, the shafts of the feathers stout and polished; back, scapulars, and wing-coverts dull brown; primaries and secondaries bright rufous, tipped with brown; tail and upper tail-coverts brownish black, with metallic green reflections; under surface of the body pale straw-colour, the shafts of the feathers very stout and glossy. Legs and beak black, irides red.

Entire length 18 inches; culmen 1·2; wing, carpus to tip, 7 to 8; tarsus 1·7.

CENTROPUS ÆGYPTIUS

Fam. UPUPIDÆ.

142. Upupa epops, Linn. *Hoopoe.*

This bird is extremely plentiful throughout Egypt and Nubia, frequenting the neighbourhood of villages, where it may be daily seen perched upon a mud wall or bough, singing its simple song of "Poop-poop-poop," or else strutting along the ground with dignified gait, stopping here and there to drive its beak into the earth after its insect food. It breeds in March and April. The Arabic name is "Hud-hud."

Head and a highly developed crest rufous, the end of each of the longer crest-feathers black, some of them having a white bar before the black. The rufous colour extends to the centre of the back and over the shoulders, but is somewhat duller; it also extends down the neck and over the chest, where it acquires a pink hue; primaries and tail black, each distinctly barred with pure white; a distinct white bar across the rump; remainder of the back and wings black barred with buff or pure white; abdomen and under tail-coverts white, the flanks marked with dusky brown. Legs brown; beak black, paler at the base; irides brown.

Entire length 12 inches; culmen 2·3; wing, carpus to tip, 6; tarsus 9.

Fig. Sharpe and Dresser, B. of Eur. part vii.

Fam. ALCEDINIDÆ.

143. Alcedo ispida, Linn. *Common Kingfisher.*

Very abundant in the Delta, and occasionally met with

throughout Egypt. I have myself seen it above Cairo upon three occasions, at Sioot, Koos, and Thebes.

Head crested; top of the head and nape black, closely barred with cobalt; lores and ear-coverts light chestnut; a patch behind the ear-coverts along the neck pure white; cheeks blue; centre of the back and upper tail-coverts brilliant cobalt; quills dusky, the outer web greenish blue; scapulars and wing-coverts green, the latter spotted with cobalt; tail blue; throat white; remainder of the underparts light chestnut, with the exception of a blue patch on each side of the upper part of the breast.

In the male the bill is entirely black, while in the female it has an orange patch on the lower mandible. Legs red; irides dark brown.

Entire length 6·6 to 6·8 inches; culmen 1·55 to 1·7; wing, carpus to tip, 2·9; tarsus 0·4.

The description is taken from five Egyptian specimens in my own collection.

Fig. Sharpe, Monogr. Alced. pl. 1.

144. Alcedo bengalensis, Gm. *Little Indian Kingfisher.*

This species, which chiefly differs from *A. ispida* in the greater length of its bill, may occasionally be met with both in Egypt and Nubia. Mr. Sharpe in his 'Monograph of the Kingfishers,' Part ix., has described a specimen of this bird killed by Mr. Lord at Shoobra, near Cairo, and he remarks that there is a specimen from Nubia in the Leyden Museum. Mr. Larking also obtained a specimen in Egypt. I believe it to be by no means so common there as *A. ispida.*

Plumage very similar to that of *A. ispida*, but rather brighter. It is a smaller bird, and may be most readily distinguished from the foregoing by its greater length of bill.

Entire length 5·8–6·6 inches; culmen 1·65–2; wing, carpus to tip, 2·6–2·9.

These measurements are taken from Mr. Sharpe's 'Monograph of the Alcedinidæ.'

Fig. Sharpe's Monogr. Alced. pl. 2.

145. Ceryle rudis (Linn.). *Black and White Kingfisher.*

Abundant throughout Egypt and Nubia. It may be daily seen, generally in pairs, perched upon the steep bank or the stranded roots of some tree that has been carried down by the river. At times, with beak directed downwards, it hovers over the water, into which it darts boldly after its finny prey; if unsuccessful, it will repeat the performance until it captures a fish, when it flies to the bank to enjoy the repast at its ease. Sometimes it flies slowly close over the surface of the water.

It begins breeding about the end of March, when it drills deep holes in the steep river-banks to place its nest in.

Head crested. The whole of the upper plumage, with the wings and tail pure black and white, sharply defined; under surface of the body pure silvery white, with the following markings:—in the adult female, only one large black patch on each side of the upper part of the breast, which nearly meets in the centre, and a few black marks on the flanks; the male has in addition an entire narrow black collar across the chest; in not quite adult plumage some of the feathers on the neck and crop are narrowly edged with dull black. Beak and legs black, irides dark brown.

Entire length 11·5 inches; culmen 2·3; wing, carpus to tip, 5·5; tarsus 0·5.

Fig. Sharpe's Monogr. Alced. pl. 19.

Fam. CORACIADÆ.

146. Coracias garrula, Linn. *Roller.*

This is only a bird of passage in Egypt and Nubia, arriving on its way north about the end of April. I first met with it at Koos on the 26th of that month; and two days later I killed three out of a party of four that I saw near Dendera. In the spring of the year they are not rare in Egypt. They are rather shy; but, owing to a fancy they appear to have for certain clumps of trees, they may be easily obtained by waiting near where they are first seen, and then getting them driven back by a companion. The birds which I shot at Dendera were obtained in this manner, as they had at first slipped out at the further side of the clump and settled in the open fields. The food of the three that I examined consisted entirely of beetles.

Head and neck bright bluish green; upper part of the back and scapulars chestnut; rump ultramarine, shading off to green on the tail-coverts; quills black with blue reflections, especially on the under surface; base of the quills, and all the wing-coverts bluish-green, with the exception of a broad band on the shoulders which is ultramarine; tail greenish blue, two centre feathers entirely dark green, the remaining feathers much lighter towards their ends, outer feathers tipped with black; entire underparts greenish blue. Legs reddish brown, beak black, irides brown.

Entire length 12·5 inches; culmen 1·2; wing, carpus to tip, 7·5; tarsus 0·8.

Fig. Sharpe & Dresser, B. of Eur. part i.

Fam. MEROPIDÆ.

147. Merops apiaster, Linn. *Common Bee-eater.*

This species arrives in Egypt about the 10th of April, and is then very plentifully distributed in flocks throughout the country, but is not quite so abundant as *M. ægyptius.* The greater number do not remain in Egypt to breed, but pass northwards in May, returning again about August. They are seen in flocks throughout the year, and nest in colonies in the sandbanks.

Forehead white in front, blending into bright emerald-green, which colour extends on each side, and forms a short eyebrow; a black band runs from the gape under the eye and over the ear, under which comes a narrow faint streak of green; top of the head, nape, upper part of the back, and part of the wing-coverts chestnut-brown, remainder of the back, rump, and scapulars pale yellowish-brown; primaries bright green, tipped with dusky; outer secondaries chestnut, tipped with dusky, inner secondaries green; *tail green, the two centre feathers long and pointed*; *throat yellow*, bordered by a black collar; remainder of the underparts bright bluish-green; legs dark brown; beak black; irides crimson.

Entire length 11 inches; culmen 1·4; wing, carpus to tip, 6; tarsus 5.

Fig. Gould, B. of Eur. pl. 59.

148. MEROPS ÆGYPTIUS, Forsk. *Blue-cheeked Bee-eater.*

(Plate VII. fig. 1.)

This is the most abundant of the Bee-eaters in April. It arrives in the country about a fortnight earlier in the spring than *M. apiaster*, which it resembles in size, habits, and cry; yet the two species are never found in one flock. During the day they may generally be met with perched upon the telegraph-wires, or feeding among the herds of cattle. I once observed them towards evening alight in such immense numbers upon a sandbank, that they made it look almost as green as meadow-land; they appear, however, generally to roost at night in the sont trees.

Forehead white, shading off into pale blue, which colour extends on each side of the head, and forms an eyebrow; a black band passes from the gape through the eye to the ear; the cheeks are blue; the *throat russet-brown*, fading into yellowish-white on the chin; remainder of the plumage brilliant green, except the underside of the wing, which is pale rufous; legs dark brown; beak black; irides crimson.

Entire length 12 inches; culmen 1·6; wing, carpus to tip, 6; tarsus 0·5.

Plate

1. MEROPS ÆGYPTIUS.
2. MEROPS VIRIDIS.

149. Merops viridis, Linn. *Little Green Bee-eater.*

(Plate VII. fig. 2.)

This pretty little Bee-eater is a resident in Middle Egypt throughout the year, but does not during the winter months range north of Golosaneh. They do not congregate in flocks, like the last two species, but are generally to be met with in pairs or family parties, often perched in rows on the long leaves of the date-palms, or on the outer twigs of the sont trees. In flight they look extremely beautiful, as they skim gracefully through the air with outspread wings, showing the orange colour underneath like an illuminated transparency. They breed in holes in the banks in April.

In this species a black band extends through the eye; and it has a partial black collar; remainder of the plumage brilliant green, excepting under the wings, where it is bright rufous; the two centre tail-feathers are very much elongated; legs brown; beak black; irides crimson.

Entire length 11 inches; culmen 1·1; wing, carpus to tip, 3·7; tarsus 4.

Fam. CYPSELIDÆ.

150. Cypselus melba (Linn.). *Alpine Swift.*

The Alpine Swift is a rare bird of passage in Egypt and Nubia, only met with in the more mountainous parts during the autumn and spring.

The entire plumage is very dark brown, almost black, except the throat and abdomen, which are white; beak and legs black; irides very dark brown.

Entire length 8 inches; culmen 0·4; wing, carpus to tip, 8·1.

Fig. Gould, B. of Eur. pl. 53.

151. CYPSELUS APUS (Linn.). *Common Swift.*

This is not the common Swift of Egypt; nor do I know of any authentic instance of its having been captured there. The *C. apus* of Egyptian lists refers generally, if not invariably, to the closely allied species *C. pallidus*, which is abundant and the only species which I have met with in that country up to the end of April. *C. apus* ranges throughout Africa and Europe; and as it visits Palestine, it must undoubtedly pass through Egypt; for this reason, rather than upon the testimony of others, I have included it in the present list.

Throat white, remainder of the plumage very dark brown, almost black; beak black; irides very dark brown.

Entire length 8·5 inches; culmen 0·4; wing, carpus to tip, 8; tarsus 0·6.

Fig. Gould, B. of Eur. pl. 53.

152. CYPSELUS PALLIDUS, Shelley. *Egyptian Swift.*

This species is very abundant throughout Egypt and Nubia. It has long been included in the Egyptian list as *C. apus*, from which, however, it differs in its rather smaller size, whiter throat, and general paler coloration, which latter character suggested to me the name *C. pallidus* as appropriate when I first described it (Ibis, 1870, p. 445). It may be distinguished from *C. apus* at a considerable distance; and when I first shot it I at once doubted its identity with that bird, and found on my return that Mr. E. C. Taylor agreed in my view, which made me careful, on revisiting Egypt, to procure more specimens, and I watched in vain among the many that I daily saw for one dark specimen; all were of the paler kind. It was not apparently breeding up to the beginning of May, when I last shot it. Major Irby has procured this species from Tangier, where, he says, it arrives before *C. apus*.

Above uniform brownish-grey, slightly inclining to white on the forehead and over the eye; feathers in front of the eye blackish; wing-coverts greyish brown, with an obsolete white edging; primary-coverts rather darker; quills dark greyish-brown, paler on the inner webs, the outer web (especially of the primaries) very dark (almost black on the last-mentioned feathers); tail greyish-brown, uniform with the breast; cheeks and sides of the neck pale greyish-brown; entire throat white, and under surface of the body dark greyish-brown, the feathers on the lower part of the breast having obsolete white tips.

Entire length 6·5 inches; culmen 0·3; wing, carpus to tip, 6·5 to 6·7; tarsus 0·5.

153. CYPSELUS PARVUS, Licht. *Little Grey Swift.*

Von Heuglin (Orn. N. O. Afr. p. 145) says of this species that it is a resident in Southern Egypt and Nubia throughout the year, and that he has found it breeding near Wady Halfa between the months of May and August.

Tail forked, outer feather on each side very long and

pointed; entire plumage sooty brown, with bronze reflections on the upper surface; under surface paler, especially on the throat; beak and feet black; irides very dark brown.

Entire length 6·5 inches; culmen 0·2; wing, carpus to tip, 5; tail 4·1; tarsus 0·35.

Fam. CAPRIMULGIDÆ.

154. CAPRIMULGUS EUROPÆUS, Linn. *Goatsucker.*

This species is only met with as a bird of passage in Egypt and Nubia. According to Von Heuglin (Orn. N. O. Afr. p. 125) it passes southward through Egypt in August, and returns again in March and April, at which seasons it may generally be met with in small flocks.

Male.—Upper parts rich ash-colour, shaded slightly with chestnut on the wings and with yellow on the rump, and beautifully pencilled with dusky; the centre of the feathers streaked with black, more boldly so on the crown and scapulars; quills dark brown, with imperfect sandy-coloured bars; a white patch on the three outer primaries near their tips, and a bold white tip to the two outer feathers of the tail; on the under surface there are two white patches on the sides of the throat; throat itself and crop dusky; remainder of the underparts orange-buff, barred with dusky; beak black; legs reddish brown; irides black.

Female.—No white spots on the wings or tail.

Entire length 10·5 inches; culmen 0·4; wing, carpus to tip, 7·4; tarsus 0·7.

Fig. Gould, B. of Eur. pl. 51.

CAPRIMULGUS ÆGYPTIUS.

155. Caprimulgus ægyptius, Licht. *Egyptian Goatsucker.*

(Plate VIII.)

This species, which ranges throughout Egypt and Nubia, appears to be most plentiful in spring and autumn, when it is generally in flocks. Von Heuglin (Orn. N. O. Afr. p. 128) remarks that six specimens which he killed out of a large flight of fifty were all females. In the Fayoom, in March, I met with a small party of four, all of which were males, from which it would appear that these birds travel in flocks of the same sex, and do not pair until shortly before breeding. Those that I met with in the Fayoom were sitting on the bare sand; and as they rose they frequently uttered a little snapping sound, and took refuge in some neighbouring tamarisk-bushes. I have also occasionally seen them flitting over the water towards sunset. Mr. S. Stafford Allen observes (Ibis, 1864, p. 236) that he found two distinct varieties. I agree with him that there is a considerable difference in the shade of colouring in certain individuals; for the four which I killed in the Fayoom, though perfectly like each other, were much darker than my former specimen from Aboo-fayda, so that at first I fancied that I had two species; but on comparison the markings would not justify their separation, although all five were males.

Pale variety.—Upper plumage pale sandy-brown, finely pencilled with black; inner web of the quills marked with white, and the whole of them irregularly banded with dusky; tail barred with nine or ten irregular wavy streaks; a white patch on the centre of the throat; remainder of the underparts pale sandy-brown, faintly barred on the chest with narrow streaks of dusky; greater portion of the underpart of the quills white; legs reddish-brown; beak dark brown; irides black.

Entire length 9 inches; culmen 0·6; wing, carpus to tip, 7; tarsus 0·7.

Dark variety.—Slightly larger; plumage rather more shaded with grey; some black marks on the scapulars; bars on the wings and tail more pronounced.

Order ACCIPITRES.

Fam. STRIGIDÆ.

156. ALUCO FLAMMEA (Linn.). *Barn-Owl.*

This species is frequently to be met with throughout Egypt and Nubia, generally in thick-foliaged trees or in ruins.

Upper plumage yellow, with the centres of the feathers marked and freckled with grey and white, and small oval spots of black and white; wings and tail banded with yellowish brown; face and underparts white, tinted with buff on the chest, and finely spotted at intervals with dusky; tarsus feathered about halfway down, the remainder covered with hair; feet pink; beak pale yellow; irides black.

Entire length 13·5 inches; culmen 1·3; wing, carpus to tip, 11; tarsus 2·5.

The above description is from an Egyptian specimen in my collection.

Fig. Gould, B. of Eur. pl. 36.

157. STRIX ALUCO, Linn. *Tawny Owl.*

Savigny mentions the Tawny Owl in his 'Description de

l'Egypte,' but it appears to be of very rare occurrence there, and probably never ranges south of Cairo.

Upper plumage tawny, with the centre of the feathers marked with dark brown; wing-coverts spotted with white, forming two irregular bands; quills and tail brown, barred with darker brown; underparts white, shaded with russet on the crop, and many of the feathers marked with dark brown stripes down their centres and barred with russet; legs and feet covered with creamy white down; beak yellow; irides black.

Entire length 15 inches; culmen 1·2; wing, carpus to tip, 10; tarsus 1·9.

Fig. Gould, B. of Eur. pl. 47.

158. NYCTALA TENGMALMI (Gm.). *Tengmalm's Owl.*

The present species is of very rare occurrence in Egypt. Schlegel, however, mentions it as being found in that country; and there is a specimen in the British Museum from Mr. Turnbull's collection.

In plumage it somewhat resembles the next species, but is more slender in form, greyer in plumage, with a white facial disk; it has also longer wings and tail, and more woolly feet; beak and irides pale yellow.

Entire length 10·3 inches; culmen 1; wing, carpus to tip, 6·8; tarsus 1·2.

Fig. Gould, B. of Eur. pl. 49.

159. CARINE MERIDIONALIS (Risso). *Southern Little Owl.*

This small Owl is extremely plentiful, both in Egypt and

Nubia, and remains there throughout the year. It frequents alike both trees and rocks, and is very partial to the small clumps which surround the water-wheels so abundant in Egypt. It breeds in March.

Upper plumage russet-brown, spotted with cream-colour, which forms two irregular bands on the shoulder; on the quills and tail the spots form interrupted bars; under surface of the body cream-colour, irregularly spotted with russet-brown; beak and irides pale yellow.

Entire length 8·5 inches; culmen 0·8; wing, carpus to tip, 6; tarsus 1·3.

160. Scops giu. *Scops Owl.*

This little Owl extends its range throughout Egypt and Nubia, where it may generally be met with in pairs or families. It appears to be most frequently found near Alexandria and Cairo, but is nowhere plentiful.

Head ornamented with short, thick, tufty horns; upper plumage mixed dusky grey and rufous-brown; quills and tail irregularly barred with white and dusky; under plumage yellowish grey, with bold distinct brown blotches on the chest; remainder of the feathers barred with narrow wavy lines, and occasionally streaked with brown down the centre.

Entire length 7·5 inches; culmen 0·8; wing, carpus to tip, 6·0; tarsus 1·05.

Fig. Gould, B. of Eur. pl. 41.

161. Asio otus (Linn.). *Long-eared Owl.*

This bird is, I believe, a resident in Egypt; for Dr. von

Heuglin (Orn. N. O. Afr. p. 107) mentions having killed it at Alexandria at the end of March, at which season it would probably be breeding. Mr. E. C. Taylor also shot two or three pairs (Ibis, 1867, p. 64).

It has long horns. Upper plumage buff, white, and grey, beautifully blended together, and mottled with dusky; quills and tail irregularly barred; face buff, with black round the eyes and towards the beak; under plumage buff and white, mottled with dusky; legs and feet covered with buff-coloured down; beak black; irides orange.

Entire length 14 inches; culmen 1·3; wing, carpus to tip, 11·3; tarsus 1·8.

Fig. Gould, B. of Eur. pl. 39.

162. Asio accipitrinus (Pall.). *Short-eared Owl.*

The Short-eared Owl is only a winter visitor in Egypt, although it remains as late as the end of March. I have killed it on two occasions in the fields while out Quail-shooting.

Upper plumage buff, mottled with dark brown and black; feathers round the eye black; wings and tail barred with brown; under plumage buff, mottled with dark brown on the throat and crop, and streaked with that colour on the abdomen; underpart of the wing white, excepting the tips of the feathers and a band near the middle, which are dusky; its horns are hardly distinguishable; beak black; irides orange.

Entire length 15 inches; culmen 1·3; wing, carpus to tip, 12; tarsus 1·8.

Fig. Gould, B. of Eur. pl. 40.

163. Bubo ignavus, Forst. *Eagle Owl.*

This bird appears very rarely in Egypt. Von Heuglin (Orn. N. O. Afr. p. 110) mentions having seen a fine old specimen, which was shot in the winter in the neighbourhood of Cairo. I know of no other instance of its capture in the country; but the statement of such a good ornithologist is sufficient proof that the present species does come to Egypt, though probably only as a straggler. In habits it is solitary, and frequents rocks and ruins.

It has very long and distinct horns.

Entire upper plumage yellowish brown, tinted with rufous and mottled with black, the quills and tail irregularly barred; throat white, remainder of the under plumage ferruginous buff, the feathers boldly marked with black down the centre and barred with the same colour; legs and feet covered with downy buff feathers; beak dusky; irides orange.

Entire length 24 inches; culmen 1·5; wing, carpus to tip, 16·5; tarsus 2·5.

Fig. Gould, B. of Eur. pl. 37.

164. Bubo ascalaphus, Sav. *Egyptian Eagle Owl.*

This species is distributed throughout Egypt and Nubia, and remains there the whole year. It frequents the mountains and ruins. Perhaps the best localities to meet with it are the Pyramids and the rocks near Soohay. It breeds in March.

Upper plumage buff, mottled with dark brown and white; quills and tail-feathers barred with dark brown; chin and throat white; remainder of the underparts buff, the feathers round the crop marked with large brown blotches; feathers on the abdomen, flanks, and thighs narrowly barred with russet; legs and feet covered with downy buff feathers; beak black; irides deep yellow.

Entire length 20 inches; culmen 2·1; wing, carpus to tip, 15·5; tarsus 3.

The above description is taken from a specimen I shot in the Fayoom.

Fig. Gould, B. of Eur. pl. 38.

Fam. FALCONIDÆ.

165. CIRCUS ÆRUGINOSUS (Linn.). *Marsh-Harrier.*

To be met with throughout Egypt and Nubia, but far most abundant in the Delta and the Fayoom.

I have a fine series of seven specimens in adult plumage, with grey wings and tail, from Egypt and Nubia, varying considerably in their coloration, which must be my excuse for the following long description of their plumage. I may also remark that they were all males by dissection, which inclines me to believe that the females do not assume this plumage at all; or if they do, it must be a long time before this change is completed.

Male.—Top of the head and nape of the neck white, buff, or russet, more or less streaked with dark brown down the centre of the feathers; back and wing-coverts brown, paler on the edges, especially on the shoulders; wings more or less washed with silvery grey; tail grey, and the upper tail-coverts usually marbled with white, grey, and rufous; under plumage more or less shaded with russet-brown, with the centre of the feathers marked with dark brown.

A Nubian specimen in my collection is entirely of a dark brown colour, with the following exceptions:—Base of the feathers on the head white and narrowly edged with buff; feathers on the shoulders and crop narrowly edged with pale brown; tail grey, wings washed with the same colour; cere and legs yellow; beak horn-blue; irides pale brownish yellow.

Entire length 19·5 inches; culmen 1·5; wing, carpus to tip, 15; tarsus 3·4.

Immature plumage.—Brown, with the exception of the head, nape, throat, a patch on the shoulders, and an irregular band on the chest, which are buff-coloured.

Fig. Gould, B. of Eur. pl. 32.

166. CIRCUS CYANEUS (Linn.). *Hen Harrier.*

This species is not nearly so common in Egypt as *C. pallidus*; but I have found it occasionally in rows of sont trees in Middle Egypt along with that bird. It only remains in the country during the winter months.

Male.—Upper plumage pearl-grey, slightly mottled on the nape with white; primaries black; *tail-coverts pure white*; the outer tail-feathers incline to white, and all except the two centre ones have seven dusky bars on them; throat, crop, and remainder of the underparts white; cere, legs, and irides yellow; beak black.

Entire length 19 inches; culmen 1·2; wing, carpus to tip, 13·6; tarsus 2·7.

The description is taken from a specimen I shot at Benisouef. The female is so similar to that of *C. pallidus*, that the one description will answer for both species.

Fig. Gould, B. of Eur. pl. 33.

167. Circus pallidus, Sykes. *Pale-chested Harrier.*

This species is resident in Egypt and Nubia throughout the year, where it may often be seen in small parties frequenting the rows of sont trees which are not uncommon in the neighbourhood of villages, and sometimes in company with *C. cyaneus*. The immature bird assumes a plumage which has caused it occasionally to be mistaken for *C. cineraceus.*

Male.—Similar to *C. cyaneus*, except that the *upper tail-coverts are white, barred with grey.*

Female.—Forehead and eyebrow buff; feathers under the eye white; ear-coverts brown; nape mottled with white, remainder of the upper plumage brown, all the feathers edged with pale brown; upper tail-coverts white, barred with brown; inner web of the primaries marked with buff and barred with brown; tail lightest towards the outer feathers, and barred with dark brown; under plumage buff, with the centre of most of the feathers rufous-brown; cere and legs yellow; beak horn-blue; irides brown.

Entire length 20 inches; culmen 1·3; wing, carpus to tip, 14·7; tarsus 2·8.

Immature bird.—Upper plumage similar to that of the adult female, except the upper tail-coverts, which are pure white; underneath it is of a uniform pale ferruginous-brown.

Entire length 19 inches; culmen 1·3; wing, carpus to tip, 14·1; tarsus 2·9.

Fig. Gould, B. of Eur. pl. 34.

168. Circus cineraceus (Mont.). *Montagu's Harrier.*

Von Heuglin (Orn. N. O. Afr. p. 105) calls this a bird of passage in Egypt; and several other writers upon Egyptian ornithology have included it in their lists, in some instances, to my certain knowledge, from the immature *Circus pallidus* having been mistaken for this species. I myself have shot three such specimens in Egypt. The Pale-chested Harrier, however, may easily be distinguished by the wing being shorter in proportion to the size of the bird than it is in the present species. These specimens rather closely resemble the female, but are without spots on the under surface of the body.

Male.—Upper parts and two centre tail-feathers grey; primaries black; secondaries with three dusky bars, only one of which is visible from above; two outer tail-feathers on each side white, barred with chestnut, and tipped with dusky grey; throat grey; under surface of the body white, with chestnut streaks on the centre of the feathers; legs, cere, and irides yellow; beak black.

Entire length 17 inches; culmen 1; wing, carpus to tip, 13·5; tarsus 2.

Female.—Above brown, with the centre of the feathers darker, lightest on the head; under surface pale ferruginous brown, with longitudinal chestnut spots on the centres of the feathers.

Entire length 17·5 inches; wing, carpus to tip, 13·5.

Fig. Gould, B. of Eur. pl. 35.

169. Astur palumbarius (Linn.). *Goshawk.*

The Goshawk appears to be of very rare occurrence in Egypt; and I know of no record of its having been met with in Nubia. On the 24th of March, 1868, my brother shot a fine female specimen in the sont woods near Benisouef, which has formed the subject of the following description:—

General colour of the upper plumage ashy grey; it has a white eyebrow, finely mottled with dusky; nape mottled with white; quills barred with dark brown; on the tail four distinct bars; underparts white, closely barred with brown; cere, legs, and irides yellow; beak horn-blue.

Entire length 25 inches; culmen 1·5; wing, carpus to tip, 14·6; tarsus 3·5.

Fig. Gould, B. of Eur. pl. 17.

170. Accipiter nisus (Linn.). *Sparrow-Hawk.*

The Sparrow-Hawk is very plentiful throughout Egypt and Nubia.

Adult female—Upper surface of the body, including the wings and tail, greyish brown, with a large white patch on the nape; under surface white, the feathers of the throat marked with fine longitudinal streaks; breast and abdomen thickly barred with dark brown; tail barred with dusky; cere, legs, and irides yellow; beak horn-blue.

Entire length 14 inches.

Adult male.—Smaller and brighter; upper plumage blue; underparts shaded with rufous on the breast, but especially on the flanks and thighs.

Entire length 12 inches; culmen 0·5; wing, carpus to tip, 7·2; tarsus 2·3.

Fig. Sharpe and Dresser, B. of Eur. part ix.

171. Accipiter gabar (Daud.). *Little Red-billed Hawk.*

This species may probably be met with as a rare straggler throughout Egypt and Nubia; for Mr. Edgar Larking has given me the description of a bird shot by him in Upper Egypt which agrees precisely with the present species. Although he brought the specimen home, it has unfortunately been mislaid, so that I have not been able to examine it. Von Heuglin (Orn. N. O. Afr. p. 74) gives Derr as its most northern limit on the Nile, while Schlegel says that it is plentiful near Suez.

Upper plumage slaty grey; quills barred with dusky, their inner webs white, secondaries tipped with white; *upper tail-coverts* and tip of tail white, with four broad black bands on the latter; throat pale grey; remainder of the underparts white, closely banded with narrow dusky bars; cere and legs red; beak black.

Entire length 12 inches; culmen 0·8; wing, carpus to tip, 7·5; tarsus 1·9.

Fig. Bree, B. of Eur. vol. i. p. 51.

172. Falco peregrinus, Linn. *Peregrine Falcon.*

The Peregrine ranges throughout Egypt and Nubia. It is

most plentiful in the winter, but probably remains occasionally to breed in the country; for on the 6th of May I shot a specimen at Aboo Fayda.

Upper plumage slate-colour, darkest on the head and shoulders, and changing to grey on the rump and upper tail-coverts, which are barred with dusky; feathers on the back and wings narrowly edged with dirty white; tail banded with grey, inclining to cream-colour on the inner webs, and tipped with buff. Under plumage white or cream-colour, streaked or spotted with brown on the crop and barred on the abdomen, flanks, and thighs; cere, eyelids, and legs yellow; beak horn-blue, inclining to yellow at the base of the lower mandible.

Female.—Entire length 19 inches; culmen 1·5; wing, carpus to tip, 14; tarsus 2·1.

Fig. Gould, B. of Eur. pl. 21.

173. FALCO BARBARUS, Linn. *Barbary Falcon.*

This Falcon, though a resident, is rather rare in Egypt and Nubia. At Edfoo on the 21st of April I saw a pair of Falcons which, from their small size and long pointed wings, I believe to have belonged to this species; and on the following day I shot a handsome male specimen on a sandbank near El Kab.

Top of the head grey, with dark centres to the feathers; *nape rufous*; remainder of the upper parts grey barred with dusky, most strongly between the shoulders; inner web of the primaries barred with flesh-colour; tail darkest towards the end, tipped with white and banded with irregular dusky bars; a distinct dusky moustache edged with rufous. Under parts creamy white, finely *barred on the abdomen and flanks with dusky*; cere and base of the bill yellow, remainder of the beak horn-blue; irides brown.

Entire length 13·5 inches; culmen 1·1; wing, carpus to tip, 11; tarsus 1·6.

The description is taken from the bird I shot at El Kab.

Fig. Salvin, Ibis, 1859, pl. 6.

174. Falco lanarius, Linn. *Lanner Falcon.*

This is the most abundant of the large Falcons, and remains throughout the year in Egypt and Nubia, breeding annually on the Pyramids.

Like all the true Falcons it appears very partial to the neighbourhood of water; frequently it will follow the sportsman on the look-out for wounded game. On the 19th of April I shot a female specimen in an interesting stage of plumage, from which my description of the immature bird is taken.

Adult.—Forehead nearly white; remainder of the upper part of the head and nape rufous finely marked with narrow black streaks; moustache, feathers in front of the eye, and an eyebrow extending to the nape black; remainder of the upper plumage dark slaty grey, with the feathers on the back and wing-coverts edged with buff; feathers on the rump and tail-coverts paler grey barred with dusky; primaries dusky grey distinctly barred with cream-colour on the inner webs; tail-feathers barred and tipped with cream-colour. Underparts cream-colour, streaked with brown on the crop, and spotted with the same colour on the abdomen; cere, eyelids, and legs yellow; beak horn-blue, more or less yellow towards the base according to age; irides brown.

Male.—Entire length 17 inches; culmen 1·1; wing, carpus to tip, 13·3; tarsus 1·9.

The sexes only differ in size, the female being larger.

A very old specimen in my collection has the top of the head very pale; and all the feathers on the crop and abdomen have brown streaks along the shafts, broadening into spots towards the tips of the feathers.

Immature.—Top of the head white, inclining to pale rufous towards the nape, with the centres of the feathers strongly streaked with brown; moustache, feathers round the eyes, and nape nearly black; remainder of the upper plumage uniform dusky brown; primaries marked on the inner webs with cream-coloured spots rather than bars; tail brown, two centre feathers without markings, remaining feathers faintly marked with a few small cream-coloured spots; tips of the feathers cream-colour; underparts white, with the greater part of the feathers on the crop and abdomen brown; cere, eyelids, and legs greyish yellow; beak horn-blue; irides brown.

Entire length 17 inches; culmen 1·2; wing, carpus to tip, 13·5; tarsus 2·1; middle toe 1·8.

Fig. Bree, B. of Eur. vol. i. p. 37.

175. Falco babylonicus, Gurney. *Red-naped Falcon.*

Von Heuglin (Orn. N. O. Afr. p. 26) calls this Falcon a tolerably common resident in Egypt and Nubia, frequenting the palm trees, mountains, pyramids, and ruined temples.

Plumage nearly similar to that of *F. barbarus*, but lighter and rather more rufous on the front of the head. It is the size of *F. lanarius*, with which it is most liable to be confounded, but differs from that bird in the absence of a whitish frontal band, the rufous feathers extending on to the cere and bordered behind by a broad, dark, slate-coloured band across the head, which separates the forehead from the rufous of the nape; *feathers on the back of the neck below the nape bordered with rufous*; a comparative absence of spots on the upper portion of the lower surface. *Middle toe longer than in* F. lanarius.

Entire length 17·5 inches; wing, carpus to tip, 12·8; tarsus 2; middle toe 2.

Fig. Gould, B. of Asia, pt. xx.

176. Falco saker, Schl. *Saker Falcon.*

This large species of Falcon is rather rare in Egypt and Nubia. In 1868 I obtained two specimens—one near Kom Ombo, the other near Sioot. It is called by the Arabs "Saker el hor;" and they train it to hunt the Gazelle.

Top and sides of the head white, each feather marked with a longitudinal streak of brown; remainder of the upper plumage slaty brown; primaries marked with cream-coloured spots or bars on the inner webs; tail marked with cream-colour in the form of spots on the centre feathers, inclining to bars on the outer ones; underparts white, boldly marked with large oval brown spots; legs and cere rather dull yellow; beak horn-blue, darkest towards the tip and inclining to yellow towards the base of the lower mandible; irides brown.

Entire length 22 inches; culmen 1·55; wing, carpus to tip, 15·8; tarsus 2·2.

Fig. Gould, B. of Asia. pt. xx.

177. Falco æsalon, Linn. *Merlin.*

The Merlin, which is extremely abundant in Egypt in spring, rarely extends its range so far south as Nubia. It may generally be met with in clumps of sont trees, and in some woods near Benisouef I have seen as many as thirty in a day, yet I never met with a single female specimen. This great preponderance of males, which has also been remarked by Mr. E. C. Taylor (Ibis 1859, p. 45), leads me to believe that it rarely, if ever, breeds in Egypt, although I have seen it as late as the end of April, though apparently not paired at that season.

Male.—Upper plumage bright blue-grey, the centre of the feathers streaked with black; a narrow edging of white feathers to the forehead, and a well-defined rufous collar on the nape; quills dusky, the inner webs barred with grey or white; a band an inch broad at the end of the tail dusky, the feathers tipped with white, and all but the two centre feathers barred with dusky on their inner webs; throat white, remainder of the underparts ferruginous white, darkest on the thighs and streaked and spotted with dark brown on the centres of the feathers; cere, base of the bill, and legs yellow, remainder of the beak horn-blue; irides brown.

Entire length 11 inches; culmen 0·7; wing, carpus to tip, 8; tarsus 1·4.

The description is taken from Egyptian specimens in my collection.

Fig. Gould, B. of Eur. pl. 24.

178. Falco subbuteo, Linn. *Hobby.*

The Hobby is by no means plentiful in Egypt and Nubia. Von Heuglin (Orn. N. O. Afr. p. 34) mentions three instances of its capture in that country; and I have a specimen procured for me at Damhanhoor in April.

Forehead buff, upper plumage dark slaty grey, with a patch of ferruginous colour on the nape; inner web of the quills barred with ferruginous buff; a moustachial stripe, feathers under the eye, and ear-coverts black; underparts buff, changing to rufous on the thighs and under tail-coverts; crop, chest, and under wing-coverts strongly mottled with dusky; cere and legs yellow; beak horn-blue; irides brown.

Entire length 13 inches; culmen 0·7; wing, carpus to tip, 10·5; tarsus 1·4.

The description is taken from my Egyptian specimen.

Fig. Sharpe & Dresser, B. of Eur. Part iv.

179. Falco concolor, Temm. *Sooty Falcon.*

Von Heuglin observes (Ibis, 1860, p. 409), in speaking of this bird under the name of *F. horus*, "I have observed this species rarely in the rocky deserts of Egypt and Nubia. A. Brehm has described a young specimen killed by myself in August 1852, near the so-called 'Fossil Forest,' at the Mokattam Mountains." In the Ibis for 1871 (p. 42) I included *F. eleonoræ* among the birds of Egypt on the authority of Von Heuglin (Ibis, 1860, p. 408), who writes of that species:—"Rare and only as a migrant bird in Nubia;" however, in his large work on the ornithology of North-

Eastern Africa he includes *F. eleanoræ* from those parts as synonymous with *F. concolor*, which seems to be the representative of that species in the Red Sea; for two pairs that he shot in the archipelago of Kakara, in 1857, appeared to belong certainly to *F. concolor*.

Entire plumage uniform plumbeous grey, except the primaries, which are dusky, and the shafts of the feathers, which are dark; cere and legs yellow; beak horn-blue; irides brown.

Total length 14 inches; culmen 0·75; wing, carpus to tip, 11·75; tarsus 1·3.

Fig. Finsch & Hartlaub, Vög. Ost-Afr. pl. 1.

180. Falco vespertinus, Linn. *Red-legged Falcon.*

This species ranges throughout Egypt and Nubia, but is most abundant in the Delta. According to Von Heuglin it is usually to be met with in small flocks of from six to twelve in Lower Egypt, but singly in Nubia. It is most plentiful in spring and autumn.

It feeds chiefly upon insects, and consequently is most likely to be met with while in pursuit of locusts in the corn-fields.

Male.—Plumage uniform deep slaty-grey, lightest on the wings and lower part of the chest; abdomen, thighs, and under tail-coverts rich russet brown; cere, base of the bill, skin round the eyes, and legs vermilion; remainder of the beak horn-blue; irides brown.

Entire length 11·5 inches; culmen 0·7; wing, carpus to tip, 9·8; tarsus 1·1.

The description is taken from a specimen in my collection from Damanhoor, shot in April.

Fig. Sharpe and Dresser, B. of Eur. part i.

181. Falco tinnunculus, Linn. *Kestrel.*

This is by far the most abundant Hawk in Egypt. On one occasion I saw at least one hundred in a single clump of palm-trees, doubtless attracted there by the locusts, which were passing in dense, continuous clouds beneath them. In 1870 the flight of locusts spread throughout the country, clearing whole districts of every green crop as they passed.

Possibly it was owing to the good done by the Kestrel in devouring these destructive insects that the ancient Egyptians placed this Hawk among their sacred animals.

Male.—Forehead buff; top of the head, nape, and ear-coverts grey; back and wing-coverts rich ferruginous brown spotted with black; rump and tail grey, the latter with a broad black band at the end, the extreme tip of the feathers being white; underparts ferruginous buff, spotted on the chest with black; cere, base of the bill, and legs yellow; remainder of the beak horn-blue; *claws black*; irides brown.

Entire length 13·5 inches; culmen 0·7; wing, carpus to tip, 9·3; tarsus 1·5.

The female differs in the absence of grey on its plumage, being wholly rufous, with dusky bars on the back and tail.

The young birds more or less resemble the female.

Fig. Sharpe and Dresser, B. of Eur. part ii.

182. FALCO CENCHRIS (Cuv.). *Lesser Kestrel.*

This bird ranges throughout Egypt and Nubia. It is most abundant in spring and autumn, especially around Alexandria, where Von Heuglin says that a few pairs remain to breed in the walls of that town.

I only shot it upon one occasion, in a wood near Benisouef, on the 29th of March.

Male.—Top of the head, nape, and ear-coverts, a band across the wings, rump and tail grey; remainder of the *back* and wing-coverts bright chestnut, *without spots*; tail similar to that of the Common Kestrel; throat buff; remainder of the underparts rosy buff, with small distinct black spots on the chest; cere, base of the bill, eyelids, and legs yellow, *claws yellowish-white*; remainder of the beak horn-blue; irides brown.

Female.—Plumage very similar to that of the Common Kestrel, but the *claws are yellowish white.*

Entire length 11·5 inches; culmen 0·8; wing, carpus to tip, 9; tarsus 1·2.

The description is taken from a male specimen which I shot at Benisouef.

Fig. Sharpe and Dresser, B. of Eur. part iii.

183. MILVUS REGALIS (Linn.). *Common Kite.*

Rüppell remarks of this species that it is abundant in Lower Egypt, while Von Heuglin says (Orn. N. O. Afr. p. 97) that neither he nor Brehm ever met with it there. I know of no instance of its capture in Egypt, and am therefore of opinion that Rüppell is in error, having no doubt mistaken specimens of *M. ægyptius*, which is the only Kite that is abundant in the country.

Head and neck pale grey, with brown streaks down the centres of the feathers; the whole of the upper surface ferruginous-brown, with dark brown centres to the feathers; primaries dusky; tail rich ferruginous-brown; under surface of the body pale brown or orange, shading into rufous on the flanks and thighs, with the centres of the feathers dark brown; cere and legs yellow; beak horn-blue; irides pale yellow.

Entire length 26 inches; culmen 1·5; wing, carpus to tip, 20·5; tarsus 2·4.

Fig. Gould, B. of Eur. pl. 28.

184. Milvus ægyptius, Gm. *Parasitic Kite.*

Arabic name "Hedaich."

Very abundant throughout Egypt and Nubia. They frequent every village, and indeed any place where there is a chance of their obtaining offal; and at Cairo and Alexandria great numbers may be seen flying over the town or perched upon the housetops. They are very inquisitive, and become bold when in search of food, often following the sportsman for a considerable distance; but I have never observed them capture even a wounded bird, although they will occasionally swoop at them. They begin breeding in March, usually selecting a sont tree near some village for their nest, which appears invariably to contain some pieces of old rag.

Adult.—Head and neck whitish grey, inclining more or

less to pale rufous on the top of the head and nape, the centre of each feather marked with a narrow streak of dusky brown; remainder of the upper plumage brown, with light edgings to the feathers; primaries black; tail rufous brown, darkest on the outer feathers, and crossed by nine or ten bars; underparts rufous brown, the feathers marked down their centres with dusky; tail forked; *beak*, cere, and tarsi yellow; irides pale yellowish brown.

Entire length 24·5 inches; culmen 1·8; wing, carpus to tip, 18; tarsus 2·2.

Immature plumage.—Tail often not forked; top of the head and nape sandy colour, with the centres of the feathers dark brown; remainder of the upper plumage dark brown, all the feathers, including the quills and tail, broadly edged with pale brown; underparts pale brown, mottled with dark brown, mostly on the chest; cere and legs yellow; beak black; irides brown.

Entire length 19 to 21·2 inches; culmen 1·5; wing, carpus tip, 13 to 16.

The description of the immature bird is taken from four specimens in my own collection.

Fig. Dubois, Ois. de l'Eur. pl. 14.

185. Milvus migrans (Bodd.). *Black Kite.*

Some ornithologists include under this name both the Black Kite (*M. migrans*) and the Yellow-billed Kite (*M. ægyptius*), both of which birds are met with in Egypt; but the black-billed examples are rare, excepting immature specimens, which invariably have the beak of that colour, whether they belong to *M. migrans* or to *M. ægyptius.* So great is the preponderance of the yellow-billed race, that I am not aware of having killed a single adult specimen in Egypt with a bill entirely black; and Von Heuglin and Mr. E. C. Taylor make similar observations.

This species is very similar to *M. ægyptius,* but has always an entirely black bill. The general shade of the plumage is blacker, the dark streaks down the centres of the feathers on the throat and crop are broader, and the irides, I believe, are invariably darker than in the adult *M. ægyptius.*

Entire length 23·3 inches; culmen 1·7; wing, carpus to tip, 18·5; tarsus 2·3.

Fig. Gould, B. of Eur. pl. 29.

186. Elanus cæruleus (Desfont.). *Black-shouldered Hawk.*

This pretty little Hawk is a resident in Egypt, and is very abundant as far south as Thebes, above which place and in Nubia its numbers are much more limited. It generally frequents the sont trees; but I have rarely observed more than a pair in the same clump. The food consists of insects and mice, which I have seen it pursuing after sunset, when I have been waiting for duck. Being by no means shy, its habits may be easily observed; and I have seen a bird occasionally remaining perched upon the top bough of a sont tree for hours together, uttering at intervals a low cry to its mate, who is rarely far off. By this rather peculiar cry, which it frequently repeats while sitting on its eggs, I was attracted to its nest on one occasion. The eggs, though rare in collections, are by no means difficult to find in Egypt. It begins breeding towards the end of February, and appears invariably to select a sont tree for its nest, which is constructed of sticks and reeds, put together with some care, and smoothly lined with the dried leaves of the sugar-cane. The eggs somewhat resemble those of the Kestrel, but are rarely quite as rounded in shape, and show more of the white ground, while the brown markings look like dry paint smeared carelessly over the surface. On the 12th of March, at Golosaneh, I found a nest containing four young birds. They were of a pale ashy colour, considerably darker on the back and top of the head, where the feathers were mostly tipped with brown, and the chest was of a pale brown.

Adult.—The eyes are surrounded by black; forehead and feathers over the eyes white; remainder of the upper plumage grey, except the shoulders, which are black; the outer feathers of the tail almost white; the whole of the underparts white; cere and legs yellow; beak black; irides carmine.

Entire length 13 inches; culmen 1; wing, carpus to tip, 12; tarsus 1·3.

Immature plumage.—Head and back tinted with yellowish brown, and the feathers of the wing and tail tipped with white; chest delicately shaded with yellowish brown, with a few brown streaks on the centres of the feathers; irides pale brown, while in the nestlings they are dark brown.

Fig. Gould, B. of Eur. pl. 31.

187. PERNIS APIVORUS (Linn.). *Honey Buzzard.*

Both Hedenborg and Rüppell mention this bird as being found in Egypt. I am, however, inclined to look upon it as a mere straggler in that country.

Feathers of the head short and stiff.

Adult.—Top and sides of the head brownish grey; remainder of the upper plumage brown tinted with grey; quills barred with dusky black, and marked with white on their inner web; tail tipped with white, and marked with the same colour at the base and on the inner web of some of the feathers; tail crossed by four distinct dark brown bands at irregular intervals; under surface of the body white, with the feathers boldly mottled and barred with brown; cere and legs yellow; beak horn-blue; irides brownish yellow.

Entire length 23 inches; culmen 1·5; wing, carpus to tip, 16; tarsus 2.

Fig. Gould, B. of Eur. pl. 16.

188. Buteo vulgaris, Bechst. *Common Buzzard.*

This bird is by no means common in Egypt. The only specimen I saw was one which I killed in a wood near Benisouef on the 25th of March; and from this bird I have taken my description.

Upper plumage brown, with lighter edgings to the feathers, mottled with white on the head and neck; tail distinctly marked with numerous dark brown bars; underparts white, mottled with brown; cere and legs yellow; beak horn-blue; irides brown.

Entire length 17 inches; culmen 1·5; wing, carpus to tip, 15; tarsus 3·2.

Specimens vary considerably both in colour and size.

Fig. Gould, B. of Eur. pl. 14.

BUTEO FEROX.

189. Buteo desertorum, Daud. *African Buzzard.*

In 'The Ibis' for 1871 (p. 40) I observed that it is highly probable that this bird is to be found in Egypt; but I do not know of any authentic instance of its capture there, though I fancy that I saw it in Nubia. As it is met with in all the surrounding countries, it cannot, in my opinion, fail to occur in Egypt.

190. Buteo ferox, Gm. *Long-legged Buzzard.*

(Plate IX.)

This is the most plentiful species of Buzzard throughout Egypt and Nubia. In Lower Egypt it is less frequently met with than higher up the Nile, and does not, I believe, winter in the Delta. It appears to be less abundant in some years than others; for in 1870 I only met with one specimen, at Kom Ombo, where it was breeding at the time. This specimen, unlike any other that I have ever seen, had a brown tail distinctly barred. In 1868 it was rarely absent from any field where Quail were abundant; and in 1871 I found it very plentiful in the Fayoom. It is a bird of lazy habits, rarely flying far, even after being shot at, but soon alighting again upon some mound or heap of maize-stalks, from which it keeps watch over the fields. I have found it breeding in Egypt in April.

Specimens differ very considerably in size and coloration.

Upper surface—top of the head varying from white to cinnamon, more or less mottled with brown down the centres of the feathers, remainder of the upper plumage buff or cinnamon-brown, mottled with dark brown; primaries dark brown, inclining to grey on the outer webs, and boldly marked with white or pale cinnamon on the inner webs; tail buff or pale cinnamon-brown, sometimes faintly edged with grey on the outer feathers, and usually unbarred, or at most only exhibiting very faint signs of cross bars; but upon one occasion I met with a specimen which had the tail very distinctly marked with a number of perfect brown bars; underparts cream-colour, more or less streaked with brown or cinnamon on the throat and crop; abdomen more or less of a uniform pale chestnut; most of the underpart of the wings white; legs and cere yellow; beak dusky; irides pale yellowish brown.

Entire length 22 to 25 inches; culmen 1·6 to 1·8; wing, carpus to tip, 17·5 to 18·7; tarsus 3·5 to 4.

191. Circaëtus gallicus (Gm.). *Short-toed Eagle.*

Tolerably plentiful throughout Egypt and Nubia, frequenting mountainous districts. On the wing it may be mistaken for the Osprey; but it is rather larger, and of a generally paler colour, while in disposition it is not nearly so shy.

Head rather broad; upper plumage ashy brown, with pale edgings to the feathers; head and neck occasionally much paler; inner web of the quills marked with pure white, and barred with dusky brown; tail tipped with white, and with three rather indistinct dusky bars, the inner web of all but the two centre feathers white; underparts white, spotted and barred with pale brown, chiefly on the upper part of the chest; *tarsus bare*; *cere and legs yellow*; beak horn-blue; *irides yellow.*

Entire length 28 inches; culmen 2; wing, carpus to tip, 20·5; tarsus 3·5.

The description is taken from specimens shot by myself in Egypt.

Fig. Gould, B. of Eur. pl. 24.

192. PANDION HALIAËTUS (Linn.). *Osprey.*

The Osprey is plentiful throughout Egypt and Nubia during the winter. In the Fayoom I found it extremely abundant, and not so shy as along the banks of the Nile. In the former locality I have often watched it hover for a moment over the water; then descending on its prey with a splash, seldom without success, it would rise and, shaking the water from its feathers, fly slowly off to some suitable position to devour its captive.

Feathers on the back of the head rather long; top and back of the head white, mottled with dark brown; remainder of the upper plumage dark brown, with pale edges to the feathers; the inner web of the quills marked with white and barred with brown; tail-feathers, with the exception of the two centre ones, pale brown, inclining to white, and with five or six distinct brown bars; under plumage white, more or less mottled with brown on the crop, according to the age of the specimen; cere and legs *slaty grey*; beak horn-blue; irides brown.

Entire length 21 inches; culmen 1·8; wing, carpus to tip, 19; tarsus 2·3.

The description is taken from two specimens shot by myself in the Fayoom.

Fig. Gould, B. of Eur. pl. 12.

193. HALIAËTUS ALBICILLA (Linn.). *White-tailed Eagle.*

Von Heuglin (Orn. N. O. Afr. p. 52) states that this species is a resident in Lower Egypt, where it frequents the lakes, as, for instance, lake Menzaleh. It is usually to be seen in pairs even during the winter months, at which season its numbers appear to be recruited by visitors. He considers the Egyptian specimens to belong to a small and possibly climatic variety of the true *H. albicilla.*

Adult.—Entire plumage ashy brown, palest on the under-parts; tail pure white; beak and legs yellow; irides pale brown.

The *immature bird* has a brown tail and slate-coloured beak.

Fig. Gould, B. of Eur. pl. 10.

194. AQUILA FULVA (Linn.). *Golden Eagle.*

This species is likewise said by Von Heuglin (Orn. N. O. Afr. p. 44) to visit Lower Egypt occasionally and at irregular intervals during the winter.

Adult.—Head and neck rich rufous-brown; remainder of the plumage dark brown; cere yellow; beak horn-blue; feet yellow; irides pale brown; *tarsus covered with feathers. It has three large scales on each toe.*

Immature plumage.—Head and neck not so pronounced rufous-brown; the tail more or less barred with white at the base, and the feathers of the tarsi more or less white.

Entire length 29 inches; culmen 2·7; wing, carpus to tip, 23·5; tarsus 4·5.

Fig. Gould, B. of Eur. pl. 6.

195. Aquila imperialis, Bechst. *Imperial Eagle.*

This fine species of Eagle is not uncommon in Lower Egypt during the cooler months, but is rarely met with on the Nile above Cairo, and in Nubia appears only as an occasional straggler.

Adult.—Top of the head and back of the neck rufous; back and wings dark brown, with the exception of the scapulars, which are mostly white; tail shaded with ash-colour, and irregularly barred with black, the broadest bar being next to the buff tip of the tail; under surface of the body dark brown, shading off into rufous on the abdomen; cere and tarsus yellow; irides pale brown; beak horn-blue.

Entire length 27 inches; culmen 2·1; wing, carpus to tip, 21·5; tail 11·0; tarsus 3·8.

The immature bird is much paler on the chest, which is distinctly striped with fulvous, and without the white on the scapulars.

Fig. Gould, B. of Eur. pl. 5.

196. Aquila næviodes (Cuv.). *Tawny Eagle.*

Von Heuglin (Orn. N. O. Afr. p. 45) mentions this species as of rare occurrence in Egypt and Nubia.

Entire plumage ferruginous-brown, with the centre of the feathers of the back, scapulars, and wing-coverts darker brown; quills and tail dusky brown; legs feathered down to the feet; feet, cere, and base of the bill yellow, remainder of the beak horn-blue; irides pale brown.

Entire length 24 inches; culmen 1·8; wing 18·0; tarsus 3·2.

197. Aquila nævia, Gm. *Spotted Eagle.*

This is the most abundant species of Eagle in Egypt, but it is less plentiful in Nubia. During my visit to the Fayoom in February and March it was extremely plentiful, and was generally to be seen sitting still by the water's edge. I frequently found it devouring pieces of decomposing fish, which appeared to form its chief food in the Fayoom.

Entire plumage brown, feathers on the head and neck with pale edgings; rump boldly mottled with white and pale brown; tail narrowly tipped with pale brown, and very indistinctly barred; under tail-coverts buff, mottled with brown. In younger specimens the chest, back, and wing-coverts are marked on the centre of the feathers with cream-coloured spots. Tarsus feathered; cere and feet yellow; beak horn-blue; irides brown.

Entire length 24–28 inches; culmen 2·4; wing, carpus to tip, 18·5–20; tarsus 4.

The descriptions are taken from Egyptian specimens in my collection.

Fig. Gould, B. of Eur. pl. 8.

198. Aquila Bonellii, Temm. *Bonelli's Eagle.*

According to Von Heuglin (Orn. N. O. Afr. p. 49) this

Eagle is occasionally met with throughout Egypt and the Fayoom during the winter months; and Antinori calls it comparatively common in Egypt and Lower Nubia. I have, however, never met with it during my several visits to those countries, nor have I seen an Egyptian specimen in any collection.

Upper plumage brown, with the edges of the feathers mostly lighter; quills black; tail more or less shaded with ash-colour, paler at the tip, and somewhat irregularly barred with dusky; throat and under surface of the body white or pale ferruginous, with brown stripes down the centres of the feathers; tarsus feathered; cere and feet yellow; beak horn-blue; irides brown.

Entire length 24 to 30 inches; culmen 1·75; wing 19·8; tail 11·5; tarsus 4·3.

Fig. Gould, B. of Eur. pl. 7.

199. Aquila pennata (Gm.). *Booted Eagle.*

Plentiful at times in Egypt and Nubia. It arrives about March to breed, and leaves again in September. It appears to be rather uncertain in its visits; for I never met with it during my last two tours in the country; but in March 1868, near Benisouef, our party killed three, and we saw several others either among the clumps of sont trees or beating up and down the fields, which were at that time full of Quail.

Specimens often differ very considerably in the colour of their chests.

Forehead occasionally white; remainder of the head and

neck light brown, the centres of the feathers streaked with dusky; remainder of the upper plumage dark brown, the feathers mostly edged with paler brown; under plumage white, streaked down the centres of the feathers with brown, or else pale brown streaked with darker brown; a more or less well-defined moustache; tarsi feathered; cere and feet yellow; beak horn-blue; irides brown.

This variation in plumage, as far as is known at present, depends neither upon sex nor age.

Entire length 21 inches; culmen 1·6; wing, carpus to tip, 15·5; tarsus 2·5.

The description is taken from Egyptian specimens in my collection.

Fig. Gould, B. of Eur. pl. 9.

200. Gypaëtus nudipes, Brehm. *Southern Bearded Vulture.*

According to Rüppell this bird is found in Egypt and Nubia; and Antinori says that it breeds in the Mokattam mountains, near Cairo. Dr. A. L. Adams mentions having seen *G. barbatus* on the Pyramids (Ibis, 1864, p. 8); and this specimen probably belonged to the present species, which does not appear to be very uncommon in Egypt. Dr. von Heuglin met with it on the shores of the Red Sea, near Suez (Orn. N. O. Afr. p. 18).

On the chin a tuft of dark brown bristles 1 inch in length; feathers on the face and throat short and brown, those on the back of the head and neck long, lanceolate, and nearly black; back, wings, and upper tail-coverts paler brown, and boldly marked with dirty white spots; quill feathers of the wings and tail dark brown; the feathers on the lower part of the throat are marked with longitudinal brownish-yellow spots; remainder of the underparts pale ferruginous brown; beak dull yellow, black at the base; legs yellow; irides brown.

Entire length 40 inches; culmen 4; wing, carpus to tip, 28; tarsus 4; tail 19·5, wedge-shaped.

Fig. Rüpp. Syst. Uebers. pl. 1.

201. VULTUR MONACHUS, Linn. *Black Vulture.*

The Black Vulture ranges throughout Egypt and Nubia, but is nowhere abundant. It may occasionally be seen on the sandbanks, either singly, or, more frequently, in company with flocks of *Gyps fulvus.*

Head and upper part of the throat covered with down, and ornamented with a ruff at the base of the neck; the whole of the plumage dark brown, with the edges of the feathers paler; basal half of the beak and a bare space on the throat bluish flesh-colour, remainder of the beak black; legs bluish flesh-colour; irides brown.

Entire length 45 inches; culmen 3·7; wing, carpus to tip, 28; tarsus 5.

Fig. Gould, B. of Eur. pl. 2.

202. VULTUR AURICULARIS, Daud. *Sociable Vulture.*

Von Heuglin (Orn. N. O. Afr. p. 9) mentions this bird as plentiful in Nubia, and not uncommon in the middle and southern provinces of Egypt; he observes, however, that he has not met with it in Lower Egypt.

Head thinly covered with dusky-coloured down; neck flesh-colour, naked, and covered with wrinkles; at the back of the neck a partial collar of short stiff feathers; back and wings brown; under surface of the body paler, the feathers long and narrow; legs and cere yellowish grey; beak and irides brown.

Total length 45 inches; culmen 3·7; wing 31·5; tarsus 6·5.

203. GYPS FULVUS (Gm.). *Griffon Vulture.*

This species is plentifully distributed throughout Egypt and Nubia. At Edfoo I met with several hundreds of them around the body of a dead camel, which they were extremely unwilling to quit, and allowed my dragoman to hit at them with his stick before they would take wing. Towards the end of April I observed a pair in the mountains of Aboo Fayda, where they were probably breeding.

Head and neck covered with short white down; lower part of the neck surrounded by a ruff of long, slender, white feathers, occasionally tinged with rufous; quills and tail dusky; remainder of the plumage brown, with a slight tint of rufous on the body; legs light brown; beak slate-colour; irides hazel.

Entire length 48 inches; culmen 2·9; wing, carpus to tip, 27; tarsus 4.

Immature birds have the head and neck dirty white, varied with brown, and the rest of the plumage much lighter than in the adult, with white and grey markings.

Fig. Gould, B. of Eur. pl. 1.

204. NEOPHRON PERCNOPTERUS (L.). *Egyptian Vulture.*

Arabic "Racham."

These birds are extremely abundant throughout Egypt and Nubia, where they may be daily seen feeding in pairs or flocks upon the offal round the villages, or slaking their thirst on the opposite sandbanks.

Adult.—Head, face, and throat bare, and of a bright yellow colour; wings black, with the outer web of some of the primaries and most of the secondaries washed over with silvery white; remainder of the plumage creamy white, more or less tinted with pale brownish yellow on the neck and crop; base of the beak yellow, apical half black; legs flesh-colour; irides crimson.

Entire length 27 inches; culmen 3; wing, carpus to tip, 18·5; tarsus 3·5.

The immature bird is more or less brown all over, and has brown irides.

It appears that this species does not obtain its mature plumage and crimson irides until the fourth year (*cf.* 'Nat. Hist. and Archeology of the Nile Valley and Maltese Islands,' by A. Leith Adams, p. 104).

Fig. Gould, B. of Eur. pl. 3.

Fam. COLUMBIDÆ.

205. COLUMBA LIVIA, Linn. *Rock-Dove.*

This Dove is abundant throughout Egypt and Nubia, inhabiting rocks and ruins, and the dove-cots in the Arab villages, in a semidomesticated state. By far the greater proportion of the Egyptian Pigeons have a grey rump; and such birds I refer to the next species, *C. Schimperi*, although I consider the colour of the rump to be a rather doubtful mark of specific distinction, as one cannot feel sure of the purity of the breed of even the apparently wild race. However, there are other distinctive marks, which, though less apparent, are more to be relied upon for the recognition of *C. Schimperi* from the present species.

General plumage slate-colour; *rump white*; lower part of the neck and upper part of the breast with a metallic green and purple lustre; the slate-colour is darkest on the head, neck, breast, and upper tail-coverts, and lightest on the wings; primaries dusky; basal portion of the secondaries and greater wing-coverts black, forming two bars on the wing; tail broadly banded across the tip with dusky, and the basal half of the outer tail-feathers white; beak dusky, with a fleshy substance at the base of the upper mandible; legs blood-red; irides brownish red.

Entire length 14 inches; culmen 0·8; wing, carpus to tip, 8·6; tarsus 1·1.

Fig. Gould, B. of Eur. pl. 245.

206. Columba Schimperi, Bp. *Schimper's Pigeon.*

I unfortunately paid but little attention to the Pigeons during my travels in Egypt, yet I think there can be no doubt that there are two races mixed in the vast semi-domesticated flocks, and living more or less in a pure wild state in the cliffs which in some places border the river. The one race has a white rump, and is *C. livia*; the other, and by far the most abundant, has a slate-coloured rump, and belongs to the present species. Von Heuglin (Orn. N. O. Afr. p. 828) does not admit the specific distinctness of these two races, and considers them all to belong to *C. livia*, which is, in my opinion, an error. Mr. E. C. Taylor (Ibis, 1867, p. 66), on the other hand, includes all the Pigeons under the name *C. Schimperi*, with the following observations:—"Flocks of Pigeons, perfectly wild, frequent the precipitous rocks that here and there border the Nile. I have frequently shot examples of them, and have always found them to possess the characteristics of *Columba Schimperi*, being decidedly and conspicuously distinguishable from *C. livia* by the absence of the white rump which forms so marked a feature in that species." I have certainly shot Pigeons both with and without the white rump; the former must undoubtedly be *C. livia*, and the latter, which on many occasions had the strongest claims to be considered pure-bred wild birds, I refer to the present species, *C. Schimperi*, as they were certainly not *C. œnas*, a bird of whose capture in Egypt I entertain very strong doubts.

207. Columba œnas, Linn. *Stock-Dove.*

Von Heuglin (Orn. N. O. Afr. p. 828) observes that there is a specimen in the Berlin Museum considered to be Egyptian; but he doubts the occurrence of this species in the country, and believes that the uncoloured plate in the 'Description de l'Egypte,' though named *C. œnas*, may be referred to *C. livia*.

General colour of the plumage slaty grey, a patch on the

side of the neck metallic green, the crop tinted with claret-colour; quills dusky, *with a single row of black blotches on the wing*; a broad black band at the extremity of the tail, and the exterior web of the outer tail-feather edged with white. In adult birds the beak is yellow, with the base red; legs blood-red; irides reddish brown.

Entire length 14·5 inches; culmen 0·8; wing, carpus to tip, 8·8; tarsus 1·1.

Fig. Gould, B. of Eur. pl. 234.

208. Turtur auritus (Linn.). *Turtledove.*

(Plate X. fig. 1.)

This Turtledove is abundant throughout Egypt and Nubia in the spring, and frequently breeds in the country. I first met with it on the 20th of April at Edfoo, when it had evidently just arrived; for I afterwards saw it daily in greater abundance than either *T. senegalensis* or *T. Sharpii.* Von Heuglin (Orn. N. O. Afr. p. 840) has fallen into the same error as most previous writers upon the birds of Egypt, and has mistaken *T. Sharpei* for the present species. The accompanying plate will show the distinctness of these two Doves.

Top of the head, back of the neck, sides of the back, rump, upper tail-coverts, and outer portion of the wing-coverts smoky grey; remainder of the back brown, with dark centres to the feathers; scapulars and greater portion of the wing-coverts black, broadly edged with clear yellowish brown; quills and tail dusky, shaded with grey; exterior web of the outer tail-feather, and a broad tip to all but the two centre ones, white; sides of the face shaded with sandy brown;

Plate X.

1. TURTUR AURITUS.
2. TURTUR SHARPII.

feathers on the sides of the neck black, tipped with white, forming three distinct oblique bands of each colour; throat and chest rich purplish pink, gradually shading into pure white on the abdomen; eyelids lilac-red; beak dusky, with a reddish shade towards the base; feet red; irides red, tinted with orange.

Entire length 12 inches; culmen 0·7; wing, carpus to tip, 7; tarsus 0·8.

209. TURTUR SHARPII, G. E. Shelley. *Sharpe's Turtledove.*

(Plate X. fig. 2.)

This bird arrives in the beginning of February, and by the end of the month becomes plentiful throughout Egypt and Nubia, and may be found breeding in great numbers towards the latter end of March, some three weeks before *T. auritus* arrives in the country. It has long been confounded with the latter species, owing to the similarity of its markings; but may at once be distinguished from that bird by the absence of any blue shading on the head and back, and from its wings being one inch shorter from carpus to tip. I first described this species in 'The Ibis,' for 1870 (p. 447), and named it after my esteemed friend Mr. R. B. Sharpe, the author of the 'Monograph of the Alcedinidæ' and other ornithological works. This Dove I regard as a desert form of *T. auritus*, and in some respects as intermediate between that bird and *T. senegalensis*. It appears never to breed on the ground, as the latter bird often does, but resembles it in the habit of frequenting burial-grounds and sandy districts, frequently at some distance from trees, which is seldom the case with

T. auritus. Its egg is intermediate in size, and, from the one specimen I brought home, appears to be of a less pure white than those of the other two species. In the beginning of April it so far surpassed in numbers its congener, *T. senegalensis*, that sixty out of sixty-two specimens which I killed on an island of the First Cataract were of this species.

Its plumage differs from *T. auritus* in the following particulars :—The head is of a pale yellowish brown, lighter beneath, shading gradually on the chest into rich pink, which again fades into white towards the vent; under tail-coverts white; the rump and upper tail-coverts broadly edged with yellowish brown; the exterior web of the outer tail-feather is stained brownish black at a distance of about an inch and a half from the tip; the two middle tail-feathers broadly edged with yellowish brown, and the two or three next feathers on each side have their white tips partially marked with the same colour; beak, legs, and irides similar to those of *T. auritus.*

Entire length 11·5 inches; culmen 0·7; wing, carpus to tip, 6; tarsus 0·8.

210. TURTUR ISABELLINUS, Bp.

The type specimen of this species is in the Berlin Museum, and has been figured by Bonaparte, the original describer (Ic. Pig. t. 102); yet Von Heuglin makes no mention of it in his great work on the ornithology of North-eastern Africa. The figure is indifferent; and as I have not seen the type specimen, and do not know upon what authority its claims are based to be an Egyptian species, I shall refrain from further remarks, merely adding, that if the species is a good one, and not a variety, I doubt if its real habitat will be found in Egypt.

211. Turtur albiventris, G. R. Gray. *White-bellied Turtle-dove.*

According to Von Heuglin, this Dove is met with singly in Egypt and Nubia. It is the *T. risorius* of his 'Systematische Uebersicht' (p. 49).

Head, neck, and crop creamy pink, with a broad black collar on the back of the neck, narrowly bordered with white; back and scapulars brown, shaded with grey on the rump; tail, two centre feathers brownish slate-colour, the remainder greyer, with white ends, increasing in width towards the exterior feathers; wings brown, shaded with grey towards the shoulders; under surface of the body white, shaded with pink on the chest and with grey on the flanks; beak, legs, and irides the same as in *T. auritus.*

Entire length 9 inches; culmen 0·7; wing, carpus to tip, 5·9; tarsus 0·8.

212. Turtur senegalensis (Linn.). *Egyptian Turtledove.*

This Turtledove, the only species which remains in Egypt the whole year, is very abundant and evenly distributed throughout the country. It is very sociable and tame, and not so fast on the wing as the other species. In every palm-grove pairs may be seen sitting together on the long leaf-stems, and in the villages they may be found strutting along the mud walls which form the native houses. They have begun breeding by the end of February, both in trees and on the ground by the side of banks.

Head purplish pink; back, scapulars, tail-coverts, and two centre tail-feathers umber-brown, shading into clear yellowish brown on the inner wing-coverts; remainder of the wing-coverts smoky grey; apical half of the three outer tail-feathers white, remainder of the tail, except the two centre feathers, slate-colour, broadly marked with black; feathers on the sides and front of the neck black, with broad yellowish-brown tips, forming a collar; chest purplish pink, gradually shading into white towards the vent; eyelids, beak, legs, and irides similar to those of *T. auritus.*

Entire length 10·5 inches; culmen 0·7; wing, carpus to tip, 5·5; tarsus 0·9.

Fig. Bree, B. of Eur. iii. p. 195.

Fam. PTEROCLIDÆ.

213. Pterocles exustus, Temm. *Singed Sand-Grouse.*

This is the most abundant species of Sand-Grouse in the country, ranging throughout Egypt and Nubia; in the latter locality it may be most plentifully met with on the uncultivated tracts, where the coarse halfa-grass has been recently cut, and on fallows. It usually keeps in small flocks, and is a bird of strong flight, frequently uttering while on the wing its loud peculiar note, which may be heard at a considerable distance, especially in the early morning and towards sunset, when they leave the more barren parts to slake their thirst at the river. The localities where I met with them most abundantly were at the Fayoom, Golosaneh, Karnak, and between

Silsilis and Kom Ombo. It breeds in April in small holes which it forms in the sand and lines with dried grass.

Male.—Head, throat, back, and upper tail-coverts sandy colour, shaded with yellow on the face and neck and with brown on the back; quills and primary coverts black, the inner primaries and outer secondaries tipped with white; wing-coverts sandy colour, those nearest the shoulder strongly shaded with brown, the remainder with yellow, and the inner ones tipped with deep brown, some of the larger ones having a white spot near the end; scapulars brown, shading into sandy yellow towards the ends of the feathers; tail, two centre feathers black, shaded with sandy colour, the remainder brown, barred with black and tipped with buff; a clear narrow black belt across the chest, edged with sandy colour, which shades into chocolate-brown on the abdomen, the centre of the latter being almost black; tarsi and under tail-coverts buff; beak dusky; feet and irides brown.

Entire length 12 inches; culmen 0·5; wing, carpus to tip, 7·5; tarsus 0·9.

Female.—Upper parts sandy colour, the feathers mottled and barred with black; quills and larger wing-coverts similar to those in the male; sides of the head, throat, and upper part of the chest sandy colour, mottled with black on the lower part of the throat and crop; a narrow double black belt across the chest, the lower part of which, as well as the abdomen and thighs, are black, narrowly barred with sandy colour; tarsi and under tail-coverts buff.

Specimens vary considerably in size.

Fig. Gould, B. of Asia, part ii.

214. Pterocles senegallus (Linn.). *Senegal Sand-Grouse.*

This Sand-Grouse, which is similar to the last in habits, may easily be recognized by its paler colours and yellow throat. Though a resident in the country it is not very abundant, but may generally be met with during the Nile tour, and is often brought to the market at Alexandria.

Male.—General plumage sandy colour; lores and a broad band encircling the head grey; basal portion of the scapulars and greater wing-coverts brown; primaries dark brown, washed on the outer webs with sandy colour; tail, the two centre feathers elongated and dusky towards the tip, the remainder barred with black and broadly tipped with white; upper half of the throat, cheeks, and ear-coverts bright yellow; remainder of the throat and crop washed with grey; centre of the chest and abdomen brownish black; tarsus covered with buff-coloured feathers; feet slaty brown; beak dusky; irides brown.

Female.—Entirely of a pale sandy cream-colour, with dusky spots on all the upper parts excepting the quills and tail; primaries inclining to brown on the inner web; secondaries, except a few of the inner ones, uniform brown; upper part of the throat, cheeks, and ear-coverts yellow; remainder of the throat spotted with dusky; centre of the abdomen dark brown; the rest of the plumage the same as in the male.

Entire length 12 inches; culmen 0·5; wing, carpus to tip, 7·2; tarsus 1.

Fig. Gould, B. of Asia, part iii.

215. Pterocles coronatus, Licht. *Coronetted Sand-Grouse.*

In Egypt and Nubia this species is rare, and does not, to my knowledge, come into the Delta. Dr. A. Leith Adams (Ibis, 1864, p. 27) mentions having shot four out of a flock at the Second Cataract; and Mr. S. Stafford Allen also killed a pair at El Kab (Ibis, 1864, p. 240).

Male.—Front of the forehead and over the eye creamy white; crown of the head cinnamon, surrounded by a band of grey; *a black patch on each side of the beak*, joining on the chin, and extending down the centre of the throat; remainder of the upper part of the throat, cheeks, ear-coverts, and neck yellow, the rest of the plumage sandy colour; scapulars and wing-coverts mottled with dark brown, with a pear-shaped spot of buff at the tips of the feathers; primaries blackish brown, slightly edged with sandy colour; tail, two centre feathers sandy colour, without elongated ends, the remainder with a bar of black and broad white tips; underparts sandy colour, washed with grey on the base of the throat and fore part of the chest; beak and feet leaden black; irides brown.

Entire length 10 inches; culmen 0·6; wing, carpus to tip, 7·7; tarsus 1·2.

Female.—Generally paler, and without any black on the face and throat, and wanting the grey band; the crown much paler, and the plumage generally barred with brown on the crop, back, and wing-coverts.

Fig. Gould, B. of Asia, part iii.

Fam. TETRAONIDÆ.

216. Francolinus vulgaris, Steph. *Francolin.*

I only include this species on the authority of Rüppell, who says that it is met with singly in the Delta during the winter.

Male.—Top of the head and nape rufous, streaked with black; a large patch of white on the ear-coverts; remainder of the head black; a broad rufous-brown collar, with some of the feathers tipped with oval black spots edged with white; upper part of the back black, with white spots; scapulars and wing-coverts dark brown, the feathers broadly edged with rufous; remainder of the back, tail-coverts, and tail composed of alternate black and white transverse zigzag lines; quills rufous brown, with transverse bars and spots of dusky brown; chest, abdomen, and flanks black, with oval white spots, becoming larger on the flanks; lower part of the abdomen rufous, with white edges to the feathers; under tail-coverts rich rufous brown, also edged with white; feathers of the thighs barred with black and white, and pencilled with rufous; beak dusky black; legs reddish brown; irides brown.

Entire length 13 inches; culmen 1·3; wing, carpus to tip, 6; tarsus 2.

Fig. Gould, B. of Eur. pl. 259.

217. Ammoperdix Heyi, Temm. *Hey's Sand-Partridge.*

This species is rare in Egypt and Nubia, but is probably a resident there throughout the year, frequenting rocky districts, where it prefers running and hiding among the stones to taking wing. Mr. E. C. Taylor mentions his having obtained a specimen at Assouan (Ibis, 1867, p. 67). Canon Tristram gives a good account of its habits (Ibis, 1868, p. 214).

Male.—General plumage deep sandy buff, washed with dark grey on the crown and cheeks; rump, upper tail-coverts, and centre tail-feathers sandy buff, pencilled and barred with brown; lateral tail-feathers chestnut; primaries brown, blotched on their outer margins with buff; secondaries pencilled with black; lores and a stripe behind the eye white, bordered above and below with dusky brown; breast deep buff; remainder of the under surface of the body chestnut and white, with the sides of the feathers black; under tail-coverts reddish orange; beak orange; legs olive-yellow; irides brown.

Entire length 9 inches; culmen, 0·7; wing, carpus to tip, 4·8; tarsus 1·5.

Female.—Entire plumage greyish buff, mottled and pencilled with pale buff and black, and with a wash of reddish buff on the shoulders and back.

Fig. Gould, B. of Asia, part iii.

218. Coturnix communis, Bonn. *Common Quail.*

A few Quail remain in Egypt throughout the year. The migratory birds arrive there in abundance towards the beginning of March and again in November, the greater number only passing through the country on their way to and from Europe; but still many remain to breed. When these travellers have arrived in the country the fact soon becomes known from their peculiar call, which may be constantly heard from among the crops, especially in the early morning and towards sunset. These are the best times for shooting Quail; for during the heat of the day they retire to the thicker crops, and are very unwilling to rise.

Female.—Upper parts brown, shaded with rufous and grey, and marked with black; a buff line extends over each eye, and another one down the centre of the head; the feathers on the neck, scapulars, sides of the back, and tail-coverts have pointed streaks of buff edged with black down the centre of the feathers; wings brown, with irregular narrow bars; underparts creamy white, shaded and spotted with brown on the crop and flanks, a distinct semicircular collar of brown spots on the throat; beak brown; legs flesh-colour; irides hazel.

Male in summer.—Chin and centre of throat black; the crop and flanks more rufous and less spotted.

Entire length 7·5 inches; culmen 0·5; wing, carpus to tip, 4·5; tarsus 1.

Fig. Gould, B. of Eur. pl. 263.

219. TURNIX SYLVATICA, Desfont. *Andalusian Hemipode.*

This bird appears to be of very rare occurrence in Egypt, and probably never ranges into Nubia. Von Heuglin (Syst. Ueb. p. 52) only once met with it, in a clover-field, in Lower Egypt.

Upper plumage of a general sandy-brown colour; the top of the head has a plain sandy-coloured central line, extending on to the nape, with a dusky black and rufous line on each side; remainder of the feathers dusky, with sandy-coloured edges, and tipped with rufous; sides of the face sandy coloured, with dusky tips to the feathers; feathers on the back and scapulars finely pencilled with black, the centres stained and spotted with rufous, many of the wing-coverts having the centre of the feathers black, forming large spots; quills dusky, edged with pale brown; chin and belly cream-colour; sides of the neck, front of the chest, sides, flanks, and under tail-coverts deep sandy orange, spotted with black; beak and legs yellowish brown; irides brown.

Entire length 6 inches; culmen ·55; wing, carpus to tip, 3·75; tarsus 1.

Fig. Gould, B. of Eur. pl. 264.

Order GRALLÆ.

Fam. OTIDIDÆ.

220. Otis houbara, Gm. *Houbara Bustard.*

This fine Bustard is plentiful in most parts of Northern Africa, frequenting the desert, and ranges, I believe, throughout Egypt and Nubia. I have never myself met with it alive, but it is not uncommon in the market at Alexandria.

This species is distinguished by a long crest of white feathers and a thick ruff of long narrow ones on each side of the neck, the upper ones black and the lower ones white; the whole of the upper plumage is sandy brown, each feather marked with zigzag bars of dusky colour; primaries white at their base and dark brown towards their ends; tail barred with grey and black; throat white, freckled with brown;

some sandy-brown feathers on the chest; remainder of the under surface of the body white; beak and legs olive-green; irides brown.

Entire length 25 inches; culmen 2·1; wing, carpus to tip, 14; tarsus 4.

Fig. Gould, B. of Eur. pl. 268.

221. Otis tetrax, Linn. *Little Bustard.*

According to Von Heuglin (Syst. Ueb. p. 54) this bird is to be met with singly in the north-eastern portion of Lower Egypt.

Male.—Upper part of the head and nape black, freckled with sandy colour; throat, cheeks, and ear-coverts deep slate-colour; remainder of the neck black, with a narrow white collar descending in a V-shape in front of the throat; a broad white band at the base of the latter, followed by a narrow one of black; the remainder of the upper plumage is sandy brown, pencilled with black and grey and spotted with black; upper tail-coverts and all the tail-feathers, except the two centre ones, tipped with white; wings, the three outer primaries dark brown, the remainder white with black ends, which are again tipped with white; secondaries white, with a narrow black bar on their outer webs; the greater wing-coverts white; underparts of the body and wings white, with a patch on each side of the crop of the same colour as the back; beak yellowish brown, darkest on the culmen and towards the tip; legs yellow; irides dark brown.

Entire length 17 inches; culmen 0·9; wing, carpus to tip, 9·5; tarsus 2·5.

Female.—No black or white on the throat, which is of the

same colour as the back; feathers on the crop and flanks barred with brown, and no white ends to the upper tail-coverts.

Fig. Sharpe and Dresser, B. of Eur. part xiii.

222. Eupodotis arabs (Linn.). *Arabian Bustard.*

Von Heuglin (Syst. Ueb. p. 53) mentions this species as being met with singly in Egypt.

General colour sandy, all the feathers delicately pencilled with darker brown; quills blackish; the greater coverts and outer secondaries tipped with white, forming an oblique bar across the wing, some of the lesser coverts exhibiting an obsolete white spot; tail greyish brown, tipped with white, before which is a subterminal bar of brown pencilled with sandy, and across the middle of the tail is a broad white band; crown of the head and whole of the neck whitish, varied with minute transverse lines of blackish; a broad black band extending from above the eye backwards, and forming a crest where it joins the nape; eyebrow whitish; under surface of the body white, the outermost under wing-coverts pencilled with brown; vent and under tail-coverts brownish, with central white streaks; bill yellowish, brownish above the nostril; feet yellowish; nails horn-brown.

Total length 34 inches; culmen 3·6; wing 14·5; tail 11; tarsus 8·5.

Fam. CHARADRIIDÆ.

223. Glareola pratincola, Linn. *Collared Pratincole.*

This Pratincole arrives in Egypt in great numbers about the middle of April. I first met with it near Assouan on the 15th of that month, and afterwards saw it in great abundance as I descended the Nile, sometimes on the bare fields, but more frequently by the sides of small pools or on the numerous sandbanks of the river. The flight is very peculiar and varied, the birds at times passing rapidly through the air in flocks, like Plovers, or else floating at a considerable height with outspread wings, or again playing over the water after the manner of Terns. When I first saw a single specimen of this bird rise from a small pool, I should have taken it for a Green Sandpiper, which it closely resembled in the colour of its back and flight, had it not been for the greater length of the pinions. Probably the larger portion of these flocks do not remain in the country to breed, but pass on into Europe, returning again in October or November on their way south. When I met with them, their chief food consisted of locusts, which were extremely abundant.

Upper parts olive-brown, shaded on the nape with sandy colour; quills and greater wing-coverts brownish black; tail-coverts and tail, which is forked, white, the latter with a broad brown ending to the feathers; throat sandy colour, bordered by a narrow band of white feathers tipped with black, forming a collar; chest sandy colour, shaded on the sides with hair-brown; remainder of the body white; *under wing-coverts chestnut*; beak black, with some light red at the base; legs dusky olive; irides brown.

Entire length 10 inches; culmen 0·6; wing, carpus to tip, 7·7; tarsus 1·2.

Fig. Gould, B. of Eur. pl. 265.

224. Glareola Nordmanni, Fischer. *Black-winged Pratincole.*

Von Heuglin observes (Syst. Ueb. p. 55) that this species is to be met with throughout Egypt and Nubia in small family parties in the fields, and that in October 1851 he found it abundant in the Fayoom and Middle Egypt.

Very similar to *G. pratincola*, but easily distinguished by the entire *underpart of the wing and axillaries being black*, and by its having no red on the beak.

Entire length 9 inches; culmen 0·6; wing, carpus to tip, 7·4; tarsus 1·9.

Fig. Gurney, Ibis, 1868, pl. viii.

225. Cursorius gallicus, Gm. *Cream-coloured Courser.*

This species, although a resident, is not very abundant in either Egypt or Nubia. It is a desert bird, preferring the sandy wastes to the more cultivated parts, and is generally to be met with in small flocks, probably consisting of the last year's brood. I myself only found it on one occasion, on the 4th of February, opposite Aboo-fayda, where I had a most exciting chase, as I had recognized the birds, and was anxious to procure a specimen. They were four in number, and very shy; they, however, preferred running to flying, never remaining long on the wing. Finding that I could not stalk them in the ordinary way, I drove them towards a bush, and then making a long round got up to that piece of covert, and shot one and broke the leg of a second. This wounded bird detained the other two, and enabled me to procure one of them. The wounded one was now alone, and so shy that I had great difficulty in procuring it, which I finally succeeded in doing by walking on one side instead of directly towards it, when it couched on the sand, hoping to be passed unobserved; and thus, after an hour's pursuit, I obtained my third specimen.

Forehead sandy rufous; hinder part of the crown grey; nape black; eyebrows white, extending back to the nape, where they join a black streak running from the eye to the nape; remainder of the upper plumage sandy colour, excepting the primaries and primary-coverts, which are black, the secondaries tipped with white, with more or less black on their inner webs; the tail-feathers, all but the two centre ones, have black spots near the ends and their tips white; the sandy colour shades off lighter on the underparts, and becomes creamy white on the chin, lower part of the abdomen, and under tail-coverts; beak black; legs enamelled white; irides brown.

Entire length 10 inches; culmen 1; wing, carpus to tip, 6·3; tarsus 2·1.

Fig. Gould, B. of Eur. pl. 266.

226. Œdicnemus crepitans, Temm. *Thick-knee.*

Plentiful throughout Egypt and Nubia, in pairs and families, affecting the more desert spots in the neighbourhood of small bushes, in preference to the cultivated fields, while they are occasionally met with on the sandbanks of the river. On the first approach of danger they crouch close to the ground; and when pursued, usually fly only for a short distance, and then run with considerable fleetness.

Upper plumage sandy colour, the centre of the feathers marked with dark brown, some of the smaller wing-coverts having a band of white and one of dark brown on them, forming a distinct diagonal bar on the wing, the greater coverts also forming a white bar; quills dark brown, with a white patch on the three outer primaries, the inner ones having their base and tips white; tail white, excepting the two centre feathers, and barred and tipped with dark brown; feathers in front of and under the eye, and a streak from the lower mandible under the ear-coverts, dark brown; cheeks and upper part of the throat white; remainder of the underparts cream-colour, shaded with brown on the throat and with rufous on the under tail-coverts; lower parts of the neck and chest streaked with brown; legs and basal half of the beak yellow, remainder of the bill and edge of it black; irides yellow.

Entire length 17 inches; culmen 1·5; wing, carpus to tip, 9·5; tarsus 2·9.

Fig. Gould, B. of Eur. pl. 288.

227. VANELLUS CRISTATUS, Meyer. *Lapwing.*

Very plentiful throughout Egypt up to the end of March, at which season they pass northward, leaving but few to breed south of Cairo. In Nubia they are much less abundant.

Top of the head and crest, cheeks, ear-coverts, and a broad collar on the crop black; a broad eyebrow, extending back to the nape and throat, white; back of the neck ashy brown; back, scapulars, and wing-coverts metallic green and purple; remainder of the wing black, with a white patch near the end of the outer primaries; upper tail-coverts chestnut; tail white, with a broad black ending to all but the two outer feathers; under surface of the body white; vent and under tail-coverts rufous; beak black; legs reddish brown; irides dark brown.

Entire length 13 inches; culmen 1; wing, carpus to tip, 9; tarsus 1·9.

Fig. Gould, B. of Eur. pl. 291.

228. Hoplopterus spinosus (Linn.). *Spur-winged Plover.*

The Spur-winged Plover is one of the most abundant birds in Egypt, where it remains throughout the year. In the fields and on the sandbanks it may be constantly seen, either sitting motionless, with head depressed and shoulders up, trying to elude observation, or else standing erect, and constantly moving the body with a little spasmodic jerk. Its cry is loud and varied, and is frequently heard. In March this species commences to breed, at which season I have found as many as thirty nests close together towards the point of a sandbank; it also breeds in the fields. The nest consists of a neat circular shallow hole in the sand, roughly lined with short pieces of dried reed, just sufficient to prevent the eggs from touching the ground.

A sharp black spur on the carpal joint of the wing; upper part of the head, nape, and throat black, remainder of the head and neck white; back, scapulars, and inner half of the wing-coverts hair-brown, remainder of the wing-coverts and basal portion of the secondaries pure white; primaries and ends of the secondaries black; tail-coverts and basal half of the tail white, the remainder black; chest and sides of the abdomen black, remainder of the abdomen, flanks, and under tail-coverts white; beak and legs black; irides red.

Entire length 12 inches; culmen 1; wing, carpus to tip, 8·2; tarsus 2·1.

Fig. Gould, B. of Eur. pl. 293.

229. Chettusia gregaria (Pall.). *Social Plover.*

This species is sparingly scattered throughout Egypt and Nubia. I only fell in with it twice between Girgeh and Sioot, killing one of a pair which I saw on the 9th of March, and one on the following day, out of a flock of eight, lower down the river.

Forehead, sides of the crown, cheeks, and chin pale buff; top of the head and a streak from the gape through the eye black; back of the neck, back, scapulars, and wing-coverts stone-grey; primaries black; secondaries white; tail white, with a black mark on the feathers near the end, forming an incomplete bar; throat and ear-coverts sandy colour, verging into stone-grey on the front of the chest, and shading off to black on the abdomen, which latter terminates posteriorly in rich chestnut; thighs, vent, and under tail-coverts white; legs and beak black; irides dark brown.

Entire length 12 inches; culmen 1·1; wing, carpus to tip, 8; tarsus 2·2.

Fig. Gould, B. of Eur. pl. 292.

230. Chettusia Villotæi, Audouin *. *White-tailed Plover.*

Egypt appears to be the metropolis of this beautiful bird, as it is a resident in the country and very plentiful, being generally distributed in pairs or small flocks round the

* Although Mr. Sharpe took especial pains to unravel the intricate synonymy of this bird for the 'Birds of Europe,' and had apparently proved that the name of *leucura* should be applied to the species, he has shown me a letter addressed to him by Count Salvadori, in which he states that in his possession is an older edition of the 'Description de l'Egypt,' bearing the date of 1809, in which Audouin bestowed the name of *Villotæi*, which accordingly stands.

marshes of the Delta, the Fayoom, and near Erment, and it may also be met with in Nubia. It is essentially a marsh Plover, and may be seen either wading in the mud or shallow water, or sitting still upon some raised bank. On rising from the ground it frequently utters its cry, which consists of a single harsh note several times repeated. The bright crimson reflections on the back, which are very beautiful in a freshly killed specimen, fade slightly after death.

Head and neck hair-brown, shading off paler in front of the forehead and round the eyes, and merging into pure white on the throat; back, scapulars, smaller wing-coverts, and some of the inner secondaries of a delicate crimson shaded with brown; tail-coverts and tail pure white; primaries black; secondaries, basal half of the primary-coverts, and the ends of the greater wing-coverts white; the wing-coverts have a black bar on them next to the white, forming a band on the wing; chest slaty grey; abdomen and under tail-coverts buff; beak black; legs pale yellow; irides light red, with a tinge of orange.

Entire length 10·5 inches; culmen 1·2; wing, carpus to tip, 7; tarsus 3.

Fig. Sharpe and Dresser, B. of Eur. part ii.

231. Pluvianus ægyptius (Linn.). *Black-headed Plover.*

This species is plentifully distributed throughout Egypt and Nubia, but is most abundant in Upper Egypt, from Sioot to Thebes, being almost invariably seen in pairs. They never wander far from the river-bank; and when on the wing fly close over the surface of the water, frequently uttering their cry during flight. They look very handsome as they thus skim along the stream on outspread pinions, displaying their distinctly marked plumage to the greatest advantage.

Top and sides of the head, nape, back, and band round the chest, base and tip of the quills, and greater part of the first primary glossy black; scapulars, wings, and tail-coverts, and the whole tail excepting the tip clear grey; a band over each eye meeting at the back of the head, throat, edge of the pectoral black band, about half of each quill, and end of the tail pure white; remainder of the underparts buff; beak black, with a small grey spot near the base of the lower mandible; legs clear grey; irides brown.

Entire length 8·5 inches; culmen 0·7; wing, carpus to tip, 5·4, tarsus 1·4.

Fig. Gould, B. of Asia, part xvii.

232. Charadrius pluvialis, Linn. *Golden Plover.*

The Golden Plover only visits Egypt during the winter, and does not range south of Cairo. In the Delta I have met with it in flocks on the open ground, or by the edge of the marshes, and I have frequently killed specimens. It probably arrives about September, and leaves again in March.

Winter plumage.—Upper parts black, mottled with yellow; forehead and over the eye buff; primaries dusky black with some white on the shafts, secondaries barred on the edges with yellow; under wing-coverts and *axillary plumes white*; tail black, barred and tipped with whitish yellow; underparts white, shaded with brown on the lower part of the throat and crop, and spotted on those parts with dusky brown; beak black; legs dusky; irides dark brown.

Entire length 11 inches; culmen 1; wing, carpus to tip, 7·4; tarsus 1·5.

In summer the throat and chest become black.

Fig. Sharpe & Dresser, B. of Eur. part vi.

233. Squatarola helvetica, Linn. *Grey Plover.*

This Plover closely assimilates to the last species in its habits and distribution, and like it is only a winter visitant in Lower Egypt.

Winter plumage.—Very similar to that of *C. pluvialis*, but of a general paler colour, and the bars and spots on the upper parts are dirty white, not yellow. *The axillary plumes are black*; and it may further be distinguished by the presence of a hind toe.

Entire length 12 inches; culmen 1·2; wing, carpus to tip, 7·4; tarsus 1·5.

Fig. Sharpe & Dresser, B. of Eur. part vi.

234. Eudromias morinellus (Linn.). *Dotterel.*

Von Heuglin (Syst. Ueb. p. 56) remarks concerning this species, that it is met with during the winter in Egypt and along the shores of the Red Sea. In 1851 he saw a large flock of Dotterel on the desert between Sakkara and the Fayoom.

Winter plumage.—Top of the head, back, and scapulars brown, with sandy spots and edges to the feathers; primaries dark brown, exterior web of the outer one strongly marked with white; no other white on the primaries; tail more slaty brown, with sandy tips to the feathers; collar round the neck and underparts sandy brown, spotted on the throat and crop with dark brown; vent and under tail-coverts white; beak black; legs olive-black; irides dark brown. In summer the underparts have distinct bands of white, chestnut, and black, and the bird differs considerably from its winter plumage.

Entire length 8·5 inches; culmen 0·65; wing, carpus to tip, 6·3; tarsus 1·4.

Fig. Gould, B. of Eur. pl. 294.

235. EUDROMIAS ASIATICUS, Pall. *Asiatic Dotterel.*

This bird is mentioned by Von Heuglin (Syst. Ueb. p. 57) as frequenting the coasts of the Red Sea and Mediterranean during the winter months.

Winter plumage.—Upper parts hair-brown, forehead and over the eye white; primaries brown, with some white on the sixth and consecutive feathers; tail, all but the two centre feathers, narrowly tipped with white; underparts white with a broad collar of hair-brown; beak black; legs olive-black; irides dark brown.

Summer plumage.—Pectoral band chestnut, bounded on the chest with a few black feathers.

Entire length 7·3 inches; culmen 0·8; wing, carpus to tip, 5·6; tarsus 1·5.

Fig. Harting, Ibis, 1870, p. 202, pl. 5.

236. ÆGIALITIS GEOFFROYI (Wagler). *Large Sand-Plover.*

Although I only know of two specimens of this bird having been brought back from Egypt, one in Mr. E. C. Taylor's collection and one in my own, I do not look upon it as of rare occurrence in that country; but it is doubtless absent from most Egyptian collections on account of its habit of frequenting the sandy shores of the lakes near the sea, which are rarely visited by the Nile tourists. I saw a flock of twenty of these birds on Lake Mareotis, when I obtained my specimen, in the beginning of February; and towards the end of March, near Damietta, I again saw considerable numbers of a Plover, which was probably this bird; but, owing to its shyness, I was unable to procure a shot.

The specimen I obtained on the 6th of February has a well-defined collar of hair-brown inclining to rufous in the centre, showing that at that early season it has already begun to assume its breeding-plumage.

Winter plumage.—Upper parts, with the exception of the forehead, pale hair-brown; forehead and underparts white; lores, under the eye, ear-coverts, and a spot on each side of the breast hair-brown; primaries dusky, fifth and consecutive one marked with white on their outer web.

Summer plumage.—A black band behind the white forehead; lores, under the eye, and ear-coverts black; top of the head, nape, and pectoral collar ferruginous.

Beak and legs black; irides dark brown.

Entire length 8·7 inches; wing, carpus to tip, 5·5; beak 0·9; tarsus 1·4.

Fig. Harting, Ibis, 1870, p. 378, pl. 11.

237. Ægialitis mongolicus (Pall.). *Mongolian Sand-Plover.*

I first had my attention drawn to a specimen of this bird in the British Museum, marked as from Egypt, by Mr. J. E. Harting's paper "On rare or little-known Limicolæ" (Ibis, 1870, p. 387). The mere fact of there being a specimen in the British Museum labelled Egypt is not very positive evidence as to its locality; but I think the shores of the Red Sea near Suez are a likely place for this bird to be found. Von Heuglin (Syst. Ueb. p. 56) records it as Abyssinian, but he did not meet with it in Egypt. The following description is taken from Mr. Harting's paper above referred to:—"Similar both in summer and winter plumage to the last-described species (*Æ. geoffroyi*), but differing in size, being considerably smaller. The bill, also, is shorter, has the outline of both mandibles straighter, and is of a dark horn-colour; the iris dark yellow-brown; tarsus dull yellowish grey."

Total length 7·3 inches; culmen 0·7; wing, carpus to tip, 5; tarsus 1·3.

238. Ægialitis pecuarius (Temm.). *African Sand-Plover.*

This species is plentiful throughout Egypt and Nubia, frequenting similar localities to those of *Æ. cantianus* and *Æ. minor*, and may generally be met with in flocks. Its numbers appear to vary considerably in the same locality in different years; for in 1870 I only met with it once, near Golosaneh, although I was then anxious to procure some specimens, while in 1868 and 1871 it was one of the most abundant of the small Plovers.

I have retained the name *pecuarius* for this species, as it is probably this bird which Temminck has figured under that name (Pl. Col. 183); but this figure is by no means a good one. It appears to be identical with *Æ. Kittlitzi* of Reichenbach and Layard and *Æ. longipes* of Heuglin.

Summer plumage.—Forehead, a band from the eye round the nape, throat, under the wing, and tail-coverts white; remainder of the *underparts ferruginous brown*, darkest on the chest; top and back of the head, back, wing-coverts, centre of the tail, and two spots on each side of the chest dusky brown, the edges of the feathers tipped with rufous or hair-brown; a band across the head from eye to eye, and another from the lores under the eye and down the side of the neck, and the quills black; sixth and consecutive primaries marked with white on their outer web; legs and beak black; irides dark brown.

Winter plumage.—Underparts whiter, black markings on the head absent, and the nape ferruginous brown.

Entire length 6·4 inches; culmen 0·65; wing, carpus to tip, 4·2; tarsus 1·2.

Fig. Temm. Pl. Col. 183.

239. Ægialitis cantianus (Lath.). *Kentish Plover.*

This is a very abundant Plover both in Egypt and Nubia, frequenting the sandy flats near water, and is apparently a sociable bird, as it is always met with in flocks. Owing to the assimilation of their plumage to the ground they frequent, they are difficult to distinguish; and their presence is often first made known by the sudden rising of a flock from a spot in the immediate vicinity.

Winter plumage.—All the upper parts, lores, under the eye, and ear-coverts hair-brown, excepting the forehead and a ring round the neck, which are white; all the underparts pure white, excepting the two spots of hair-brown on the sides of the breast meeting in some specimens and forming an indistinct collar.

Male in summer plumage.—Top and back of the head rufous, which colour is separated from the white forehead by a black band; lores, under the eye, ear-coverts, and a spot on each side of the breast black.

Legs and beak black; irides dark brown.

Entire length 6·5 inches; culmen 0·6; wing, carpus to tip, 4·2; tarsus 1·1.

Fig. Gould, B. of Eur. pl. 296.

240. ÆGIALITIS HIATICULA (Linn.). *Greater Ring-Plover.*

This species is included in the 'Description de l'Egypte;' and Von Heuglin (Syst. Ueb. p. 56) observes that it is to be met with during the winter in Lower Egypt. I never found the true *Æ. hiaticula*, but have often killed *Æ. intermedius*, a very closely allied form, which has frequently been confounded with the present species.

Breeding-plumage.—Back of the head and all the upper parts hair-brown; remainder of the plumage and a ring round the back of the neck white, with the following exceptions:—a band over the base of the beak, lores, under the eye, ear-coverts, a band across the head from eye to eye, and a broad collar extending round the back of the neck, all of which parts are black; quills dusky, *fifth and consecutive primaries marked with white on their outer web*; tail brown, lighter towards the base and broadly edged with white, excepting on the two centre feathers; legs orange; *beak orange, with a broad black tip.*

In winter plumage and in the immature birds the black markings are less distinct and occasionally all but absent.

Entire length 7·5 inches; culmen 0·6; wing, carpus to tip, 5·3; tarsus 0·9.

Fig. Gould, B. of Eur. pl. 296.

241. ÆGIALITIS INTERMEDIUS (Ménétr.). *Middle Ring-Plover.*

· The present species is not uncommon in Lower Egypt, where I have shot it on several occasions near Damietta, and frequently seen it. I have also received several specimens from a collector at Alexandria. In the Fayoom I never met with it, nor do I know of an instance of its capture above Cairo. It is very closely allied to *Æ. hiaticula*, from which it chiefly differs in being rather smaller.

Plumage similar to *Æ. hiaticula*, but with only *a narrow patch of orange on the base of the bill.*

Entire length 6·2 inches; culmen 0·5; wing, carpus to tip, 4·4; tarsus 0·9.

242. ÆGIALITIS MINOR, Meyer & Wolf. *Little Ring-Plover.*

The Little Ring-Plover is a resident and very abundant throughout Egypt and Nubia, frequenting alike the river-banks, canals, pools, and marshes, either singly or more often in small flocks.

Very similar to *Æ. hiaticula*, but smaller. It has no yellow on the beak, no white patch on any of the primaries, the shaft of the first primary only being white.

Entire length 6·5 inches; culmen 0·55; wing, carpus to tip, 4·6; tarsus 0·95.

Fig. Gould, B. of Eur. pl. 297.

243. Hæmatopus ostralegus, Linn. *Oyster-catcher.*

This well-known bird is of rare occurrence on the Egyptian coast, but may be occasionally met with on the Mediterranean and Red Seas during the winter. Mr. E. C. Taylor (Ibis, 1867, p. 69) and Von Heuglin (Syst. Ueb. p. 57) have both observed it there.

Entirely black above, and on the throat and upper breast; lower part of the back, rump, and upper tail-coverts, as well as the rest of the under surface of the body, pure white; base of the tail white, tip black; lesser wing-coverts black, like the back; wings black, with a white bar across the primaries, and the tips of the greater coverts white, forming a very distinct patch on the wing; the innermost long secondaries entirely black; legs lake-colour; bill orange-red at the base, shading into yellow to the tip.

Entire length 14 inches; culmen 3; wing, carpus to tip, 9·7; tail 4; tarsus 2·1.

Fig. Gould, B. of Eur. pl. 300.

244. Numenius arquata, Linn. *Curlew.*

The Curlew is plentiful throughout Egypt and Nubia, where it frequents the sandbanks on the river and the marshes of the Delta and the Fayoom. I have seen it in Upper Egypt as late as the end of April, but found it most plentiful in the Fayoom and Lower Egypt, where I have frequently killed specimens.

Head, neck, and chest brownish buff, with dark brown centres to the feathers on these parts and on the flanks; chin, upper part of the throat, and remainder of the under-parts white, the axillaries with a few brown marks near the ends of some of the feathers; back and scapulars dark brown, edged with buff; wings dark brown, edged and barred with buff on the inner half, and with white on the outer half, except on the exterior web of some of the outer primaries; rump and upper tail-coverts white, the latter with dark brown centres to the feathers; tail white, barred with brown and shaded with buff; beak fleshy brown shading into dark brown towards the tip; legs dusky; irides brown.

Entire length 22 inches; culmen 4 to 6; wing, carpus to tip, 12; tarsus 3·2.

Specimens vary considerably in size, the females being generally the largest and having the longest bill.

Fig. Gould, B. of Eur. pl. 302.

245. Numenius phæopus, Linn. *Whimbrel.*

The Whimbrel is to be met with on the banks of the Nile in small flocks in the winter (Von Heuglin, Syst. Ueb. p. 62).

Somewhat similar in plumage to *N. arquata*, but of a smaller size, and differing in the following points:—*top of the head brown*; tail-coverts more distinctly barred with brown; *axillaries distinctly barred with brown*; flanks barred with brown, and lower part of the chest slightly so.

Entire length 17·5 inches; culmen 3·5; wing, carpus to tip, 8·2; tarsus 2·2.

Fig. Gould, B. of Eur. pl. 303.

246. Numenius tenuirostris, Vieill. *Slender-billed Curlew.*

The present species is usually to be met with on the Nile during the spring and autumn; yet, according to Captain Loche, it breeds there in the marshes amongst the grass. In habits it is shy and usually frequents the more desert flats by the side of large lakes. Von Heuglin mentions having seen a large flock in the desert near Alexandria (Syst. Ueb. p. 62).

Very similar in plumage to *N. arquata* but much smaller and more mealy-looking. The chest is white, and the spots on the underparts are pear-shaped. It may at once be recognized from *N. phæopus* by its not having a dark crown, as well as by the colour of the axillaries and under wing-coverts, which are pure white.

Entire length 14·8 inches; culmen 3; wing, carpus to tip, 9; tarsus 2·3.

Fig. Sharpe and Dresser, B. of Eur. part iii..

247. Limosa ægocephala (L.). *Black-tailed Godwit.*

The present species is a winter visitant, ranging throughout Egypt and Nubia, and is by no means uncommon in Lower Egypt and the Fayoom, where I have frequently shot it. It is generally to be met with in small flocks, though often singly, feeding in company with Redshanks, Ruffs, and other

Waders; but on the wing it keeps separate from them. I have rarely been to Sakkara without meeting with this bird on some of the larger pools, where, as they often return to the same spot and are not more shy than Redshanks, they may easily be obtained.

Winter plumage.—Upper parts hair-brown, lightest on the head and back of the neck, and darkest towards the rump; the latter as well as the upper tail-coverts white, with the ends of the latter black; tail brownish black, with white bases to the feathers increasing in breadth towards the outer ones; quills dark brown, with some white only on the inner web of the first four, the remainder of the quills having a broad white base; underparts white, washed on the neck and crop with ashy brown; beak brownish flesh-colour, shading into black towards the tip; legs dusky black; irides dark brown.

Entire length 19 inches; culmen 4·8; wing, carpus to tip, 8·8; tarsus 3·5.

In summer the breast and throat become ferruginous brown, and the upper parts are mottled with that colour and black.

Fig. Sharpe and Dresser, B. of Eur. part xiii.

248. Machetes pugnax (Linn.). *Ruff.*

The Ruff is very abundant throughout Egypt and Nubia from August till May, more especially in the Fayoom and the Delta, where it may generally be met with in large flocks, frequenting the flooded fields in preference to the marshes.

Male in winter plumage.—Upper parts hair-brown, the centre of the feathers darker; tail-coverts white, excepting a few of the centre ones; quills dark brown; underparts white, shaded with hair-brown on the lower part of the throat, crop, and sides of the chest; beak brownish black; legs olive-brown; irides dark brown.

Entire length 12 inches; culmen 1·5; wing, carpus to tip, 7·5; tarsus 1·9.

Female in winter.—Differs only from the male at that season in being smaller and in having the legs pale yellowish brown. Entire length 10 inches.

In summer the male puts on the broad ruff from which the bird takes its name, and varies immensely in its plumage, no two specimens being exactly alike.

Fig. Gould, B. of Eur. pl. 328.

249. Scolopax rusticola, Linn. *Woodcock.*

The Woodcock appears to be only an accidental straggler in Egypt. During my last tour I heard of a specimen having been captured in the Delta, and am also glad to find the locality "Egypt" given to the species in Mr. G. R. Gray's 'Hand-list of Birds.'

Forehead and top of the head greyish brown, hind part and nape rufous, with four broad black bands; from the gape to the eye a streak of deep brown; chin white; on the side of the neck a patch of brown; the upper parts are a mixture of rufous brown, black, yellow, and grey, with zigzag transverse lines and pencillings of black, darkest on the back and scapulars; rump and tail-coverts chestnut, with paler tips and narrow transverse bars of black; tail black, varied with chestnut and tipped with grey above and white beneath, quills dusky, with chestnut bars; underparts greyish white, tinged with yellowish brown and barred with dusky pencillings; under tail-coverts yellowish, with black triangular central spots; legs flesh-colour, tinged with grey; beak flesh-colour at the base, shading into dusky at the tip; irides deep brown.

Entire length 13·8 inches; culmen 2·8; wing, carpus to tip, 7·8; tarsus 1·4.

Fig. Gould, B. of Eur. pl. 319.

250. GALLINAGO MAJOR (Gm.). *Solitary Snipe.*

This Snipe is not uncommon in Lower Egypt during the winter, but does not range, to my knowledge, south of the Delta, though it appears to me highly probable that it is to be found in the Fayoom.

Top of the head black, with pale brown markings and a central line of the same colour; in front of the eye a dark brown patch; sides of the head and throat white, speckled with dusky; nape pale rufous with black spots; back and scapulars dark brown, the feathers partly edged with rufous brown; wings dusky, the greater wing-coverts edged with white; *tail consisting of* 16 *feathers*, which are tipped with white and barred with black and chestnut; underparts varied with transverse triangular bars of dark brown, and shaded on the chest and flanks with ferruginous brown; beak flesh-colour at the base, shading into dusky brown at the tip; legs olive; irides dark brown.

Entire length 12·5 inches; culmen 2·4; wing, carpus to tip, 5·5; tarsus 1·4.

Fig. Gould, B. of Eur. pl. 320.

251. Gallinago media, Leach. *Common Snipe.*

The Common Snipe ranges throughout Egypt and Nubia, and is very abundant wherever there is suitable ground for it, as, for instance, throughout Lower Egypt, the Fayoom, and around the lake near Erment. There are perhaps few localities better suited to this bird than the large marshes of Lower Egypt, where, in February, I have killed over forty couple in a day. By the end of that month their numbers rapidly decrease; yet towards the end of March I one day killed twenty couple in the same marsh. Up the Nile at Dendera I have met with them as late as the 24th of March.

Top of the head, back, and scapulars black, streaked with chestnut and yellow; quills black; wing-coverts dusky, edged with buff; underparts white, more or less shaded with ferruginous brown on the cheeks, throat, and upper part of the chest, the latter parts spotted with dusky; thighs also barred with dusky; tail, which consists of 14 feathers, black, tipped with white and barred with ferruginous brown; beak brown, shading into dusky at the tip and flesh-colour at the base; legs greenish slate-colour; irides dark brown.

Entire length 11·5 inches; culmen 2·8; wing, carpus to tip, 4·9; tarsus 1·2.

Fig. Gould, B. of Eur. pl. 321.

252. Gallinago gallinula (Linn.). *Jack Snipe.*

The Jack Snipe has the same range in Egypt as the last species; and I have likewise procured it near Dendera as late as the 24th of March.

Crown of the head black, the feathers edged with rufous; a buff band extending from the beak over the eye and down the nape; a brown patch in front of the eye; cheeks white, with the tips of the feathers brown; back and inner web of the scapulars black and rufous, with purple and green reflections; outer webs of the scapulars cream-colour, forming two bands down the back; wings dusky, the coverts edged with pale brown and tipped with white; tail dusky, the feathers edged with very pale rufous; underparts white, strongly mottled with brown on the throat, crop, and flanks; beak pale fleshy brown, shading into dark brown towards the tip; legs pale brown; irides dark brown.

Entire length 8 inches; culmen 1·6; wing, carpus to tip, 4; tarsus 0·9.

Fig. Gould, B. of Eur. pl. 322.

253. Rhynchæa capensis, Linn. *Painted Snipe.*

(Plate XI.)

The present species ranges throughout Egypt and Nubia, and is not uncommon at times in the Delta and the Fayoom, where it may occasionally be met with in flocks, though more often singly. It remains in the country throughout the year, and breeds in May. It somewhat resembles the Jack Snipe in habits, being difficult to flush, and in only flying for a short distance; but it is slower on the wing than that species.

Secondaries long in proportion to the primaries, giving the wings a very rounded appearance.

RHYNCHŒA CAPENSIS.

Female.—Head and neck rufous brown, inclining to greenish black on the top of the head; a buff mark extending from the base of the beak to the crown; a white patch encircling the eye, and extending backwards through the ear-coverts; back and scapulars bronzy; wing-coverts green; rump, tail, and quills slaty grey, inclining to dark brown at the base of the outer web of the primaries, the whole pencilled and barred with wavy black lines; *the quills have numerous clear buff spots, forming rows when the wings are extended*; the neck shades into black at the base, which colour is bordered by a clear white collar, extending round the shoulders; remainder of the underparts creamy white, with a large dusky patch on each side of the chest next to the collar; beak flesh-colour, shading into dusky brown at the base, and into rufous brown on the culmen and towards the tip; legs olive-green; irides brown.

Male.—Neck brownish grey, mottled with white on the throat; feathers round the eye and collar buff; a buff band down the scapulars; some broad black bars on some of the feathers; wing-coverts pale green, mottled with buff; beak darker; remainder of the plumage similar to the female.

Entire length 9·3 inches; culmen 2; wing, carpus to tip, 5; tarsus 1·8.

254. TRINGA MINUTA, Leisler. *Little Stint.*

The Little Stint is a winter visitor to Egypt and Nubia, and is extremely abundant in some parts. It may usually be met with in flocks, frequenting the marshy ground, and on the sandbanks of the river.

Winter plumage.—Upper parts hair-brown, the centre of the feathers darker; tail-coverts dark brown, with narrow pale edges; tail, two centre feathers dark brown, the remainder pale stone-grey; wings dark brown, the coverts with pale edges, the greater ones tipped with white, forming a narrow bar on the wing; forehead and underparts pure white; beak and legs olive-black; irides dark brown.

Summer plumage.—Upper parts mottled with rufous and black.

Entire length 5·5 inches; culmen 0·7; wing, carpus to tip, 3·8; tarsus 0·8.

Fig. Sharpe and Dresser, B. of Eur. part vii.

255. TRINGA TEMMINCKII, Leisler. *Temminck's Stint.*

This Stint ranges throughout Egypt and Nubia, but is not so plentiful as the last species, being usually met with singly or in pairs.

Upper parts dusky olive, with narrow dark streaks on the centres of the feathers; wings dusky black, coverts with pale edges, the greater ones tipped with white, forming a narrow bar on the wing; underparts white, strongly shaded on the lower part of the neck and crop with dusky; legs and beak olive-black; irides dark brown.

Entire length 5·5 inches; culmen 0·65; wing, carpus to tip, 3·8; tarsus 0·7.

Fig. Sharpe and Dresser, B. of Eur. part vii.

256. TRINGA ARENARIA, Linn. *Sanderling.*

This species is to be met with in Lower Egypt in small flocks during the winter months, according to Von Heuglin (Syst. Ueb. p. 63).

Winter plumage.—Upper parts grey, with dusky shafts to the feathers, shading into dark brown on the rump and centre tail-feathers, the remainder of the tail much lighter; a small dusky spot just in front of the eye; quills dusky black, much paler on the inner web, some of the smaller primaries having the basal portion of the outer web and a great part of the inner secondaries white; wing-coverts dusky, with pale edges, and the ends of the greater coverts white, forming a narrow bar on the wing; front and sides of the face and all the underparts white; beak and legs olive-black; irides dark brown.

Entire length 7 inches; culmen 1; wing, carpus to tip, 5; tarsus 0·9.

Fig. Gould, B. of Eur. pl. 335.

257. TRINGA CINCLUS, Linn. *Dunlin.*

We are informed by Von Heuglin (Syst. Ueb. p. 63) that the present species is found on the Mediterranean and Red Sea coasts from October till the end of May. It frequents shingly beaches, where it may generally be met with in flocks.

Winter.—Upper parts dark brown, with pale brown edgings to the feathers; base and tips of the inner secondaries white; tail dusky grey; throat, chest, abdomen, under the wing, and under tail-coverts white; neck and crop pale brown, spotted with dark brown; sides of the chest likewise spotted; beak and legs black; irides dark brown.

In summer the upper plumage becomes more rufous and black, and the centre of the chest and abdomen are black.

Entire length 6·8 inches; culmen 1; wing, carpus to tip, 4·4; tarsus 0·9.

Fig. Gould, B. of Eur. pl. 329.

258. Tringa subarquata, Güld. *Curlew Sandpiper.*

This species is a winter visitant in Egypt, where it is not very plentiful. I shot the only specimen that I saw, at Golosaneh, on the 8th of May, and have one other specimen, procured for me at Alexandria in February. Its habits are similar to those of *T. minuta*, and it may occasionally be met with in the same flock as that bird.

In winter the upper parts are hair-brown, darker in the centre of the feathers; wings dusky brown, with pale margins; tail-coverts white, with brownish-black bars; underparts white, shaded with hair-brown on the base of the neck and crop; beak, which is slightly curved downwards, black; legs olive; irides dark brown.

In summer the back becomes mottled with black and chestnut, and the chest becomes rich ferruginous brown, more or less mottled with white and dusky according to the season.

Entire length 8 inches; culmen 1·6; wing, carpus to tip, 5; tarsus 1·1.

Fig. Gould, B. of Eur. pl. 328.

259. Totanus calidris, Linn. *Redshank.*

Rare on the Nile above Cairo, but very abundant in the Delta and the Fayoom, where it is generally to be met with in scattered flocks throughout the more marshy districts. On the wing it may easily be recognized by the amount of white which it displays, and especially by the white band on the wings, which is very distinct. Its cry, consisting of two short whistling notes, may be easily imitated, and is very effective in calling the birds round within shot.

Upper plumage hair-brown, with a greenish shade, many of the feathers finely streaked or barred with dusky; rump pure white; tail and tail-coverts white, barred with dusky; primaries dusky; secondaries nearly pure white, forming a distinct white band on the wing, which is very apparent during flight; underparts white, with the throat, crop, and flanks more or less streaked with dark brown; beak dark brown, shading off to pale reddish brown towards the basal half; legs transparent red; irides brown.

Entire length 11 inches; culmen 1·7; wing, carpus to tip, 6·2; tarsus 2.

Fig. Gould, B. of Eur. pl. 310.

260. Totanus fuscus, Leisler. *Dusky Redshank.*

This bird ranges throughout Egypt and Nubia, but appears to be rather sparingly distributed; for we only met with it on one occasion, near Sakkara, on the 7th of April, where we killed several birds out of a large flock that had been feeding in a small muddy pool. From these birds I have taken the following description :—

Winter plumage.—Upper parts hair-brown; lower half of the back and rump pure white; tail-coverts white, with well-defined dusky bars; tail dusky, with numerous white bars, *the white on the outer tail-feathers not so pure as in* T. calidris; wing-coverts and secondaries edged with white and barred with brown; underparts white; *beak long, slender, and straight*, slightly hooked at the point, of a dark brown colour, inclining to pale reddish brown towards the base of the lower mandible; legs brownish red; irides brown.

Specimens vary considerably in plumage according to season, changing in summer to a deep slate-colour more or less barred with white.

Entire length 12 inches; culmen 2·4; wing, carpus to tip, 6·5; tarsus 2·2.

Fig. Gould, B. of Eur. pl. 309.

261. Totanus canescens (Gm.). *Greenshank.*

The Greenshank is plentifully distributed throughout Egypt and Nubia, where it frequents the Nile banks, canals, and pools, usually singly or in pairs, and is rarely met with in the larger marshes of the Delta, where the Redshank abounds. Its well-known call consists of three whistling notes, which may be easily imitated, and will rarely fail to attract the bird within reach of the gun.

Winter plumage.—Head whitish, with dusky black centres to the feathers on the crown; ear-coverts and in front of the eye, back of the neck, scapulars, and inner secondaries greyish ash-colour, with a dark streak next to the shafts, and the edges of the larger feathers paler and barred with dark brown; wings brownish black, paler on the inner coverts and secondaries; remainder of the plumage white, the upper tail-coverts barred with dusky; tail, the centre feathers shaded with ashy, and the whole partially barred with dusky; legs green; beak dusky olive; irides dark brown.

Entire length 13·5 inches; culmen 2·2; wing, carpus to tip, 7·5; tarsus 2·3.

Fig. Sharpe and Dresser, B. of Eur. part v.

262. Totanus stagnatilis, Bechst. *Marsh-Sandpiper.*

The Marsh-Sandpiper ranges throughout Egypt and Nubia, but is not very plentiful on the Nile above Cairo, where we generally met with it singly or in company with the Wood-Sandpiper. In Lower Egypt and the Fayoom it is far more numerous, and in these districts I may have seen as many as a hundred in one day. It is by no means shy, and comes readily when its whistle is imitated, the cry consisting of one note, which is easily acquired. It is active and graceful in its movements; and when it sees an intruder it will generally stand motionless in the water, apparently hoping to pass unobserved.

Winter plumage.—Upper parts ashy grey, inclining to white on the forehead; many of the feathers streaked in the centre with dark brown; lower part of the back and rump pure white; tail and tail-coverts white, barred with dark brown; primaries dusky; underparts white; sides of the neck and flanks sparingly marked with narrow brown streaks.

Summer plumage.—The top of the head and back becomes browner, and the upper plumage is generally strongly marked with black spots and bars; under plumage spotted on the lower part of the throat and crop; beak black, inclining to green at the base; legs pale yellowish green: irides dark brown.

Entire length 9 inches; culmen 1·6; wing, carpus to tip, 5·5; tarsus 2.

Fig. Sharpe and Dresser, B. of Eur. part i.

263. Totanus ochropus (Linn.). *Green Sandpiper.*

This Sandpiper is abundant and very evenly distributed throughout Egypt and Nubia, frequenting canals and pools in preference to marshes, but generally to be observed wherever there is water. It rarely takes long flights, but if driven from one pool will almost invariably fly to the nearest piece of water, along the edge of which it runs, constantly stopping to pick up some shell or worm, but always keeping a sharp look out upon the sportsman.

Upper plumage dusky green, finely spotted with dull white; upper tail-coverts and tail white, the latter distinctly marked with dusky black bars; quills dusky; underparts white, spotted on the lower part of the neck and crop with dusky; flanks dusky, narrowly barred with white; beak and legs deep greenish black; irides brown.

Entire length 9·5 inches; culmen 1·4; wing, carpus to tip, 5·5; tarsus 1·3.

Fig. Gould, B. of Eur. pl. 315.

264. TOTANUS GLAREOLA (Linn.). *Wood-Sandpiper.*

This Sandpiper ranges throughout Egypt and Nubia, where it is, properly speaking, only a winter visitant, though, according to Von Heuglin (Syst. Ueb. p. 62), a few remain in the country throughout the year. In its visits it appears to be somewhat irregular; for although in 1870 and 1871 I found it one of the most abundant of the wading birds in Lower Egypt and the Fayoom, and also shot several in Nubia, in 1868 I did not fall in with it once, to my knowledge, above Cairo, and Mr. E. C. Taylor also found it rare during his visits.

Upper parts dusky olive, with the feathers edged or partially barred with white or brownish white; rump and tail white, the latter barred with black; underparts white, spotted with dusky on the cheeks and neck, and barred with that colour on the sides of the crop, flanks, and under tail-coverts: beak olive; *legs pale yellowish green*; irides dark brown.

Entire length 7·5 inches; culmen 1·3; wing, carpus to tip, 4·9; tarsus 1·5.

Fig. Gould, B. of Eur. pl. 315.

265. ACTITIS HYPOLEUCOS (Linn.). *Common Sandpiper.*

This species is a resident in the country and ranges throughout Egypt and Nubia, where it is very abundant and evenly distributed. It prefers the banks of the river and canals, where it is generally met with singly.

Upper plumage bronzy green, feathers more or less streaked and barred with dusky; quills dusky, with a white patch on the inner webs; base and tips of the secondaries white; tail, exterior web of the two outer feathers and end of all but the centre ones white, barred with dusky; underparts white, shaded and streaked with brown on the crop and sides of the throat; beak dusky; legs olive-brown; irides dark brown.

Entire length 7·5 inches; culmen 1; wing, carpus to tip, 4·2; tarsus 0·9.

Fig. Gould, B. of Eur. pl. 318.

266. Himantopus candidus, Bonn. *Black-winged Stilt.*

Abundant both in Egypt and Nubia, but more especially so in the Delta, where it may be almost daily seen in small flocks, striding about the shallow pools which are so frequent near the villages, perfectly undisturbed by the presence of man; for the natives never molest it.

Top of the head, nape, a band across the upper part of the back, and wings black, with green reflections; remainder of the plumage white, with a delicate pink blush on the breast; legs pink; beak black; irides orange-red.

Entire length 14 inches; culmen 2·5; wing, carpus to tip, 9·8; unfeathered portion of the leg 8.

Fig. Gould, B. of Eur. pl. 289.

267. Recurvirostra avocetta, L. *Avocet.*

The Avocet is a winter visitant to Egypt and Nubia, and is moderately abundant. I have met with large flocks of these birds on two occasions,—once in the Delta in February, when they were too shy to allow of my approach within shot, and on the second occasion at Golosaneh in March, when I obtained two specimens. According to Von Heuglin (Syst. Ueb. p. 63) they are very abundant on the shores of the Red Sea.

Entire plumage white, except the following parts—top of the head and back of the neck, a band between the shoulders, inner part of the scapulars, wing-coverts, and primaries, which are brownish black; beak, the apical half of which is curved upwards, black; legs slaty grey.

Entire length 17 inches; culmen 3·7; wing, carpus to tip, 9; tarsus 3·6.

Fig. Gould, B. of Eur. pl. 289.

268. Ibis æthiopica (Lath.)*. *Sacred Ibis.*

I can find no authenticated instance of this bird having been seen in Egypt in modern times, although there can be no doubt that it once lived in that country; for the food found in many of the mummied specimens consists of shells, insects, and reptiles now common in Egypt. Some authors imagine that the Ibis was brought into the country by the ancient Egyptians; but this appears to me highly improbable, as it would be the only instance of an animal not indigenous to Egypt having been made an object of general worship by that people.

This bird is now plentiful higher up the Nile at Khartoom; and I think it probable that it may yet be found in Egypt proper, for it breeds at Wady Halfeh according to Von Heuglin (Syst. Ueb. p. 61).

* *Ibis religiosa* of authors.

Head and neck bare and black; end of the primaries black, with metallic green reflections; secondaries elongated, forming a plume over the tail, which is black, with purple reflections; remainder of the plumage pure white; legs and beak black; irides dark brown.

Entire length 28 inches; culmen 5·5; wing, carpus to tip, 14; tarsus 3·5.

Fig. Savigny, Descr. de l'Egypte, pl. 7, fig. 1.

269. Ibis falcinellus, Linn. *Glossy Ibis.*

The Glossy Ibis ranges throughout Egypt and Nubia, where it remains during the year, but is not very abundant. I only met with it on one occasion, near El Kab, in April, where I saw three feeding together in a small pool, and procured two of them.

Top of the head and cheeks, back, wings, tail, flanks, and under tail-coverts bright metallic green and purple; remainder of the plumage, upper part of the back, and a broad band on the wing-coverts bordering the shoulders bright ferruginous brown; beak and legs olive-black; irides dark brown.

Entire length 22 inches; culmen 5·8; wing, carpus to tip, 11·5; tarsus 4.

The female is similar in plumage but rather smaller than the male.

Fig. Gould, B. of Eur. pl. 311.

270. Tantalus ibis, Linn. *African Wood-Ibis.*

This bird wanders northward into Upper Egypt during the time of the inundations, according to Von Heuglin (Syst. Ueb. p. 61).

Entire face and pouch without feathers and of a bright scarlet; plumage white, with a roseate shade on the body, strongest on and under the wings; quills, primary-coverts, and tail black, with a bright metallic bronzy-green gloss; beak yellow; legs dusky olive; irides dark brown.

Entire length 34 inches; culmen 8·5; wing, carpus to tip, 17, tarsus 7·7.

Fig. Wolf, Zool. Illustr., 2nd series, pl. 46.

271. GRUS CINEREA, Bechst. *Common Crane.*

This is a common winter visitant both in Egypt and Nubia, arriving in October and leaving again in March.

During their stay they may frequently be met with in flocks on the sandbanks and desert spaces by the river, or in the wide plains of halfa grass. When on the wing they fly in long lines one behind the other, at even distances, frequently uttering their cry, which may be heard at a considerable distance. They are extremely watchful and very difficult to approach.

Forehead covered with black hairs; top of the head naked and red; back of the head and front of the throat dark slaty grey; remainder of the plumage pale slaty grey; the secondaries very much elongated and forming a large pendent plume, which covers the tail and is darkest towards the points of the feathers; beak olive-green, inclining to red at the base of the lower mandible; legs black; irides reddish brown.

Entire length 46 inches; culmen 5; wing, carpus to tip, 26; tarsus 10.

Fig. Gould, B. of Eur. pl. 270.

272. Grus virgo, Pall. *Demoiselle Crane.*

This Crane ranges throughout Egypt and Nubia, but is far less plentiful than the last species and nearly as shy. On the 2nd of April I met with a large flock near Beni-souef, when, after in vain trying to stalk them for more than an hour, I obtained a long shot as they flew over my head. I am not aware of having seen them upon any other occasion.

Scapulars elongated and pointed, reaching beyond the tail. The plumage is ashy grey, with the following exceptions:—a tuft of elongated feathers behind the eye white; sides of the head, throat, front part of the neck, primaries, and tips of the scapulars black; beak black at the base, yellow at the tip; legs brownish black; irides reddish brown.

Entire length 39 inches; culmen 2·5; wing, carpus to tip, 25; tarsus 7.

Fig. Gould, B. of Eur. pl. 271.

273. Platalea leucorodia, Linn. *Spoonbill.*

Very plentiful throughout Egypt and Nubia. It may constantly be been in flocks on the sandbanks of the river and in the great marshy lakes of Lower Egypt and the Fayoom.

Beak long and flat, much widened at the tip.

Breeding-plumage pure white, excepting a long buff-coloured crest, the pouch and a collar round the crop, which are yellow; beak deep slate-colour, irregularly barred with black and having a yellow patch on its wider part; legs black; irides crimson.

Immature birds have the beak smooth and pale brown.

Entire length 36 inches; culmen 8·8; wing, carpus to tip, 16; tarsus 6.

Fig. Gould, B. of Eur. pl. 286.

274. Ciconia alba, Bechst. *White Stork.*

The White Stork visits Egypt and Nubia during migration, and at such times is extremely abundant. In March and April I have seen these birds drawn up along the river-bank like an army, and in such numbers that whole islands appeared white with them.

Wings black; the wing-coverts and remainder of the plumage pure white; beak, legs, and the bare skin around the eyes and on the pouch bright red; irides dark brown.

Entire length 44 inches; culmen 8; wing, carpus to tip, 24; tarsus 9.

Fig. Gould, B. of Eur. pl. 283.

275. Ciconia nigra (Linn.). *Black Stork.*

The present species ranges throughout Egypt and Nubia, but is not very plentiful. It is an unsociable bird, never congregating in flocks or associating with other species. I saw it occasionally on the sandbanks, but could never get within range, as it is extremely wary and always keeps to the open.

Adult.—Head, neck, chest, and all the upper parts black, with purple, green, and bronzy reflections; underparts white; the naked space around the eyes and on the throat, beak, and legs vermilion; irides brown.

Entire length 42 inches; culmen 7·5; wing, carpus to tip, 19; tarsus 11.

Fig Gould, B. of Eur. pl. 284.

Fam. ARDEIDÆ.

276. Ardea cinerea, Linn. *Common Heron.*

The Heron is to be met with throughout Egypt and Nubia, especially on the sandbanks, often in considerable numbers, and in company with Spoonbills, Pelicans, and other Waders.

Adult.—Forehead, top of the head, neck, a tuft of long plumes on the crop, centre of the abdomen, and under tail-coverts white; a broad black band over the eye; back of the head and two long crest-plumes black; back, wing-coverts, and tail grey; primaries and most of the secondaries black; a narrow line of black spots down the centre of the throat; feathers on the crop and on each side of the abdomen black; flanks grey; beak and irides yellow; legs black.

Entire length 38 inches; culmen 5; wing, carpus to tip, 18·5; tarsus 6·5.

Fig. Gould, B. of Eur. pl. 274.

277. Ardea purpurea, Linn. *Purple Heron.*

This Heron is a resident in the country, and is very plentiful in some parts of Lower Egypt and the Fayoom. I met with great numbers on the desert side of Birket el Korn, among the thick banks of sedge that grow in the lake. They are not nearly so shy as the Common Heron, and always frequent the dense reeds; on being disturbed they would rarely go straight away, but generally flew round over the same spot several times, so that they were easily shot.

Top of the head, nape, and a crest of two long feathers slaty black; neck rufous brown, with a black streak running down the back and one on each side of it; throat white; remainder of the upper plumage slaty grey, strongly shaded with rufous on the wing-coverts; the ends of the scapulars long and narrow, and of a light rufous and pale grey colour; quills browner; tail shaded with olive; feathers on the crop elongated, of a creamy colour, shaded with rufous and boldly streaked with black; remainder of the underparts deep rufous brown, lighter on the thighs, and shaded on the flanks with grey; centre of the abdomen and under tail-coverts black, chestnut, and white mixed; a bare patch in front of the eye and beak yellow, the latter shaded with brown towards the culmen; legs greenish yellow, with the shins and upper part of the toes black; irides yellow.

Entire length 36 inches; culmen 5·3; wing, carpus to tip, 14·5; tarsus 5.

Fig. Gould, B. of Eur. pl. 274.

278. Herodias alba (Linn.) *Great White Heron.*

The Great White Heron is plentiful in Lower Egypt and the Fayoom. On lake Marcotis I have frequently observed very large flocks of this species wading in the shallows at a considerable distance from the land; and on Birket el Korn, in the Fayoom, I have seen single specimens on several occasions; but, as it is a very shy bird, I was never able to approach within shot. I have also seen it in the collections of other travellers from Egypt.

Winter.—Entire plumage pure white; a bare space in front of and behind the eye yellowish green; beak yellow, shaded with brown; legs olive-black, shaded with yellow towards the feathered part of the thigh and on the soles of the feet; irides yellow.

In the summer plumage the feathers on the back are hair-like, and extend beyond the tail, and the feathers on the crop are elongated.

Entire length 42 inches; culmen 5; wing, carpus to tip, 16·5; tail 7; tarsus 7·6.

Fig. Gould, B. of Eur. pl. 276.

279. Herodias garzetta (Linn.). *Little Egret.*

This graceful little bird is abundant both in Egypt and Nubia, and is a resident in those countries throughout the year. It is usually to be met with singly by the edge of the water, and is equally partial to both the river and pools, feeding almost exclusively on fish. Early in April it begins to put on its breeding-plumage.

Entire plumage pure white. In the breeding-season it assumes a crest of two long narrow plumes; the feathers on the crop are elongated; and those on the back are long, extending rather beyond the tail, and are of a very peculiar hairy structure; a bare space in front of the eye of a greenish shade; legs and *beak black*; feet dirty yellow; irides pale yellow.

Entire length 23 inches; culmen 3·5; wing, carpus to tip, 11·5; tarsus 4.

Fig. Gould, B. of Eur. pl. 277.

280. Ardeola russata (Wagl.). *Buff-backed Heron.*

This species is very abundant in Egypt, especially in the Delta, where flocks may be daily seen feeding among cattle without the least fear of man. On the ground it is graceful, but looks awkward on first taking wing. It is a useful bird to the natives, as it causes great havoc among the locusts and other insects, in this respect replacing the Sacred Ibis, for which bird it is usually made to do duty with the tourist. In August it breeds in large flocks in the sont woods.

Winter.—Entire plumage pure white, shaded with *buff on the crown.*

Summer.—Top of the head and nape, crop, and back buff, such parts of the plumage being composed of hairs rather than feathers; a bare patch in front of the eye and *beak yellow*; legs olive-black; irides pale yellow.

Entire length 20·5 inches; culmen 2·4; wing, carpus to tip, 3·2.

Fig. Gould, B. of Eur. pl. 278.

281. Ardeola comata (Pall.). *Squacco Heron.*

The present species is distributed in small numbers throughout Egypt and Nubia, where it is a resident. I have shot it on the banks of the river near Dendera in May, and saw it in flocks at Damietta and in the Fayoom in February. Von Heuglin observes that he encountered it in numbers between Assouan and Dongola in June and July.

Chin, upper part of the throat, abdomen, wings, rump, and tail white, shaded with buff on the wing-coverts; *a long crest of white feathers with black edges*; head, neck, and chest brownish buff, the feathers on the crown more completely edged with dusky black than those of the neck; back light yellowish brown, shaded with purple; a bare patch in front of the eyes green; beak black, shaded with yellow towards the base and keel of the lower mandible; legs olive; irides pale yellow.

Entire length 18·5 inches; culmen 2·6; wing, carpus to tip, 8·5; tarsus 2·2.

Fig. Gould, B. of Eur. pl. 275.

282. NYCTICORAX GRISEUS (Linn.). *Night-Heron.*

The Night-Heron is abundant throughout Egypt, usually in flocks, frequenting clumps of sont- and palm-trees. They are not shy, and are often difficult to drive out of the thicker-foliaged trees. When disturbed they rise awkwardly, a few at a time; but when once fairly started they mount high, and fly for a considerable distance.

Adult.—Upper plumage: forehead, eyebrow, and two long plumes starting from the head white; top and back of the head, back, and greater wing-coverts black, with a bright metallic green lustre; wings and tail grey; underparts white; beak black, inclining to greenish yellow towards the base of the lower mandible; legs pale brown; irides crimson.

Immature.—Entire upper plumage ashy brown, streaked with pale yellowish brown on the head and neck, and spotted with white on the back and wings; underparts white, mottled with pale brown; legs and beak greenish black; irides brown.

Entire length 21 inches; culmen 2·8; wing, carpus to tip, 12; tarsus 3.

Fig. Gould, B. of Eur. pl. 279.

283. Botaurus stellaris (Linn.). *Bittern.*

Very plentiful in Lower Egypt and the Fayoom, but less common in other parts of Egypt and Nubia. This scarcity is probably to be accounted for by the absence of reeds in those parts. It feeds chiefly at night, and reposes during the day amongst the rank marsh vegetation, where it is very easily approached. In the Fayoom I got within a few yards of a flock of about twenty that were perched up in the reeds, reposing, as is their habit, during the day.

Feathers on the top of the head and neck long; crown of the head and nape black, a brownish-black patch extending from the gape under the ear-coverts; remainder of the plumage sandy buff, mottled with brown, chin and centre of the throat palest; back strongly mottled with blackish brown; quills and primary-coverts dusky brown, irregularly barred and marked with rufous buff; remainder of the wing-feathers and tail irregularly barred with brown; down the centre of the throat the brown forms irregular lines and bars on the sides of the neck; legs olive; beak yellowish brown, shading into dark brown towards the culmen; irides brown.

Entire length 28 inches; culmen 2·9; wing, carpus to tip, 12·5; tarsus 3·7.

Fig. Gould, B. of Eur. pl. 280.

284. Botaurus minutus (Linn.). *Little Bittern.*

The Little Bittern ranges throughout Egypt and Nubia, but is of rather rare occurrence. I only shot it on one occasion, near Koos, on the 26th of April, when I met with it sitting motionless by the river-bank, with its neck stretched out in a straight line, making itself look as tall as possible.

Top of the head and nape, back, scapulars, and tail greenish black; quills black; greater wing-coverts creamy white, remainder of the coverts sandy colour; the rest of the plumage sandy brown, inclining to cream-colour on the sides of the chin, the lower part of the abdomen, and under tail-coverts; ear-coverts washed with grey; legs olive; beak yellowish brown, shading into dark brown on the culmen; irides brown.

Entire length 12 inches; culmen 1·9; wing, carpus to tip, 5·5; tarsus 1·6.

The immature birds have the feathers on the back and scapulars brown, edged with sandy colour, with some brown streaks on the throat; abdomen and greater wing-coverts sandy colour.

Fig. Gould, B. of Eur. pl. 281.

Order ANSERES.

Fam. PHŒNICOPTERIDÆ.

285. PHŒNICOPTERUS ANTIQUORUM, Bp. *Flamingo.*

The Flamingo is rather rare on the Nile itself, but is extremely abundant in the great brackish-water lakes of Lower Egypt, and is not uncommon in the Fayoom. On lakes Mareotis and Menzaleh large flocks of these birds may generally be seen wading far out in the shallow water. They are very shy and difficult to approach within gun-shot, and when disturbed make a great clamour with their loud harsh voices. On the wing they look very peculiar, as they fly with their long necks and legs stretched out.

Head, neck, body, and tail white, delicately shaded with pink; quills black; scapulars bright pink; upper and under wing-coverts brilliant vermilion; legs and two thirds of the bill pink, remainder of the bill jet-black; irides pale yellow.

Entire length 45 inches; culmen 5·7; wing, carpus to tip, 16; unfeathered part of the leg 19; tarsus 19.

Fig. Gould, B. of Eur. pl. 287.

Fam. RALLIDÆ.

286. Rallus aquaticus, L. *Water-Rail.*

This species is a winter visitant, and is plentiful in Lower Egypt and the Fayoom, where I have frequently killed it, but has not been met with, to my knowledge, in Nubia. It frequents the sedgy districts, and when disturbed only flies a short distance to the nearest patch of thick covert.

Entire upper parts brown, with dark centres to the feathers; underparts uniform slaty grey, excepting on the flanks, sides of the abdomen, and under tail-coverts, which in the female are black, barred with white; in the male the vent and under tail-coverts are buff; beak red, shading into black on the culmen and towards the tip; legs reddish brown; irides red.

Entire length 10 inches; culmen 1·6; wing, carpus to tip, 4·6; tarsus 1·5.

Fig. Gould, B. of Eur. pl. 339.

287. ORTYGOMETRA CREX (Linn.). *Corn-Crake.*

The Corn-Crake is a winter visitor to Egypt, where it may be met with singly in the clover-fields, but is not plentiful.

Upper plumage and tail pale brown, with dark centres to the feathers; wing-coverts chestnut; quills dark brown, with a rufous shade, outer web of the first primary white; sides of the head and neck yellowish brown without spots; upper part of the throat and abdomen white; remainder of the underparts sandy colour, shading into rufous on the flanks and under tail-coverts, where the feathers are mottled and barred with that colour; beak and legs flesh-colour; irides pale brown.

Entire length 10·5 inches; culmen 0·95; wing, carpus to tip, 5·8; tarsus 1·5.

Fig. Gould, B. of Eur. pl. 341.

288. PORZANA MARUETTA, Leach. *Spotted Crake.*

The Spotted Crake is probably a resident in Lower Egypt and the Fayoom, where one or two specimens may generally be met with during a day's sport in the marshes. They frequent chiefly the low sedge, and are very similar to the Water-Rail in habits and appearance on the wing.

Centre of the crown, back of the neck, back, tail, and scapulars olive-brown, with black centres to the feathers; wings brown, without the olive shade, the carpal margin of the shoulders white; remainder of the head, neck, and crop slaty grey, shaded with olive on the latter part; neck and crop spotted with white; back, wings, and tail spotted and streaked with the same colour; abdomen white; flanks strongly barred with brown; under tail-coverts buff; beak yellow, greenish at the tip, and shading into scarlet towards the base of the upper mandible; legs olive; irides brown.

Entire length 8·5 inches; culmen 0·8; wing, carpus to tip, 4·7; tarsus 1·3.

Fig. Gould, B. of Eur. pl. 343.

289. PORZANA PYGMÆA (Naum.). *Baillon's Crake.*

I have no other authority than that of Rüppell for including the present species among the birds of Egypt.

Upper parts, including the wings and tail, olive-brown; back, scapulars, and wing-coverts marked with oval and triangular white spots surrounded with black, and some of them having a black spot in the centre; outer edge of the first primary white; sides of the head, throat, chest, and abdomen bluish slate-colour; flanks, vent, and under tail-coverts black, transversely barred with white; beak olive; legs pinkish brown; irides red.

Entire length 6·5 inches; culmen 0·7; wing, carpus to tip, 4; tarsus 1·1.

Fig. Gould, B. of Eur. pl. 344.

290. GALLINULA CHLOROPUS (Linn.). *Moor-Hen.*

The Moor-Hen is very plentiful in some parts of Lower Egypt and the Fayoom, but I have not met with it elsewhere in Egypt, although it probably ranges throughout the country.

Head, neck, and underparts deep slate-colour, shaded with dull white on the centre of the abdomen; under tail-coverts white; quills and tail brownish black; remainder of the upper surface deep olive-brown; the wings narrowly edged with white, and some of the feathers on the flanks having white streaks down their centres; the frontal shield and beak red, tipped with yellow; legs olive-green, with a red and yellow patch below the feathered part; irides brown.

Entire length 14 inches; culmen 1·1; wing, carpus to tip, 7·2; tarsus 2.

Fig. Gould, B. of Eur. pl. 342.

291. Porphyrio Alleni. *Allen's Gallinule.*

This Gallinule, which is of smaller size and more graceful form than *P. hyacinthinus*, has been found by Mr. S. Stafford Allen in Lower Egypt; and an immature specimen, which he procured near Alexandria, is now in the collection of Messrs. Sharpe and Dresser, who have kindly lent it to me for description in the present work.

Adult.—Back, wings, and tail green; under tail-coverts white; remainder of the plumage indigo-blue, inclining to black on the head, neck, rump, and abdomen; beak and frontal shield red, tinged with orange; irides reddish brown; legs pink.

Immature plumage.—Top and sides of the head clear brown; back and scapulars sandy brown, with olive-brown centres to the feathers; rump and tail dark brown, the feathers of the latter edged with paler brown; quills dark brown, primaries shaded with olive on their outer webs; wing-coverts olive, edged with sandy colour; chin, centre of the chest, and abdomen white; remainder of the underparts sandy, excepting the flanks and thighs, which are indigo-blue; irides light brown.

Entire length 9·3 inches; culmen 1·45; wing, carpus to tip, 5·8; tarsus 2.

292. Porphyrio hyacinthinus, Temm. *Violet Gallinule.*

The present species is abundant in the Fayoom, where I have frequently shot it, but have never met with it elsewhere in Egypt, although it is probably plentiful also in some of the lakes of Lower Egypt. It frequents the thick beds of reeds and half-sunken bushes, and, like the Common Moor-Hen, is very partial to perching up in them, and if unobserved, will remain there motionless until the sportsman has passed, before taking wing.

Back of the head, neck, and wings ultramarine, with the exception of the inner web of the quills; back and scapulars green; cheeks and throat bluish green; chest indigo; abdomen black; under tail-coverts white; legs pink; beak and shield on the forehead red; irides ferruginous brown.

Entire length 17 inches; beak, from the underpart of the shield, 2·8; wing, carpus to tip, 9·7; tarsus 3·5.

Fig. Gould, B. of Eur. pl. 340.

293. Fulica atra, Linn. *Common Coot.*

This species ranges throughout Egypt and Nubia, and is extremely abundant on all the lakes.

Entire plumage dark slate-colour, shading into black on the neck and head; the wings have a narrow white edging to them, and the secondaries are slightly washed with that colour towards their tips; beak and frontal shield pure white; legs dusky white, shaded with yellow next to the feathers and on the sides of the tarsi, the joints and soles of the feet shaded with black; irides brownish red.

Entire length 16 inches; culmen 1·2, with frontal plate 2·3; wing, carpus to tip, 8; tarsus 2·2.

Fig. Gould, B. of Eur. pl. 338.

294. Fulica cristata, Linn. *Crested Coot.*

The Crested Coot appears to be plentiful at times in Egypt, and extends, I believe, throughout Nubia. I never met with a specimen while in the country; but a resident informed me that they are abundant during the inundations.

Similar in size and plumage to *F. atra*, but distinguished by having two red knobs on the white frontal plate.

295. Cygnus olor, Linn. *Mute Swan.*

According to Von Heuglin (Syst. Ueb. p. 65) both this and the next species come into Lower Egypt singly or in small flocks in the winter, being especially noted in the neighbourhood of Damietta.

Entire plumage white; beak orange, with its edges, as

well as a large tubercle next to the forehead and lores, black; irides brown.

Entire length 60 inches; culmen 3·5; wing, carpus to tip, 25; tarsus 4·25.

Fig. Gould, B. of Eur. pl. 354.

296. CYGNUS MUSICUS, Linn. *Hooper.*

A winter visitant, like the last.

Entire plumage white; beak and lores pale yellow, with the tip and edges of the former black.

Entire length 58 inches; culmen 4·1; wing, carpus to tip, 22; tarsus 4·25.

Fig. Gould, B. of Eur. pl. 355.

297. CHENALOPEX ÆGYPTIACUS (Linn.). *Egyptian Goose.*

This species is very evenly distributed throughout Egypt and Nubia. It is a very wary bird, and difficult to shoot; and will oftentimes avoid a boat by walking away from the river, and taking up a position from whence it can see the approach of danger. It breeds very early in the fields by the river; for in the beginning of May I shot some fair-sized flappers, and while in pursuit of them the old birds tried their best to draw me away by feigning to be wounded, but still carefully kept out of shot.

Centre of the head light brown; upper part of the throat and cheeks white, the whole shading into brown on the nape; forehead, region of the eye, some of the feathers on the throat, and remainder of the neck bright ferruginous brown, ending abruptly at the base of the neck; upper parts of the back, chest, and flanks ferruginous buff, darkest on the back, the whole finely barred with dusky; middle of the back and scapulars darker, the larger feathers of the latter changing to chestnut; primaries black, outer web of the secondaries brilliant metallic green; wing-coverts white, with a well-defined narrow black line across the wing; lower half of the back and tail black; centre of the chest marked with a broad chocolate-coloured patch; centre of the abdomen white; under tail-coverts buff; legs deep pink; beak brownish flesh-colour; irides brown.

Entire length 26 inches; culmen 2; wing, carpus to tip, 16; tarsus 3·2.

Fig. Gould, B. of Eur. pl. 353.

298. Anser albifrons, Gm. *White-fronted Goose.*

This is the most abundant Goose in Egypt, where it may usually be met with in flocks, but does not remain in the country later than March. When on the wing they fly in a wedge-shaped flock, and frequently utter a loud harsh cry, which may be heard at a considerable distance. They are generally on the move just before sunrise and sunset, and as they are very regular, taking the same line of flight and feeding at the same spot each day, they may be most readily obtained by lying in wait for them. If once fired at, the flock generally leaves the neighbourhood altogether.

Forehead and front of the cheeks white; whole of the neck brown; upper part of the back and scapulars darker brown, with paler edgings to the feathers; remainder of the back and tail dusky brown, with the tail-coverts and end of the tail white; quills black; wing-coverts grey, the larger ones tipped with white; under surface of the body and tail white in winter, while in spring the breast becomes more or less mottled and banded with deep chocolate-brown; flanks brown, with the feathers broadly edged with white; legs and beak orange; irides brown.

Entire length 28 inches; culmen 1·8; wing, carpus to tip, 16; tarsus 1·4.

Fig. Gould, B. of Gr. Br. part xix.

299. Bernicla brenta, Pall. *Brent Goose.*

Von Heuglin (Syst. Ueb. p. 66) states that this bird is found in Lower Egypt in small flocks during the winter.

Head, neck, front of the chest, and upper parts, including the wings, black, with a patch of white on each side of the neck and upper tail-coverts; upper part of the back, scapulars, and wing-coverts shaded with brown, with paler edges to the feathers; vent and under tail-coverts white; remainder of the underparts dusky ash-colour, each feather margined with stone-grey; beak and legs black; irides dark brown.

Entire length 24 inches; culmen 1·5; wing, carpus to tip, 14; tarsus 2·7.

Fig. Gould, B. of Eur. pl. 352.

300. Tadorna vulpanser, Fleming. *Common Sheldrake.*

The present species appears to be rarer than the Ruddy Sheldrake; for it is not so often found in the market at Alexandria. I have met with it on two occasions—once near Sioot, and once in the Fayoom.

Head and greater part of the neck brilliant dark green; remainder of the neck and body white, with the following exceptions—upper part of the back and chest chestnut; primaries black; secondaries tipped with white, and with their outer webs brilliant metallic green; scapulars mostly black; wing-coverts white; tail black; and a dark brown band down the centre of the chest and abdomen; legs and beak orange; irides brown.

Entire length 26 inches; culmen 1·2; wing, carpus to tip, 13; tarsus 2·2.

Fig. Gould, B. of Eur. pl. 357.

301. Tadorna rutila (Pall.). *Ruddy Sheldrake.*

The present species is rarely met with on the river, but is not uncommon on the lakes of Lower Egypt and the Fayoom, and is frequently brought to the Alexandrian market. I met with it twice on Lake Menzaleh, which appears to be its favourite habitat in the country.

Head very pale rufous; neck darker rufous, surrounded near its base by a more or less distinct black ring; upper part of the back, scapulars, and the entire under surface of the body rich ferruginous brown; primaries black; outer web of the secondaries brilliant metallic green; wing-coverts white; upper tail-coverts and tail black; beak and legs black; irides brown.

Entire length 25 inches; culmen 1·7; wing, carpus to tip, 14; tarsus 2·1.

Fig. Gould, B. of Eur. pl. 358.

302. Anas boschas, Linn. *Common Wild Duck.*

The Wild Duck is distributed throughout Egypt and Nubia, and is everywhere plentiful.

Male.—Head and neck rich metallic green, the lower part surrounded by a white ring; lower neck and fore part of the breast chocolate-brown; upper part of the back chocolate-brown, with pale edges to the feathers; scapulars grey and brown, pencilled with dusky; lower part of the back, rump, and upper tail-coverts black, with green reflections; tail black, edged with white, except the four centre feathers, which are curled up; primaries dusky brown; secondaries deep metallic blue, shading into black and tipped with white; greater wing-coverts barred with white and tipped with black, remaining wing-coverts brown; abdomen greyish white, shaded with yellow and pencilled with dusky; legs orange; beak yellow; irides dark brown.

Entire length 24 inches; culmen 2·3; wing, carpus to tip, 10·8; tarsus 2.

Fig. Gould, B. of Eur. pl. 361.

303. Anas strepera, Linn. *Gadwall.*

The Gadwall ranges throughout Egypt and Nubia, and is moderately abundant, frequenting the large sheets of water in preference to the small pools and canals. I have shot it in Lower Egypt, the Fayoom, and up the Nile at El Kab.

Feathers on the top of the head and nape dusky, barred and edged with brown; remainder of the head and neck dirty white, thickly freckled with brown; base of the throat and crop dusky black, with white semicircular bars and edges to the feathers; upper part of the back, outer half of the scapulars, and sides of the body dusky, with narrow undulating white bars; remainder of the scapulars brown, with pale edges to the feathers; back dark brown; rump and tail-coverts black, with a metallic gloss; tail stone-grey, with cream-coloured edges; wings, *some of the smaller coverts stone-grey, the greater part chestnut*, some of the larger ones tipped with black; primaries brown, becoming very pale on the inner web; secondaries greyish brown, some with black on the outer web, and many with the outer web white; centre of the chest and abdomen white; beak black; legs orange-brown; irides brown.

Entire length 19 inches; culmen 1·8; wing, carpus to tip, 11·4; tarsus 1·3.

Fig. Gould, B. of Eur. pl. 366.

304. Dafila acuta (Linn.). *Pintail Duck.*

The Pintail is very abundant in Lower Egypt and the Fayoom, but much less common on the Nile above Cairo. It may usually be met with in large flocks on the lakes, or feeding, in company with other kinds of Duck, along the banks of the canals, and more rarely in the small pools.

Two centre tail-feathers long and pointed; neck long.

Male.—Head brown, a white band commencing on each side of the nape and joining the white on the throat; back of the neck ashy brown, almost black towards the nape; remainder of the throat and under surface of the body white, shaded with grey on the abdomen; back and smaller scapulars grey, owing to the feathers being evenly barred with dusky and white, and the flanks coloured in the same manner; the larger scapulars are black, elongated, and broadly edged with grey and buff; primaries brown; secondaries tipped with white, and with their outer webs brilliant metallic green; wing-coverts grey, the larger ones tipped with rufous, forming a band on the wing; legs black; beak slate-colour, with the tip and a broad band down the culmen black; irides brown.

Entire length 23 inches; culmen 2; wing, carpus to tip, 10·5; tarsus 1·5.

The female is a pale mottled brown bird, having the tail pointed, but not so much elongated as in the male.

Fig. Gould, B. of Eur. pl. 365.

305. Rhynchaspis clypeata (Linn.). *Shoveller.*

The Shoveller is a resident in Egypt and Nubia, and is one of the most abundant species of Duck in the country. They prefer the smaller pools and the banks of the lakes and river, are less shy than the other species of water-fowl, and are therefore most frequently shot, though they are very inferior eating. They are very late in assuming their breeding plumage; for I have frequently shot them in April still in moult.

Beak long and widening out towards the end; head and neck dark metallic green; front part of the chest and greater part of the scapulars white; centre of the back brown, with paler edgings to the feathers; lower part of the back, tail-coverts, and tail black, with green and purple reflections; outer feathers of the tail edged with white; remainder of the scapulars elongated, and coloured blue, white, and black; primaries brown, the secondaries having their outer webs metallic green; greater wing-coverts brown, edged with white, the other wing-coverts blue-grey; remainder of the chest and abdomen chocolate-brown; legs orange; beak black; irides brown.

Entire length 20·5 inches; culmen 2·6; wing, carpus to tip, 9; tarsus 1·3.

Fig. Gould, B. of Eur. pl. 360.

306. QUERQUEDULA CRECCA (Linn.). *Common Teal.*

This is the most abundant species of water-fowl throughout Egypt and Nubia, being met with on nearly every small pool or canal, preferring these haunts to the larger sheets of water.

Male.—Head and neck rich ferruginous brown, with a large patch of bright metallic green encircling the eye and extending over the ear-coverts down the sides of the neck, ending in a steel-blue patch at the back of the neck; a white streak passes from the beak between the green and brown of the cheeks; remainder of the neck, upper part of the back, a portion of the scapulars, and sides of the body dusky, the feathers being composed of alternate narrow streaks of white and black; remainder of the scapulars white, with a border of velvety black on their outer webs; remainder of the back and tail dusky brown; quills dusky, exterior web of the outer secondaries black, of the inner ones metallic green; wing-coverts brownish ash-colour, the larger ones tipped with creamy white; underparts white, spotted with black on the crop, and shaded with dusky on the abdomen; under tail-coverts buff, the centre ones black; beak and legs black; irides brown.

Entire length 15·5 inches; culmen 1·4; wing, carpus to tip, 7·2; tarsus 1·1.

Fig. Sharpe and Dresser, B. of Eur. part i.

307. Querquedula circia (Linn.). *Garganey Teal.*

The Garganey Teal is moderately abundant throughout Egypt and Nubia, and is a resident in the country. We met with a considerable number at El Kab towards the end of April; but it appears to be most plentiful in the Delta, for I have seen it frequently in the market at Alexandria.

Top of the head dark brown, margined by a white streak on each side, which commences over the eyes and joins on the nape; chin black; remainder of the head and neck rufous brown, finely spotted with white on the centre of each feather; front of the chest pale brown, with semicircular black bars on each feather; back and tail brown, often tinted with grey, and with pale edgings to the feathers; quills brown, secondaries tipped with white, and with their outer webs brilliant metallic green; greater wing-coverts broadly tipped with white; remainder of the wing-coverts and outer web of the scapulars grey, the rest of the scapulars black, with a clear white streak down their centres; abdomen nearly white, the flanks finely barred with black; legs and beak nearly black; irides brown.

Entire length 15 inches; culmen 1·6; wing, carpus to tip, 7·5; tarsus 1.

Fig. Sharpe and Dresser, B. of Eur. part v.

308. Mareca penelope (Linn.). *Widgeon.*

The Widgeon is plentiful in Lower Egypt in the winter, where I have shot it twice and frequently seen it, and it is generally to be found in the market at Alexandria. Up the Nile it appears to be of rare occurrence; for I have not observed it above Cairo nor in the Fayoom.

Forehead and top of the head buff; remainder of the head and neck chestnut; back grey, owing to the feathers being evenly barred with black and white; tail-coverts black, edged on their inner web with white; tail dusky; primaries brown; secondaries black, with the lower half of the outer web metallic green; greater wing-coverts tipped with black; remainder of the wing-coverts white, except on the carpal bend, where they are dusky; fore part of the chest ferruginous pink, remainder of the chest and abdomen white; flanks grey like the back; beak grey, tipped with black; legs black; irides brown.

Entire length 21 inches; culmen 1·4; wing, carpus to tip, 10·3; tarsus 1·3.

Fig. Gould, B. of Eur. pl. 359.

309. Nyroca leucophthalma (Bechst.). *Ferruginous Duck.*

This Duck ranges throughout Egypt and Nubia, but is most plentiful on the large lakes of the Fayoom and Lower Egypt. On Birket el Korn I daily saw immense flocks of many thousands together far out on the centre of the lake, which when disturbed rose with a running flight, striking the water rapidly with their feet, and making a noise in so doing which could be distinctly heard at a couple of miles' distance.

Head, neck, fore part of the chest, and sides of the body rich ferruginous brown; a ring round the neck, back, wings, and tail dark brown; secondaries and inner primaries shading into white on their inner webs; chest white, shading into brown on the abdomen; under tail-coverts white; beak slaty grey with a black tip; legs olive-black; irides white.

Entire length 16 inches; culmen 1·8; wing, carpus to tip, 7·5; tarsus 1·1.

Fig. Gould, B. of Eur. pl. 368.

310. Fuligula ferina (Linn.). *Pochard.*

The Pochard ranges throughout Egypt and Nubia, but is most plentiful in the Delta. It prefers open water to the more reedy districts, and on the approach of danger will rather swim out of its way than take to the wing.

Head and neck rufous brown; upper part of the back and front of the chest black; centre of the back and scapulars pale grey, finely pencilled with dusky; remainder of the back and tail almost black; primaries brown, secondaries narrowly tipped with white; wing-coverts brownish grey; underparts of the body dirty white, ending in black towards the tail; legs dark slate-colour; beak grey, tipped with black; irides brown.

Entire length 19 inches; culmen 2; wing, carpus to tip, 8; tarsus 1·4.

Fig. Gould, B. of Eur. pl. 367.

311. Fuligula marila (Linn.). *Scaup Duck.*

This species comes into Lower Egypt in the winter, and remains there until May, according to Von Heuglin (Syst. Ueb. p. 67). It frequents the large brackish-water lakes near the sea, and probably never ascends the Nile; nor has it been met with, to my knowledge, in the Fayoom.

Male.—Head and neck dark metallic green; base of the neck, upper part of the back and crop, rump, vent, and tail-coverts black; tail dusky brown; back and scapulars white, with fine undulating dusky bars; wing-coverts dusky grey, pencilled with black; primaries dusky brown; secondaries white, with broad black ends; chest and abdomen white, sides shaded with brown, the feathers narrowly barred with undulating dusky lines; beak slaty blue, with the nail black; legs pale slaty grey; webs of the feet inclining to black; irides yellow.

Entire length 20 inches; culmen 1·9; wing, carpus to tip, 8·5; tarsus 1·5.

Female.—Fore part of the face and a patch on the ear-coverts white; remainder of the head, neck, crop, upper part of the back, and tail-coverts brown.

Fig. Gould, B. of Eur. pl. 371.

312. Fuligula cristata (Linn.). *Tufted Duck.*

This Duck is most plentiful in Lower Egypt and the Fayoom, where I have occasionally shot it. It frequents the open water, but is not very shy.

Male.—Head, which is crested, and neck deep greenish purple; remainder of the neck, front of the chest, back,

ERISMATURA LEUCOCEPHALA.

scapulars, wings, and tail black; primaries shading into white on the inner web; vent, under tail-coverts, and thighs black; chest and abdomen white; beak slaty grey, with a black tip; legs black; irides yellow.

The female has no crest, and is generally browner in colour.

Entire length 16 inches; culmen 1·6; wing, carpus to tip, 8; tarsus 1·3.

Fig. Gould, B. of Eur. pl. 370.

313. Erismatura leucocephala (Scop.). *White-headed Duck.*

(Plate XII.)

The White-headed Duck is tolerably plentiful in Lower Egypt; but I am not aware of its having been met with on the Nile above Cairo. Its favourite haunts are the great brackish-water lakes of Mareotis and Menzaleh; and it is probably to be met with in the Fayoom, though I do not know of an instance of its capture there. It is an extremely good diver, and prefers to keep to the water instead of taking to flight, unless very closely pursued. I only met with it alive on one occasion, on Lake Mareotis; when I shot one on the water, believing at the time that it was wounded. I have also seen it occasionally in the Alexandrian market.

The description is taken from one of my Egyptian specimens, the colour of the beak, legs, and irides having been noted at the time.

Beak swollen at the base; tail-feathers long, narrow, and stiff; head white, all except the top, which is black: back of the neck below the nape black; remainder of the plumage ferruginous brown, freckled with pale brown and dusky, darkest on the fore part of the chest, flanks, and upper tail-coverts; lower parts of the chest and abdomen dirty white; tail black; legs black; beak blue-grey, without a spot; irides brown.

Entire length 18 inches; culmen 1·8; wing, carpus to tip, 6; tarsus 1·3.

314. ŒDEMIA FUSCA (Linn.). *Velvet Scoter.*

According to Von Heuglin (Syst. Ueb. p. 67) the present species is to be met with singly in Lower Egypt in the winter.

Male.—Entire plumage velvety black, excepting a patch behind the eye and a bar across the wing, which are pure white; beak orange, with its margin and a swelling near the nostrils black; legs bright red; irides yellow.

Entire length 23 inches; culmen 1·7; wing, carpus to tip, 11; tarsus 1·8.

Female.—Blackish brown, with the under surface of the body dirty white, streaked and spotted with brown; on the sides of the head some irregular patches of brownish white, and a white bar across the wing; beak dusky; legs brownish red.

Fig. Gould, B. of Eur. pl. 377.

Fam. PELECANIDÆ.

315. PELECANUS CRISPUS, Bruch. *Dalmatian Pelican.*

The present species is abundant throughout Egypt and Nubia, frequenting the sandbanks in the river, often in large flocks. It appears to be more plentiful than the other species of Pelican, and was the only one I met with in the Fayoom, where I frequently killed specimens.

Feathers on the forehead terminating in a curved line, which is concave towards the middle of the culmen; entire plumage white, with the following exceptions:—primaries dark brown; upper part of the back, scapulars, and wing-coverts stone-grey, with their edges more or less white; tail-feathers brown and grey, edged with white; legs and pouch flesh-colour; *irides greyish white.*

Entire length 72 inches; culmen 18·5; wing, carpus to tip, 28; tarsus 5·2.

The description is taken from a specimen in my collection, shot in February.

Fig. Gould, B. of Eur. pl. 406.

316. PELECANUS ONOCRATALUS, Linn. *White Pelican.*

This Pelican is very abundant in Egypt and Nubia. On the 20th of April, 1870, below Edfoo, we met with an immense flock of several thousands, passing low along the river on their way north; and although fired at several times they still kept streaming onwards in one continuous flock, without diverging from their course. Mr. Adderley procured a specimen out of this flock; and as it does not agree in the colour of the legs with former descriptions of this species,

I give the following notes as they were made by me at the time:—

Feathers on the forehead come to a point towards the culmen; pouch pure pale yellow; legs olive-black; irides crimson; primaries black; remainder of the *plumage white, with a very faint roseate blush.*

Entire length 60 inches; culmen 16; wing, carpus to tip, 26; tarsus 4·5.

Fig. Gould, B. of Eur. pl. 405.

317. PELECANUS MINOR, Rüpp. *Lesser Pelican.*

Von Heuglin (Syst. Ueb. p. 72) observes that according to Rüppell this bird is abundant in Lower Egypt; and Mr. D. G. Elliot (P. Z. S. 1869, p. 581) likewise gives the locality Egypt for this species.

It is very similar to *P. onocrotalus*, but slightly smaller. The *feathers on the forehead come to a point towards the culmen*; crest long and pendent; primaries black; remainder of the *plumage pure white.*

Entire length 55 inches; culmen 12; wing, carpus to tip, 24; tarsus 5.

318. SULA CYANOPS, Sundev. *Masked Gannet.*

Mr. E. C. Taylor tells me that he met with a Gannet on the Red Sea, near Suez, which must have belonged to the present species, as it is the only one that inhabits those waters.

Naked skin on the face and pouch slate-colour; quills,

greater wing-coverts, and tail dark brown; remainder of the plumage white; beak yellow; legs slaty grey; irides yellow.

Fig. Gould, B. of Australia, vol. vii. pl. 77.

319. PHALACROCORAX CARBO (Linn.). *Cormorant.*

The Common Cormorant is very plentiful throughout Egypt, especially in the Fayoom; and I have shot as many as twenty in one evening during their flight from the lake to their roosting-place in the rocks, where I believe they breed. On the Nile they are more plentiful in the winter than later in the season.

Entire plumage deep glossy green, with the following exceptions:—part of the pouch which is without feathers greenish blue; a white crescent-shaped patch on each side of the head, covering the cheeks, joining underneath and coming to a point on the pouch; feathers on the head and neck more or less white according to age; centres of the feathers on the upper part of the back, wing-coverts, and secondaries paler, and of a brownish hue; a patch of pure white on the flanks; legs black; beak black on the culmen and tip, shading off to yellow on the remainder of the bill; irides green. The younger birds have no white on the head and neck, and have the breast more or less white.

Entire length 36 inches; culmen 3; wing, carpus to tip, 13·5; tarsus 1·5.

Fig. Gould, B. of Eur. pl. 407.

320. PHALACROCORAX PYGMÆUS, Temm. *Little Cormorant.*

The only locality in which I found this bird was the

Fayoom, where it was not uncommon on the desert side of the great lake of Birket el Korn, and I shot two specimens. It is a far more active bird than the Common Cormorant, and much more shy, but very similar in its habits; for as I paddled among the reeds I frequently saw it sitting upright on the half-sunken bushes, or diving actively in pursuit of fish. It appears to be a sociable species; for I generally noticed it in pairs or small flocks, possibly family parties; but it never flew in company with other birds.

The following description is taken from my Egyptian specimens shot in February:—

Upper plumage black, glossed with green, with the following exceptions—sides of the neck shading off to brown; wing-coverts almost grey, with the ends of the feathers black, narrowly edged with white; underparts white, shaded with brown on the neck and crop; flanks and under tail-coverts black; legs black; culmen brown; remainder of the beak and bare part of the crop yellow; irides brown (noted at the time).

Entire length 22·5 inches; culmen 1·4; wing, carpus to tip, 8·5; tarsus 1·2.

Fig. Gould, B. of Eur. pl. 409.

321. STERNA CASPIA, Pall. *Caspian Tern.*

The Caspian Tern is tolerably abundant in Lower Egypt, but does not, to my knowledge, extend its range up the Nile. Mr. E. C. Taylor tells me that he has observed it on several occasions at Port Saïd and at Damietta.

Adult in breeding-plumage.—Top of the head, nape, and around the eye black; back and wings pearl-grey; ends of the quills dusky; remainder of the plumage white; beak vermilion; legs black; irides dark brown.

Entire length 21 inches; culmen 2·8; wing, carpus to tip, 16·5; tarsus 1·5.

Fig. Gould, B. of Eur. pl. 414.

322. Sterna anglica, Montagu. *Gull-billed Tern.*

The present species is one of the most abundant Terns in Egypt. Though most plentiful in Lower Egypt and the Fayoom, I have met with it frequently as far up the Nile as Sioot.

Breeding-plumage.—Top of the head and nape glossy black, remainder of the upper plumage pale pearl-grey; under plumage white; legs and *entire beak black*; irides dark brown.

In winter the top of the head is white, streaked or mottled with black; nape and in front of the eye darker.

Entire length 14 inches; culmen 1·5; wing, carpus to tip, 13; tarsus 1·35.

Fig. Gould, B. of Eur. pl. 410.

323. Sterna cantiaca, Gm. *Sandwich Tern.*

This Tern appears to be more confined to Lower Egypt than *S. anglica*, and is by no means so common, though it cannot be considered a rare species in that country.

My description is taken from a specimen obtained at Alexandria in February.

The plumage is very similar to that of *S. anglica*; the bill, however, is longer and more slender, and is tipped with dull whitish yellow.

Entire length 15·7 inches; culmen 1·9; wing, carpus to tip, 10·4; tarsus 1.

Fig. Gould, B. of Eur. pl. 415.

324. STERNA MEDIA, Horsf. *Allied Tern.*

This species of Sea-Swallow is plentiful in Lower Egypt, where it remains throughout the year.

Summer plumage.—Top of the head and nape black; back, scapulars, wings, and tail pearl-grey, the primaries having a dusky border on the inner web next to the shafts; remainder of the plumage white; beak yellow; legs black.

Entire length 16·2 inches; culmen 2·2; wing, carpus to tip, 12·5; tarsus 1.

The description is taken from a specimen shot at Alexandria on the 2nd of June, 1865, by Mr. S. Stafford Allen.

Fig. Bree, B. of Eur. vol. iv. p. 87.

325. STERNA BERGII, Licht. *Swift Tern.*

The present species is not uncommon in Lower Egypt, where it is a resident.

Top of the head white, mottled towards the back with black, nape entirely of that colour; remainder of the neck and underparts white; back, scapulars, and wing-coverts pale pearl-grey, fading almost into white on the rump and tail; first three primaries nearly black, remainder of them deep grey, with a white border on the inner web; beak yellow; legs black; irides dark brown.

Entire length 16·5 inches; culmen 2·3; wing, carpus to tip, 13·5; tarsus 1·2.

Fig. Cretzschm. in Rüpp. Atlas, t. 13.

326. Sterna fluviatilis, Naum. *Common Tern.*

This Tern may be occasionally met with in pairs along the Mediterranean coast in the winter and spring, according to Von Heuglin (Syst. Ueb. p. 70).

Breeding-plumage.—Upper part of the head and nape black; remainder of the head, neck, under surface of the body, and the edges of the carpal band white; the rest of the plumage pearl-grey, with the first primary partially edged with black; beak and legs coral-red, the former shaded with black towards the tip; irides dark brown.

In winter the head is mottled with white towards the forehead.

Entire length 15 inches; culmen 1·3; wing, carpus to tip, 10; tarsus 0·8.

Fig. Sharpe & Dresser, B. of Eur. part vii.

327. Sterna hirundo, Linn. *Arctic Tern.*

The present species is to be met with singly along the Egyptian coast, as stated by Von Heuglin (Syst. Ueb. p. 70).

Tail in the adult longer than in *S. fluviatilis*, and the tarsus always shorter.

Summer plumage.—Upper part of the head and nape black; entire plumage, including the *inner webs of the quills, grey*, shading into white on the throat, cheeks, ear-coverts, and towards the extremities of the tail-feathers; the exterior web of the first primary and outer tail-feathers dusky; beak and legs coral-red; irides dark brown.

Entire length 15 inches; culmen 1·4; wing, carpus to tip, 11; tarsus 0·6.

Fig. Gould, B. of Eur. pl. 419.

328. Sterna minuta (Linn.). *Lesser Tern.*

This small Tern is a winter visitor, but appears to be of rare occurrence in Egypt; for I have only seen one specimen from that country, which was shot by Mr. Baird on the Nile, and is now in his collection.

A streak extending from the lores over the eye, top of the head, and nape black; back and wings pearl-grey; outer primaries dusky; remainder of the plumage white; beak yellow, tipped with black; legs orange; irides dark brown.

Entire length 8·7 inches; culmen 1·3; wing, carpus to tip, 7; tarsus 0·7.

Fig. Gould, B. of Eur. pl. 420.

329. Hydrochelidon fissipes (Linn.). *Black Tern.*

Von Heuglin (Syst. Ueb. p. 71) says that this Tern is met with on the Nile.

Head, neck, and breast dusky black, shading into slate-colour on the upper parts and on the abdomen; vent and under tail-coverts white; beak black, shaded with deep red towards the base; legs dusky red; irides dark brown.

Immature plumage.—Forehead, cheeks, and under surface of the body white; back, wings, and tail leaden grey intermingled with brown.

Entire length 10 inches; culmen 1; wing, carpus to tip, 8; tarsus 0·7.

Fig. Gould, B. of Eur. pl. 422.

330. Hydrochelidon nigra (Linn.). *White-winged Black Tern.*

Von Heuglin (Syst. Ueb. p. 71) mentions this Tern as not uncommon during winter and spring on the coasts of both the Mediterranean and the Red Sea.

Summer plumage.—Head, neck, scapulars, and chest black; rump, tail-coverts, tail, and vent white; wings grey, with white edges to the shoulders; outer primary nearly black; beak dusky black, tinged with red at the base; legs red; irides dark brown.

Entire length 9 inches; culmen 1; wing, carpus to tip, 8·7; tarsus 0·9.

Fig. Gould, B. of Eur. pl. 423.

331. Hydrochelidon leucopareia (Natt.). *Whiskered Tern.*

This is a very abundant species on the Nile, ranging throughout Egypt and Nubia. I met with small flocks on several occasions as far up as El Kab, and on the 1st of May shot several at How. In the Delta and the Fayoom they are extremely abundant, and by no means shy, often flitting gracefully backwards and forwards over the small ponds close to the villages.

Breeding-plumage.—Top of the head and nape black; upper surface pearl-grey; cheeks and throat white; underside of the wings and under tail-coverts white; remainder of the under surface leaden grey; beak and legs coral-red; irides dark brown.

Entire length 9·5 inches; culmen 1·2; wing, carpus to tip, 9; tarsus 0·9.

Fig. Gould, B. of Eur. pl. 424.

332. Rhynchops flavirostris, Vieill. *Scissor-billed Tern.*

(Plate XIV.)

I first saw some of these curious birds flitting over the sandbanks near Edfoo on the 1st of April; on the 4th a small flock passed our boat near Philæ, and we met, I believe, the same party again ten days later among the rapids of the First Cataract. Afterwards we saw these Terns frequently in considerable numbers, and killed several near Erment, where I believe they were beginning to breed on the sandbanks. They were not shy, and afforded me plenty of opportunities of watching their graceful evolutions as they played together.

Mr. S. Stafford Allen (Ibis, 1864, p. 243) mentions having seen the Scissor-billed Tern once near Thebes, and speaks of its having been killed at Damietta, which appears to

RHYNCHOPS FLAVIROSTRIS.

me very possible; for when I met with them they had evidently just arrived on their migration down the Nile, and probably some intended to continue their journey.

Beak very much flattened at the sides and much deeper than it is broad, *lower mandible longest.*

Top of the head, nape, back, centre tail-coverts, two middle tail-feathers, and wings dusky brown; forehead and remainder of the plumage white; secondaries tipped with white; inner web of the tail-feathers shaded with dusky; legs and beak vermilion, the latter shading off to yellow towards the end; irides brown.

Entire length 17 inches; beak, from the gape, upper mandible 3·1, lower mandible 3·9 to 4·4; wing, carpus to tip, 14; tarsus 1·1.

Description taken from three specimens shot by myself in Upper Egypt.

Fam. LARIDÆ.

333. Larus marinus, Linn. *Greater Black-backed Gull.*

According to Von Heuglin (Syst. Ueb. p. 69) this species is met with singly on the Mediterranean coast throughout the year.

Head, neck, tail, and underparts white; back, scapulars, and wings deep slate-colour; primary coverts white, the primaries, secondaries, and scapulars tipped with white; eyelids red; beak yellow, with a scarlet patch on the lower mandible; irides pale yellow.

Entire length 30 inches; culmen 3·5; wing, carpus to tip, 20; tarsus 3·1.

Fig. Gould, B. of Eur. pl. 430.

334. LARUS FUSCUS, Linn. *Lesser Black-backed Gull.*

This Gull ranges up the Nile into Nubia, where I frequently saw it in small flocks, generally towards sunset, passing northward in April. On the 24th of that month, near Erment, I shot a specimen out of a small flock, apparently the same that I had seen on several consecutive evenings during our return journey down the river. I have taken my description from this specimen.

Entire plumage pure white, except the back and wings, which are deep slate-colour, with the primaries black; a large white spot on the first primary near the tip; ends of the quills and greater scapulars white; legs and beak yellow, with the base of the gape and a spot on the lower mandible vermilion; irides pale yellow; eyelids vermilion.

Entire length 23 inches; culmen 2·3; wing, carpus to tip, 17; tarsus 2·5.

Fig. Gould, B. of Eur. pl. 431.

335. LARUS LEUCOPHÆUS, Licht. *Mediterranean Herring-Gull.*

This Gull is a very abundant resident in Egypt and Nubia. I believe it to have been the species of which I saw flocks occasionally in Nubia, apparently migrating northward in April. Von Heuglin (Syst. Ueb. p. 69) probably refers to this species under the name of *L. argentatus*, which he declares is met with singly along the Nile up to Kartoom.

This bird is very similar to *L. argentatus*, from which it differs in the grey back being a shade darker, and in the legs of the adult being yellow.

Entire plumage white, excepting the back, scapulars, and greater part of the wings, which are grey; the greater part of the primaries black, with white tips and a white spot on the outer one; scapulars and secondaries tipped with white; beak yellow, with a scarlet patch on the lower mandible; *legs bright yellow*; irides pale yellow; eyelids scarlet.

Entire length 22 inches; culmen 2·4; wing, carpus to tip, 17; tarsus 2·5.

Immature birds have the legs flesh-colour.

336. LARUS ARGENTATUS, Brünn. *Herring-Gull.*

Von Heuglin (Syst. Ueb. p. 69) says that this Gull is very abundant on the Mediterranean coast, and is found singly up the Nile as far as Kartoom.

Similar to *L. leucophæus*, but the grey on its plumage is of a paler tint, and the *legs in the adult are flesh-colour*.

Entire length 22 inches; culmen 2·4; wing, carpus to tip, 16·5; tarsus 2·5.

Fig. Gould, B. of Eur. pl. 434.

337. LARUS CANUS, Linn. *Common Gull.*

I only met with a single specimen of this Gull, on the 27th of February, near Damietta. According to Von Heuglin

(Syst. Ueb. p. 69) it is to be found singly on the Mediterranean coast in the winter.

Winter plumage.—Head white, with fine dusky streaks on the upper part; neck, rump, tail, and underparts white; back, scapulars, wing-coverts, and secondaries pearl-grey, with a white edging to the shoulders and white tips to the greater wing-coverts and secondaries; primaries black, with white tips, excepting the outer two, which have a white patch near their ends; beak yellow, shaded with grey towards the base; legs yellow; irides brown.

The following measurements are taken from the specimen I shot in Egypt:—

Entire length 16·3 inches; culmen 1·3; wing, carpus to tip, 14; tarsus 1·9.

Fig. Gould, B. of Eur. pl. 437.

338. Larus cachinnans, Pall.

According to Von Heuglin (Syst. Ueb. p. 69) this Gull is to be met with on the Red Sea and near Damietta.

From an examination of specimens, in which I have been assisted by Mr. Howard Saunders, who is making an especial study of the *Laridæ*, this species appears to be perfectly identical with *Larus leucophæus* (*anteà*, p. 304), and I have, therefore, not given a description of the bird.

339. Larus gelastes, Licht. *Slender-billed Gull.*

This Gull ranges throughout Egypt, and is probably a resident in the country. Mr. E. C. Taylor (Ibis, 1867, p. 72) mentions that his party procured a specimen out of a small

LARUS ICHTHYAETUS

flock they saw near Keneh, in Upper Egypt. This is the most southern point on the Nile that I am aware of its having been met with.

Head, neck, tail, outer border of the wing, and greater part of the first four primaries white; outer web of the first primary, inner border of the first four, and ends of all black; remainder of the upper plumage pearl-grey; underparts white, beautifully shaded with pink; beak and legs coral-red; irides very pale yellow.

Entire length 16 inches; culmen 1·6; wing, carpus to tip, 11·5; tarsus 1·9.

Fig. Bree, B. of Eur. vol. iv. p. 98.

340. Larus ichthyaëtus, Pall. *Great Black-headed Gull.*

(Plate XIII.)

This fine species ranges throughout Egypt and Nubia, and is far from uncommon. In the Fayoom I met with it daily on Birket el Korn, and frequently shot it in full plumage in February, and have also noticed it as high up the Nile as El Kab. It is likewise abundant on the coast of the Red Sea and Mediterranean.

Entire head and upper part of the neck black, with a small white patch above and below the eye; remainder of the neck, upper part of the back, tail-coverts, tail, and under surface of the body white; back, scapulars, and greater part of the wing-coverts pearl-grey; primaries white, with a large patch of clear black near the ends of the feathers and on the outer web of the first one, the smaller ones being grey, with white tips; the outer secondaries white, the inner ones grey tipped with that colour; beak yellow, with a broad red patch crossing it, and a black bar near the tip; gape and eyelids vermilion; legs yellow; irides dark brown.

Entire length 25 inches; culmen 3; wing, carpus to tip, 19; tarsus 1·9.

341. LARUS LEUCOPHTHALMUS, Licht. *White-eyed Gull.*

The present species is to be met with on the Egyptian coast, but does not appear to be at all plentiful.

Head, nape, and throat black, with a small white patch above and below the eye; a white border to the black on the neck, shading into dusky ash-colour on the back and sides of the chest; back and scapulars ashy brown; tail-coverts and tail white; wings dusky brown, with white tips to the secondaries; remainder of the underparts white; beak red, tipped with black; legs brownish red; irides white.

Entire length 15·5 inches; culmen 1·8; wing, carpus to tip, 12·5; tarsus 1·7.

Fig. Bree, B. of Eur. vol. iv. p. 95.

342. LARUS MELANOCEPHALUS, Natt. *Mediterranean Black-headed Gull.*

This species is moderately plentiful in Lower Egypt, especially in the neighbourhood of Alexandria, but is, according to Von Heuglin (Syst. Ueb. p. 69), only a winter and spring visitant.

Summer plumage.—Entire head deep black, with a small white patch above and below the eye; back and wings pearl-grey; primaries tipped with white, and the outer web of the first one black for three quarters of its length; remainder of the plumage white, with a delicate pink blush on the chest; beak, eyelids, and legs coral-red; irides dark brown.

Mr. Howard Saunders (Ibis, 1872, p. 79) has given some remarks on the distinctions between this species and the common Black-headed Gull, which may be useful to my readers:—"In the adult plumage this species is distinguishable at a glance from *L. ridibundus*; and even immature birds of the former show a stronger bill and somewhat larger tarsi; still the best distinction exists in the first primary. In young *L. melanocephalus* that portion of the inner web which lies *next* to the shaft is *smoke-coloured* on both upper and under sides, whereas in *L. ridibundus* it is *white*, as is also the shaft. This holds good until *L. melanocephalus* has lost all colour on the inner web of the first primary, when the dark edging of the same feather in *L. ridibundus* forms a still more marked distinction. A further peculiarity of this species is, that although it assumes the black head in its second spring, when it commences to breed, yet it does not acquire the full white primaries until the third spring."

Entire length 15 inches; culmen 1·3; wing, carpus to tip, 11·3; tarsus 1·7.

Fig. Gould, B. of Eur. pl. 427.

343. Larus ridibundus, Linn. *Black-headed Gull.*

This Gull is extremely abundant in Lower and Middle Egypt, where it remains the whole year; but I know of no instance of its capture in Nubia. During March 1870, when there was a plague of locusts in the land, we met the present species far up the river in large flocks, busily engaged in devouring these insects.

Adult in breeding-plumage.—Head and throat dark brown, with a small white patch above and below the eye; neck, upper part of the back, tail-coverts, tail, and under surface of the body white; remainder of the back, scapulars, secondaries, inner primaries, and greater part of the wing-coverts pearl-grey; carpal bend of the wing, outer wing-coverts, and greater part of the four outer primaries white; the outer web of the first primary, the tips of all, and part of the inner web of the larger ones black; legs, beak, and eyelids brownish red; irides dark brown.

In winter.—The head white, a dusky patch in front of the eyes, and often some dusky feathers on the back of the head.

Entire length 15 inches; culmen 1·5; wing, carpus to tip, 12·5; tarsus 1·6.

Fig. Gould, B. of Eur. pl. 425.

344. Larus minutus, Pall. *Little Gull.*

This species is to be met with in the Delta, and I one day saw it on Lake Mareotis in great numbers. On the large lake of the Fayoom I also believe that I saw a pair in company with *L. ridibundus.*

My description is taken from a specimen obtained at Alexandria on the 28th of February.

Winter plumage.—Back and wings pearl-grey, with the tip of the quills white; remainder of the plumage white, the breast suffused with a pink blush; beak brownish red; legs vermilion; irides brown.

In summer plumage the head is black.

Entire length 10·4 inches; culmen 0·9; wing, carpus to tip, 8·8; tarsus 0·9.

Fig. Sharpe and Dresser, B. of Eur. part iv.

Fam. PROCELLARIIDÆ.

345. PUFFINUS KUHLII, Boie. *Cinereous Shearwater.*

This is probably the species intended by Von Heuglin (Syst. Ueb. p. 68) under the name *Nectris macrorhyncha*, Heugl., which, he says, is not rare on the Mediterranean coast of Egypt.

Upper surface ashy grey, the feathers slightly edged with lighter grey, especially on the rump, the head darker; wing dark brown, the greater coverts decidedly lighter margined; quills and tail blackish brown, with a slight shade of grey; under surface of the body entirely white, with an appearance of ashy grey on the sides of the face and neck; bill yellowish, darker on the lower mandible, inclining to bluish a little way off the tip; feet yellowish, web lighter yellow, outer toe darker.

Total length 20 inches; culmen 2·05; wing, carpus to tip, 12·8; tail 5·3; tarsus 1·95.

Fig. Kuhl's Proc. t. 11, 12.

346. Puffinus anglorum, Temm. *Manx Shearwater.*

Von Heuglin (Syst. Ueb. p. 68) calls this bird rare on the north coast of Egypt, where he mentions that he found a specimen that had been washed up by the tide.

We know that this bird is extremely plentiful throughout the Mediterranean, where it is resident; and after carefully comparing a specimen from Malta with others from Ireland (all in the collection of Mr. Howard Saunders), it is difficult to admit the specific distinction of *P. Baroli*, Bonelli, and *P. yelkouan*, Acerbi, names which have been applied to the Mediterranean bird.

Above sooty black, underneath entirely black; the sides of the face as far as the upper part of the breast shaded with grey; bill black, under mandible somewhat lighter; feet yellowish; outer toe blackish.

Total length 13 inches; culmen 1·35; wing 9·2; tail 3·7; tarsus 1·6.

Fig. Gould, B. of Eur. pl. 443.

Fam. PODICIPIDÆ.

347. Podiceps cristatus (Linn.). *Great Crested Grebe.*

This Grebe is rare in Egypt; yet I have certainly seen it on two occasions in the Fayoom, and believe that I have also observed it on the Nile near Keneh. In habits it is extremely shy, diving at the first glimpse of danger, so that it is very difficult to approach, especially as it usually frequents the open sheets of water.

Breeding-plumage.—Top of the head and ear-tufts dusky;

round the neck a broad frill of chestnut, edged with black; cheeks and throat white; upper plumage dusky brown, with a white bar across the wings; underparts silvery white, becoming ferruginous brown on the flanks; legs olive-black; beak dusky; irides red.

In winter the ear-tufts and frill are absent.

Entire length 21 inches; culmen 1·9; wing, carpus to tip, 7·2; tarsus 2·2.

Fig. Gould, B. of Eur. pl. 388.

348. Podiceps nigricollis, Sundev. *Eared Grebe.*

This is probably the bird referred to by Von Heuglin (Syst. Ueb. p. 68) under the name *P. auritus*, Briss., which, he states, is to be met with in Lower Egypt during the winter.

Feathers behind the eye and ear-coverts elongated, and of a light chestnut-colour; remainder of the head, throat, and upper parts, including the wings, olive-black; secondaries white; under surface of the body silvery white, shading into chestnut-brown on the sides; beak black; legs olive; irides red.

Entire length 12 inches; culmen 0·9; wing, carpus to tip, 5; tarsus 1·6.

Fig. Gould, B. of Eur. pl. 391.

349. Podiceps griseigena, Bodd. *Red-necked Grebe.*

According to Von Heuglin (Syst. Ueb. p. 68) this species

comes into Lower Egypt in the winter, where it is met with singly.

Summer plumage.—Tufts on the head, upper part of the head, and back of the neck black; remainder of the upper parts, including the wings, olive-black, the secondaries white; chin and sides of the head white; neck chestnut; remainder of the under surface of the body white, shading into dusky black at the vent; beak olive-black, shaded with yellow at the gape; legs dusky olive; irides red.

Entire length 17·5 inches; culmen 1·7; wing, carpus to tip, 7·9; tarsus 1·2.

Fig. Gould, B. of Eur. pl. 389.

350. Podiceps minor (Linn.). *Little Grebe.*

The present species is plentiful in Lower Egypt and the Fayoom, where I have shot it on several occasions, but have never observed it on the river.

Front of the face, upper part of the throat, and the whole of the upper plumage olive-black; wings brown, with a large portion of the secondaries white; ear-coverts and front of the neck rich ferruginous brown; underparts white, shaded with dusky on the crop, sides, and vent; beak olive-black, shading into yellow at the tip and gape; legs olive; irides brown.

Entire length 10 inches; culmen 0·9; wing, carpus to tip, 4; tarsus 1·4.

Fig. Gould, B. of Eur. pl. 392.

351. Colymbus septentrionalis, Linn. *Red-throated Diver.*

Von Heuglin (Syst. Ueb. p. 68) mentions that he once observed this species in Lower Egypt in the winter.

Summer plumage.—Forehead, sides of the head, and neck slate-colour, with a ferruginous brown patch down the centre of the throat; back of the head and hinder part of the neck black, streaked with white; remainder of the upper parts dusky, more or less spotted with white; underparts white; beak and legs black, the latter tinted with olive; irides red.

Entire length 22·5 inches; culmen 2; wing, carpus to tip, 11·5; tarsus 2·5.

Fig. Gould, B. of Eur. pl. 395.

Order STRUTHIONES.

Fam. STRUTHIONIDÆ.

352. Struthio camelus, L. *Ostrich.*

A perfect monograph of the Ostrich has been published by Drs. Finsch and Hartlaub in the 'Vögel Ost-Afrika's,' and I translate from thence the following particulars as to its occurrence in Egypt:—"They are no longer found on the plains of El Mograh, between Cairo and Suez, where Burckhardt met with wild Ostriches in 1816. Von Heuglin looked in vain for it both on the Libyan plains and in Central Egypt; but a very trustworthy hunter, Prince Halim Pacha, assured him that he had found fresh-disturbed breeding-places of the

Ostrich a few days' journey distant from Cairo. Formerly it was often referred to as occurring there. Pocock states that it inhabited the hilly desert to the south-west of Alexandria. Sonnini often saw fresh tracks in the desert of Bahireh; and Minutoli observed flocks of from ten to fifteen individuals on the route from Alexandria to Suvah and Dernah."

CONCLUDING REMARKS.

Having reviewed in the foregoing part of this work all the different species of birds that have been included in the Egyptian lists by former writers, as well as those that have come under my own observation, it will, perhaps, be of service briefly to determine the value of the evidence on which they have been inserted, and the true claim to specific distinction of the more closely allied species. In the former pages I have included over 350 birds as having some feasible claim to be considered inhabitants of the Egyptian district, bounded on the north by the Mediterranean, on the south by the Second Cataract, and on the east and west by the Arabian and Libyan deserts.

Fam. Turdidæ.—Among the Thrushes, *Turdus viscivorus* has probably never occurred in Egypt; for no traveller on the Nile more recent than Rüppell records it from that country. *T. torquatus*, I have little doubt, is met with in Lower Egypt. The true *Pycnonotus nigricans* (Vieill.) never could have come to Egypt, as stated by Von Heuglin (Orn. N. O. Afr. p. 399). The bird referred to by him is doubtless *P. xanthopygius*, the Palestine form, differing only from *P. nigricans* in the absence of a red eyelid; and for that reason I have included it in my work under the name of *P. xanthopygius*.

Fam. Sylviidæ.—*Saxicola philothamna* has almost crept into Egyptian lists on account of Mr. E. C. Taylor's *S. erythropygia* having been referred to that species; but the latter bird is apparently referable to *S. mœsta*, Licht. *S. xanthomelæna* is an undoubtedly good species, with which *S. Finschi* is identical (vide *suprà*, p. 74). *S. homochroa*, of which I have only seen females, may, I think, only be a sexual or seasonal plumage of *S. deserti*. *S. lugens* and *S. leucomela* of Von Heuglin's large work are doubtfully separable; while his *S. syenitica* is probably only a stage of *S. leucopygia*, depending on the age of the specimen. *Pratincola Hemprichii* is mentioned as Egyptian for the first time by Von Heuglin (Orn. N. O. Afr. p. 339). It may have been remarked by some of my readers that although many species of Warblers are included in my previous list, several still hold their claim to being Egyptian birds upon rather unsatisfactory evidence. This, I think, arises from the nature of the country, the dryness of the climate, and the great absence of bushes, which are especially unfavourable to birds of this family, and cause their numbers to be limited, while it does not entirely exclude their occasional occurrence. Thus we find *Ruticilla semirufa*, naturally a very local species, only collected in Egypt by Hemprich and Ehrenberg, though, according to Canon Tristram, it is not uncommon in Palestine.

Again, our Hedge-Sparrow, *Accentor modularis*, has only been observed by Von Heuglin. *Bradypterus Cettii* appears a somewhat doubtful Egyptian species, although I fully believe that it does occur there. *Pseudoluscinia fluviatilis* is included upon still more uncertain authority; but as both these last species are found in Palestine, one may naturally conclude that they do visit Egypt. *Calamodyta aquatica* is stated by Von Heuglin to be common at times in company with *C. schœnobænus*; but I have never met with it, although I have taken some pains to search for it. *C. melanopogon* is perhaps more abundant in the Nile Delta than in any other part of its range, yet it has been strangely omitted by Von

Heuglin in his work; and this has rather shaken my confidence in his remarks upon the *Calamodytæ*, as I think he must have confounded it with some of the more nearly allied species. *Calamoherpe arundinacea*, the Reed-Warbler, probably escaped my notice owing to its being a bird of passage; although during my tours I have spent about two months at different times in February and March in the marshes of the Delta. *C. palustris* is a bird which neither myself nor Von Heuglin ever met with; but it is included as a bird of both Egypt and Nubia upon the authority of Rüppell and Lichtenstein; the determination is, however, in my opinion, open to question. *Acrocephalus pallidus* of Von Heuglin (Orn. N. O. Afr. p. 294), said by him to be a resident both in Egypt and Nubia, puzzles me as to what species it should be referred. I do not know of an *Acrocephalus* to which the name of *pallidus* could be applied; and he especially remarks that it is not the *Hypolais pallida* of Gerbe. I have referred it, in a footnote (p. 100), to *Hypolais elæica*.

Of the three species of true *Acrocephalus*, *A. turdoides* appears to me of doubtful occurrence; *A. arabicus*, Von Heuglin, I only know from his description (Orn. N. O. Afr. p. 289); but it seems to me to be probably a good species and to occur in Egypt.

Hypolais olivetorum has been collected by Mr. Rogers near Alexandria. I mention it here as it is new to the country. *H. elæica* is a common Egyptian and Nubian species; it is included by Von Heuglin under a collective specific name, *H. languida*, of which he recognizes five subspecies, and includes his *Acrocephalus pallidus*, which a few pages previously he referred to a different genus. Owing to this apparent indecision of the author I have refrained from adding *H. pallida*, Gerbe, to the Egyptian lists, although it is probably the species which Von Heuglin considers to be found in Egypt, but which I could only include upon his authority, no positive instance of its capture in that country being recorded. I may remark, however, that it is a Warbler very likely to occur there. *Phyllopneuste hippolais*, the Melodious Willow-Warbler, appears to have good claims as an Egyptian species; while *P. Eversmanni*, though mentioned by Mr. G. R. Gray in his 'Hand-list of Birds' (vol. i. p. 215) as Egyptian, has not been observed by Von Heuglin as occurring in any part of North-eastern Africa.

Curruca orphea is undoubtedly Egyptian, and likewise *C. atricapilla* and *C. hortensis*, although they are all of rare occurrence. *C. melanocephala*: the Egyptian race of Black-headed Warblers I have kept under this name, as I cannot find that they differ sufficiently from the European specimens that I have examined to justify their separation; yet Von Heuglin (Orn. N. O. Afr. p. 303) has separated them from the European species under the name of *Sylvia melanocephala minor*. There appears to me to be a slight difference; but I should wish to see a large series before considering them distinct, for I think perhaps the differences are accidental. *Melizophilus sardus* is included upon very positive authority, though Mr. Sharpe informs me that he still requires proof as to its occurrence out of the island of Sardinia. I am not surprised to find *Melizophilus provincialis* as a migratory species in Egypt; but I should have expected to find *Sylvia conspicillata* included by Von Heuglin among the birds of North-eastern Africa, as it is a likely bird to occur in that region.

Fam. NECTARINIIDÆ.—One beautiful species of this tropical

family comes within the scope of my present work, and is far from being uncommon above the First Cataract.

Fam. CERTHIIDÆ.—This family has only been represented in the preceding pages by one species, the Wall-creeper, *Tichodroma muraria*; and the authority upon which that bird has been included is so far from convincing, that I do not hesitate to express my doubts as to its occurrence in Egypt.

Fam. LANIIDÆ.—Of this family I have included six species, three of which are plentiful; two, *Lanius minor* and *L. collurio*, are rare; the other, *L. excubitor*, notwithstanding Von Heuglin's very positive assertion, appears to me a species so extremely unlikely to be found in Egypt, that I cannot consider it to be an undoubtedly Egyptian bird.

Fam. MUSCICAPIDÆ.—The three species of Flycatchers are only met with during their migrations.

Fam. HIRUNDINIDÆ.—*Cotyle rupestris* has been included upon the authority of Brehm; but is, in my opinion, not to be met with in Egypt. *C. minor* appears to me a very doubtfully good species; the other Swallows, except *Hirundo rufula* and *Chelidon urbica*, are extremely abundant.

Fam. MOTACILLIDÆ.—Amongst the Wagtails, *Motacilla sulphurea* is perhaps the rarest species in Egypt, while *M. vidua* is almost exclusively confined to the neighbourhood of the First Cataract. Of the Yellow Wagtails, I have recognized three species as Egyptian; for they are, in my opinion, specifically distinct, *Budytes flava* and *B. cinereocapilla* being more easily distinguished when alive than when viewed as skins in a collection.

Of the Pipits, *Anthus pratensis* is far from common, though undoubtedly Egyptian. *A. Raalteni* is included for the first time as Egyptian in this work. If properly identified, it is doubtless only met with as a straggler, and is interesting as being the most northern point at which the bird has yet been met with.

Fam. ALAUDIDÆ.—I have included twelve species of Larks, although I consider some to be of very doubtful specific value. *Ammomanes lusitana* and *A. fraterculus* appear to me to be only local varieties, imperceptibly blending into each other towards the confines of their respective ranges. *A. arenicolor*, though included upon somewhat meagre data, I look upon as very probably Egyptian. *Galerita rutila*, mentioned by Mr. G. R. Gray (Hand-list of Birds, ii. 119) as Egyptian, I have not included, but have only remarked upon at the end of *G. cristata*, as I think the specimen from which the locality "Egypt" has been taken may prove to be only *G. cristata*, or else have a wrong locality marked on it. Again, I am inclined to doubt Brehm's authority when he includes *Alauda arborea* as Egyptian. *Alauda intermedia*, Swinhoe, the common Egyptian form of *A. arvensis*, is a good instance of a constant race or subspecies. *Calandrella reboudia* appears to me a somewhat similar constant subspecies of *C. brachydactyla*, while I cannot find any good specific distinction between *C. pispoletta* and the last-named bird. *Melanocorypha calandra* is probably only met with as a straggler; and the remarkable desert form *Rhamphocoris Clot-Bey*, though undoubtedly Egyptian, is extremely rare.

Fam. EMBERIZIDÆ.—Among the Buntings I have only to mention *Emberiza intermedia*. I have retained this name as determined by Von Heuglin; but the only specimen I know of from Egypt being a female, I cannot feel certain of its distinctness from *E. palustris*.

Fam. FRINGILLIDÆ.—*Passer Italiæ* and *P. montanus* are

both included upon Von Heuglin's authority. *Coccothraustes vulgaris* is here mentioned for the first time as Egyptian, and its claims rest upon good authority. I am very sceptical as to the Lesser Redpole, *Ægiothus rufescens*, ever having been met with in Egypt. *Estrelda melanorhyncha*, included upon the authority of Von Heuglin, is the only instance we have of a species of this genus being found in the country.

Fam. STURNIDÆ.—*Pastor roseus* is of very rare occurrence, for I only know of a single instance of its capture.

Fam. CORVIDÆ.—I have included *Corvus monedula* and *Pica caudata* upon very unreliable authority; in fact, in my opinion, they have probably never been met with there in a wild state. As regards *Pyrrhocorax alpinus*, though there is no reason why this bird should not be found in Egypt, the only authority we have for its occurrence is most unsatisfactory.

Fam. CUCULIDÆ.—Although Herr F. Heine distinctly tells us (Journ. f. Orn. 1863, p. 350) that *Chrysococcyx cupreus* is found in Egypt, I think we may feel quite certain that it never by any chance ranges into that country.

Fam. ALCEDINIDÆ.—*Alcedo bengalensis* is, in my opinion, rather a subspecies of *A. ispida* than specifically distinct.

Fam. MEROPIDÆ.—*Merops viridis*: this includes *M. viridissimus* of authors; for I can find no difference between the Egyptian and Indian specimens, unless it be in the generally slightly longer tail of the former bird.

Fam. CYPSELIDÆ.—*Cypselus apus* I have never met with in Egypt, although it must undoubtedly come there. The bird usually referred to this species from Egypt is *C. pallidus*, which I first described (Ibis, 1870, p. 445). *C. parvus* I likewise see no reason to doubt being found in Upper Egypt and Nubia, though I have not seen a specimen of it from those parts.

Fam. STRIGIDÆ.—*Strix aluco*, the Tawny Owl, is included on the authority of Savigny, who mentions it in his 'Description de l'Egypte.' *Nyctala Tengmalmi* appears to be very rare, but is, I think, undoubtedly Egyptian; nor can we doubt *Bubo ignavus* being met with out there after the very positive evidence of Von Heuglin (Orn. N. O. Afr. p. 110). The other six species of Owls are not uncommon in Egypt.

Fam. FALCONIDÆ.—Among the Harriers, I am very sceptical as to *Circus cineraceus* ever having been met with in Egypt. *Accipiter gabar* I have no doubt is found, but is certainly of very rare occurrence in that country, though probably more plentiful in Nubia. Among the true Falcons, Von Heuglin includes *Falco babylonicus*, which he calls tolerably common in Egypt and Nubia. It is a rare and not very well-known bird; so I think it may have been confounded with *F. lanarius*, as a similar error has caused *F. cervicalis* to have been included by some authors in the Egyptian lists. Besides, Von Heuglin has on several occasions confounded *F. concolor* with *F. eleonoræ*, which mistake he has corrected in his large work; so that *F. eleonoræ* no longer holds a place as an Egyptian bird. The absence of this Falcon, I think, may be accounted for by there being no cliffs on the Mediterranean coast; and towards the Red Sea it is replaced by *F. concolor*. Of the remainder of the Falcons in my list I have specimens from the country in my own collection. Of the Kites, I feel certain that *Milvus regalis* has never been met with in Egypt, although Rüppell goes so far as to call it common about Alexandria. *M. ægyptius* and *M. migrans* are considered by some ornithologists to be varieties of the same species; but I do not agree in this theory. *Pernis apivorus* has probably been met with in Egypt, though it is open to doubt. *Buteo desertorum* is also probably Egyptian, but I can find no positive evidence of its having occurred there. *Haliaëtus albicilla* opens up a subject for investigation whether it be the true *H. albicilla*, a small subspecies, as Von Heuglin asserts, or a new species. I include *Aquila fulva*, *A. nævioides*, and *A. Bonellii* upon Von Heuglin's authority. The immature *A. imperialis* has been occasionally mistaken for *A. nævioides*; and I do not feel certain that Von Heuglin may not have fallen into this same error.

Gypaëtus nudipes, I think, may be safely considered to be the only representative of that genus in Egypt.

Fam. COLUMBIDÆ.—*Columba livia* and *C. Schimperi*, I believe, are both plentiful in Egypt and Nubia, while I think there are good reasons to doubt *C. œnas* being found there.

Turtur Sharpii is not only distinct from *T. auritus* in plumage and measurements, but decidedly so in its habits. *T. albiventris* is included on the authority of Von Heuglin, and I have no doubt he is correct. *T. isabellinus* rests on the authority of Bonaparte (Ic. Pig. t. 102). As I only know it from the figure, I am unable to decide its claims to a place in the Egyptian avifauna; but it appears to me very possible that the locality may have been wrongly given to the specimen which formed the subject of that plate. The type is in the Berlin Museum.

Fam. TETRAONIDÆ.—The Francolin appears very doubtfully Egyptian, being only included upon Rüppell's list, which is, perhaps, the most untrustworthy authority we have upon Egyptian birds.

Turnix sylvatica, the Andalusian Hemipode, is a widespread species, so that its occurrence in Egypt is not surprising.

Fam. Otididæ.—*Otis tetrax* barely claims a place in the present work, as it appears only to be met with in the desert east of Port Saïd. *Eupodotis arabs* is included solely upon Von Heuglin's note (Syst. Ueb. p. 53).

Fam. Charadriidæ.—*Eudromias morinellus* and *E. asiaticus* are entered on Von Heuglin's authority. *Ægialitis mongolicus* bases its claim upon a specimen in the British Museum. One cannot always rely on a labelled museum specimen; but it is not an unlikely bird to find its way into Egypt by the Red Sea. *Æ. hiaticula* is included upon the authority of Savigny's 'Description de l'Egypte,' and Von Heuglin (Syst. Ueb. p. 56), where the latter author also recognizes *Æ. intermedius*; yet I think that it may possibly prove to be identical with the latter species, which I have frequently killed in Egypt without ever meeting with the true *Æ. hiaticula.*

Fam. Scolopacidæ.—*Numenius tenuirostris* is undoubtedly Egyptian; and *N. phæopus,* though included upon less authority, is, in my opinion, also met with there. *Scolopax rusticola* is, though rare, undoubtedly to be found in Egypt. *Tringa arenaria* and *T. cinclus* are both stated by Von Heuglin to be Egyptian.

Fam. Tantalidæ.—*Ibis æthiopica* breeds at Wady Halfeh, and has therefore a right to a place in the present work, although it does not appear to wander into Egypt proper.

Tantalus ibis is only an occasional visitor.

Fam. Rallidæ.—*Ortygometra crex,* the Corn-Crake, is found in Egypt, according to Von Heuglin; and this appears very probable. *Porzana pygmæa* is also a likely bird to be met with, but rests solely upon Rüppell's statement. *Porphyrio Alleni* has undoubtedly occurred; and I think that there need be no hesitation in admitting *Fulica cristata*.

Fam. Anatidæ.—*Cygnus olor*, *C. musicus*, *Bernicla brenta*, *Fuligula marila*, and *Œdemia fusca* are included upon the authority of Von Heuglin; the others I have shot myself in Egypt.

Fam. Pelecanidæ.—*Pelecanus minor* is undoubtedly Egyptian, as is also *Sula cyanops*, which is here included for the first time.

Fam. Laridæ.—Among the Terns I have included *Sterna fluviatilis*, *S. hirundo*, *Hydrochelidon fissipes*, and *H. nigra*, upon the authority of Von Heuglin. *S. nilotica* of the latter's 'Systematische Uebersicht,' p. 71, I refer to *S. anglica*; while Mr. G. R. Gray, in his 'Hand-list of Birds' (iii. p. 119) considers *S. nilotica* as the oldest name for this species; but that name is anterior to 1766, and cannot be employed.

Larus marinus, included upon Von Heuglin's authority, is probably correct. *L. argentatus* and *L. affinis* of that author's first list I believe to be nothing else than *L. leucophæus*, the Mediterranean Herring-Gull; for I much doubt the true Herring-Gull of the Atlantic ever visiting Egypt. *L. cachinnans* of Von Heuglin's list I believe to be only a variety of *L. leucophæus*, of very doubtful specific value.

Fam. Procellariidæ.—*Nectris macrorhyncha* of Heuglin is probably synonymous with *Puffinus Kuhlii*, Boie, which is the older name. This, as well as *P. anglorum*, have fair claims to be Egyptian birds, though the latter would appear to be of very rare occurrence.

Fam. PODICIPIDÆ.—*Podiceps nigricollis, P. griseigena*, and *Colymbus septentrionalis* are included upon Von Heuglin's authority.

With the exception of some two or three species of which I have seen undoubted Egyptian specimens, all the remaining birds included in the present work have been collected by myself in that country.

INDEX.

THE END.

Printed by TAYLOR AND FRANCIS, Red Lion Court, Fleet Street.

www.ingramcontent.com/pod-product-compliance
Lightning Source LLC
Chambersburg PA
CBHW030904270326
41929CB00008B/571